The
Scottish Sketches
of
R. B. Cunninghame Graham

Selected and edited with
Introduction, Notes, Glossary
and Bibliography

by

JOHN WALKER

EDINBURGH
SCOTTISH ACADEMIC PRESS

Published by
Scottish Academic Press Ltd.
33 Montgomery Street, Edinburgh EH7 5JX

ISBN 0 7073 0288 9

Printed in Great Britain by
Clark Constable Ltd, Edinburgh

CONTENTS

Preface   vii

Editor's Foreword   ix

Introduction   I

SECTION I: LANDSCAPES AND PLACES   17

Editor's Preface   19

Pollybaglan (*Progress*)   20

Mist in Menteith (*A Hatchment*)   24

Snow in Menteith (*Progress*)   28

Lochan Falloch (*Faith*)   31

The Craw Road (*Charity*)   34

The Grey Kirk (*His People*)   38

The Laroch (*Progress*)   41

Tobar Na Réil (*His People*)   44

Inch Cailleach (*Redeemed*)   48

SECTION II: THE SCOTTISH CHARACTER   51

Editor's Preface   53

A Vigia (*Hope*)   54

Salvagia (*The Ipané*)   57

A Survival (*The Ipané*)   62

Euphrasia (*Redeemed*)   68

SECTION III: SCENES AND SITUATIONS   71

Editor's Preface   73

A Braw Day (*Charity*)   74

Falkirk Tryst (*A Hatchment*)   79

At Dalmary (*Hope*)   84

Fidelity (*Brought Forward*)   89

With the North-East Wind (*Brought Forward*)   93

SECTION IV: TYPES AND FIGURES   97

Editor's Preface   99

Heather Jock (*The Ipané*)   101

Miss Christian Jean (*His People*)   106

The Beggar Earl (*A Hatchment*)   115

A Fisherman (*Success*)   120

A Traveller (*Progress*)   125

A Retainer (*Hope*)   129

SECTION V: THE SCOTS ABROAD   133

Editor's Preface   135

A Pakeha (*Thirteen Stories*)   137

M'Kechnie v. Scaramanga (*Progress*)   140

A Convert (*Progress*)   148

Christie Christison (*Charity*)   156

SECTION VI: SCOTTISH STORIES   165

Editor's Preface   167

Beattock for Moffat (*Success*)   168

Ha Til Mi Tuliadh (*His People*)   175

Caisteal-na-Sithan (*Charity*)   180

At the Ward Toll (*Faith*)   185

A Princess (*Charity*)   189

Brought Forward (*Brought Forward*)   194

GLOSSARY   198

BIBLIOGRAPHY   202

PREFACE

Cunninghame Graham's involvement with Scotland became manifest when he became the first President of the Scottish National Party in 1928. Many of us will have seen pictures of him with Hugh MacDiarmid and the Duke of Montrose (an unlikely trio!) in the early days of the modern Scottish national movement. Nevertheless, because of the remarkably varied nature of his career —traveller and writer of travel books, Radical M.P. for North-West Lanarkshire, Scottish laird, long time resident of South America, married to a Chilean poetess, soaked in Spanish culture—the nature and quality of his Scottish interests are not often clearly seen, and the man himself, with his combined Hispanic and Scottish background, remains something of a puzzle to most writers on Scottish literature.

The sketches and stories collected here give a vivid picture of Cunninghame Graham both as prose stylist and as a recorder of Scottish scenes and Scottish people. The combination of observation and memory on the one hand with a hauntingly imaginative sense of the past on the other, gives a special flavour to his evocations of Scottish scenes and Scottish manners. For one who was born outside Scotland he shows an impressive command of spoken Scots in his dialogue, however limited its range. That dialogue, like his sense of place, reflects his sensuous awareness of those parts of Scotland he knew well. The same awareness is shown in his depiction of Scottish characters abroad. Imagination and moral feeling are there too. The result is a distinctive contribution to Scottish literature that is now made available to the reader.

DAVID DAICHES

EDITOR'S FOREWORD

Robert Bontine Cunninghame Graham is one of those writers people claim to have heard of, but have never read. A reason for his comparative obscurity in Scotland is that, being a man of so many parts, his other attributes and interests —politics, travel, equestrianism, etc.—have tended to overshadow his literary qualities. In other words, the image of the "character" has been cultivated to the detriment of the writer.

This is understandable, given the exciting life he led, the great feats of daring he achieved in several continents, and the heights of adventure to which he rose.[1] Cunninghame Graham was a fascinating man, with a propensity for the headlines, and a philosophy of life that sprang from his great sense of justice, contempt for hypocrisy and cant, and his support of the underdog, whether it be little country, lost cause, oppressed minority or downtrodden individual.

It was the man that first attracted me, as I grew up in Graham territory in Dumbarton, where, not only are streets named after him, but a monument created to his memory became a focal point in our childish games. Sadly, that monument has fallen prey over the years to the vandals and has recently been removed and re-erected at Gartmore (May 1981), but the family home at Ardoch still stands, overlooking the Clyde. It was a constant reminder to us of the Graham myth. Although the legendary Don Roberto had already died (in 1936) when we played our young lives away on the banks of the Clyde, our elders remembered clearly with affection the spry, wiry figure of Graham moving actively around his Ardoch estate.

I was first attracted to the literary Graham not for his Scottish sketches, but for his sketches and histories of Spain and especially Latin America, regions that he frequented and knew so well. Whilst contributing to a rehabilitation of Cunninghame Graham as a painter of pampa customs and as an apologist of the gauchos,[2] I have come more and more to appreciate his Scottishness and his qualities as a Scottish writer.[3]

During my research on Graham over the years, I have travelled to libraries and institutes in North America, South America, Spain, London, Edinburgh, and to the various Graham estates, especially Ardoch, in my search for, and investigation of, materials. I have also collected a vast library of Graham publications, books, pamphlets, prefaces, translated into several languages (especially Spanish), and I pride myself in having the best "private" collection, outside the main Graham centres. Apart from books and critical articles, my studies have produced several bibliographies of scholarship on Graham, including his Scottish writings.[4] All of this has convinced me of two facts. First, Cunninghame Graham is a sadly neglected writer, who has not received just recognition for his literary efforts, especially in Scotland. I am pleased to report, however, that there has been a recent, if mild, upsurge of interest in Graham, the writer as well as the man. Admiral Sir Angus Cunninghame Graham (who died 14 February 1981) and his daughter, Lady Polwarth, who have done so much to perpetuate the name of Don Roberto, inform me in our frequent meetings of an increasing number of scholars showing an interest in Graham's work. Apart from my own efforts, good work has been done by Cedric Watts (in Sussex), Andrew Maitland (in Edinburgh), Laurence Davies (now in U.S.A.) and Richard Haymaker (also in U.S.A.), and Lady Polwarth herself. I am sorry to acknowledge the recent death of Herbert West, a pioneer Graham scholar (with Tschiffely) in the thirties. A recent BBC radio play by Alanna Knight, based on the life of Graham, and a dramatic presentation on Don Roberto, staged at Stirling University, have done something to redress the balance, and suggest that perhaps Graham is beginning to come into his own.

However, the second fact, inextricably bound up with the first, is that, even if Graham were to become slightly known to a reading public—popularity he never craved—it would be difficult to find his books, all of which are long out of print and almost impossible to obtain. Even when accessible in the antiquarian market, the prices are prohibitive. One of my ambitions has been to make Graham's work readily available to a general reading public. To this end I have already produced a critical edition of his South American sketches,[5] with other collections promised on his sketches of Spain, North Africa, and Mexico/Texas/South-West U.S.A. These Scottish sketches offer to the reader a sample of Graham's production on his own country.

In his literary career Graham wrote almost a book a year for forty years, many of them collections of sketches. Out of the total of about two hundred sketches, some fifty were about Scotland, all published in various collections throughout his life. In 1914, early in his literary career, several of his Scottish sketches that had appeared before that date were gathered and published.[6] That selection is of only a part of Graham's work, and, besides being incomplete, is not representative, since many sketches of superior quality were omitted, whilst others of inferior quality were included.

As always with Graham, the problem is deciding which sketches to leave out. Obviously the complete *Scottish Sketches* would have been desirable, but not practical for economic reasons. I have tried to give a representative selection, choosing the best, whilst keeping an eye on the chronological sequence which will provide some idea of Graham's literary evolution.

To give shape and uniformity to the work, rather than offer a straightforward chronological treatment, I have divided the sketches into groups. This arrangement is for the convenience of the reader. My intention is to facilitate a better comprehension of Graham's Scottish work as a whole, and of the sketches in particular. The reader will note that each group is meant to introduce and illuminate the succeeding group, and that within the various divisions the

sketches have been arranged in an order that will make sense. After careful study
I settled on the following pattern:

     I. Landscapes and places.
     II. The Scottish character.
     III. Scenes and situations.
     IV. Types and figures.
     V. The Scots abroad.
     VI. Scottish stories.

Obviously, there is a certain overlapping within the groups, since some
sketches on types and figures (IV) reveal much of the Scottish character (II), and
some of the scenes and situations (III) depict something of the landscape (I), and so
on. The division is one of convenience, but within its framework there is a
decided progression and a certain logic. Any thematic or subject grouping, of
course, runs the risk of clashing with the chronological order of publication.
Fortunately, in most cases they coincide. Within the groups I have tried to maintain the chronological sequence as far as possible, as long as it does not destroy the
overall picture. In this way we have a complete, systematic view of Graham's
treatment of certain themes or topics, and we also see something of his evolution
and maturing as a writer.

Apart from an attempt to achieve balance between the sections and the
work as a whole, I have omitted certain sketches which, although interesting, are
only marginally Scottish ("My Uncle," "The Colonel," "The Admiral," "In A
German Tramp") or of inferior quality as *sketches* ("Loose and Broken·Men"). For
the curious reader I have appended the bibliographical details not only of all of
Graham's books, but of all the sketches, anthologised or omitted.

I should like to express my thanks to the late Admiral Sir Angus and Lady
Cunninghame Graham and their daughter Lady Polwarth for their great help,
generous hospitality, unfailing co-operation and spirited encouragement over
the years; also for their permission to reproduce the sketches, and to scrutinise,
reproduce and quote from the Graham material at Ardoch (now at Harden), the
National Library of Scotland, Edinburgh, and elsewhere; to the National Library
itself, Dartmouth College Library, and Douglas Library, Queen's University; to
the Canada Council, and the School of Graduate Studies and Research, Queen's
University, for their generous travel and research grants which have facilitated
the investigation and publication of this and other Graham material over the
years; to my daughter Clare, who typed and my wife Irene who proof-read the
manuscript; and to Sylvia Warder for valuable secretarial assistance.

NOTES

1. For the adventurous side of his life see A. F. Tschiffely, *Tornado Cavalier,*
   London, Harrap, 1955.

2. See my articles "R. B. Cunninghame Graham: Gaucho Apologist and Costumbrist of the Pampa," *Hispania*, LIII, No. 1, March 1970, 102-6; "Cunninghame Graham and the River Plate Region," *The Bulletin* (Buenos Aires), XXII, No. 8, April 1977, 11-15; "The Scotsman who Loved the Life of the Pampas," *Glasgow Herald*, 9 July 1966, 8; "Don Roberto in the New World," *Scottish Field*, CXVII, No. 808, April 1970, 25-7; "A Wandering Scotsman in the 'Purple Land,'" *Buenos Aires Herald*, 20 April 1979, 2.

3. See my *Cunninghame Graham and Scotland: An Annotated Bibliography*, Dollar, Douglas Mack, 1980.

4. "R. B. Cunninghame Graham: An Annotated Bibliography of Writings About Him," *English Literature in Transition*, Vol. 22, No. 2, 1979, 77-156; "A Chronological Bibliography of Works on R. B. Cunninghame Graham (1852-1936)," *The Bibliotheck*, Vol. 9, Nos. 2 & 3, 1978, 47-64.

5. *The South American Sketches of R. B. Cunninghame Graham*, Norman, University of Oklahoma Press, 1978.

6. *Scottish Stories*, London, Duckworth, 1914.

INTRODUCTION

CUNNINGHAME GRAHAM AND SCOTLAND

THE MAN AND HIS LIFE

Robert Bontine Cunninghame Graham was born in London in 1852 and died in Buenos Aires in 1936. During his lifetime he travelled extensively, visiting North and South Africa, Ceylon, France, Spain, Italy, Mexico, Texas, SouthWest U.S.A., and especially South America, where he is probably more appreciated than in his native Britain. Although his exploits abroad have tended to underline the image of the great cosmopolitan figure, which he undoubtedly was, all his life Graham, despite neglect by his compatriots, considered himself a Scotsman, by temperament, heritage and upbringing—a Scottishness that manifested itself not only in his life but also in his writings.

Robert was born on 24 May 1852 in London, where his father, Major William Bontine, an officer in the Scots Greys, was stationed. Young Robert was part of a complex genealogical tree that saw amongst his forebears many of the famous Grahams of Scottish history—Sir John of the Bright Sword, who sacrificed himself on Wallace's behalf at the Battle of Falkirk; Sir Robert Graham, slayer of James I, variously labelled assassin and patriot; Nicol Graham, who challenged the power of Rob Roy; and his famous predecessor, Sir Robert Graham, named for his memorable verses as "Doughty Deeds," whom Graham immortalised in the biography of the same name.[1] Graham himself, as the rightful Earl of Menteith, could legitimately lay claim to the throne of Scotland by descent from Robert II, given the illegitimacy of the Stuart line. At least this is the theory that I heard advanced when I was growing up in Dumbarton, where Don Roberto was often referred to by the older people as the "uncrowned King of Scotland"—a claim supported by antiquarian scholars like Andrew Lang.

If Graham was less interested in the titles associated with the earldoms of Menteith and Glencairn (the territory of the Cunninghames), the lands he did inherit from his illustrious family were to play an important role in his formative years. Spanning ten thousand acres, they included parts of four counties (Perthshire, Stirlingshire, Dumbartonshire and Renfrewshire). He was brought up on his father's estates in Finlaystone (Renfrewshire), Gartmore (Perthshire) and Ardoch (Dumbartonshire), where he acquired a life-long passion for riding. Thus in his ancestry and upbringing were sown the seeds of his feeling for, and appreciation of, things Scottish.

He occasionally visited his Spanish grandmother in the Isle of Wight and in

Cádiz. Perhaps less to his liking, but typical of the aristocratic education of the period, were his stays at Harrow and in Brussels, where he learned fencing and French, to add to his horse-riding and Spanish. The Spanish side, mostly through his mother, herself the product of the union of Scottish and Spanish noble families, influenced his decision at the age of seventeen to set out on a ranching enterprise to Argentina in 1870, rather than follow his father into the army. Though a failure financially, it provided young Robert with lots of adventure, valuable experience and much raw material for his future writing. It was in the New World also that Don Roberto, as he was affectionately called, first acquired the spirit of radicalism, seeing abuses and injustice everywhere, with the poor and the oppressed at the mercy of unscrupulous dictators. These early travels motivated his later association with apparently unlikely companions, social reformers like Keir Hardie, John Burns, and the like.

Home again in 1878, he visited Spain and France, where he met Gabrielle de la Balmondière, his future wife, whom he rescued in true chivalrous and quixotic fashion from her unhappy circumstances, and married on 24 October 1878. They returned to Gartmore, which they found in worsening condition because of the rash behaviour of Major Bontine, now suffering increasingly from the injuries of an earlier military accident. The young couple, more and more frustrated since the power of attorney was still in his father's hands, set out for Texas to try and make their fortune and improve the Gartmore situation. After ranching there for two years and also losing everything in an Indian raid, they embarked on another profit-making scheme, selling cotton in Mexico City. After a short spell in a fencing academy, Robert earned enough money to enable him to return to San Antonio where he found his ranch invaded by the Indians. These experiences did not deter him from defending vigorously the Indian against certain extermination.

With the death of his father in 1883, Don Roberto returned home from Spain to face debts of £100,000. His experiences in the New World had inculcated in him feelings for the oppressed and the underdog, and the desire to write about them. Not only was he a kind and courteous laird towards his own tenants, but in 1886 he was elected Liberal M.P. for West Lanarkshire, and achieved a certain notoriety for his radical spirit, fiery speeches and progressive ideas that were the stuff of the twentieth century—universal suffrage, free secular education with a free meal, an eight-hour working day, nationalisation of land, graduated income tax, triennial parliaments, abolition of the House of Lords, and prison reform, as well as opposing capital and corporal punishment.[2] Never really appreciated by either side—his peers called him an eccentric traitor and a cowboy dandy, whilst the working classes could never quite trust an "aristo"—he lost his seat in Parliament in 1892, tried half-heartedly to regain it several times, and eventually became disillusioned with the "official" labour movement.

After his political demise, the eccentric in him inspired a profitless gold hunt in Spain, based on Pliny's description of ancient Lusitania. In 1897 he tried to reach Tarudant, the Forbidden City of Morocco, previously unentered by a Christian.

Besides being an embarrassment to the British government, which was in a delicate political situation in Africa at the time, he endangered his own life. However, he never lost his sense of humour, and once, when ambushed and asked the vital question, "Are you a Christian?," he replied with a straight face, "No, I'm a U.P." His Arab captors, ignorant of the abbreviation for United Presbyterian, seemed satisfied with his answer. Eventually he was captured by a kaid, or chief, suspected of being a British agent, but finally released without reaching his objective. This stranger-than-truth adventure was recounted in *Mogreb-el-Acksa* (1898), recognised as one of the most exciting travel books ever written, and the acknowledged source of George Bernard Shaw's *Captain Brassbound's Conversion*.[3]

On his return from Morocco in 1889 he settled down to what might be called his literary period, attaining the incredible production of almost a book a year for forty years till his death in 1936. They were mostly collections of stories, essays and sketches, based on his experiences in Africa, the Americas, Spain, and, of course, Scotland, plus histories, biographies and travel books, mostly about Latin America. In 1901 he suffered the first of two tragic losses, the sale of the beautiful family estate at Gartmore, following closely on the disposal of Finlaystone. The loss of the ancestral home at Gartmore was a bitter experience, exceeded only by the death of his wife, the mysterious mystic poetess, Gabriela, on a visit to Spain in 1906.[4] After her death, though allegedly of Chilean-French extraction, she was buried, as she requested, in the ruins of the Augustinian priory on the island of Inchmahome, on the Lake of Menteith.[5]

Left only with the family home at Ardoch, situated between Dumbarton and Cardross, he spent most of his time between London, where, close to his mother and literary acquaintances, he indulged in his passion for riding in Rotten Row every day, and Scotland, where the quiet of Ardoch afforded him the opportunity to produce collections of sketches (for example, *Faith, Hope* and *Charity*) and histories of Latin America, before war broke out in 1914, the year which saw the publication of his *Scottish Stories*. Though bitterly anti-imperialist and anti-war, Graham, at the age of sixty-two, offered his services as a Rough Rider, a firm rebuff to those who had openly doubted his patriotism because of his earlier radical views on the Irish Home Rule question, the Turkish issue and the Zulu Wars. Rejected by the authorities, he accepted as a poor substitute a distasteful mission to South America to buy horses and cattle for the government —justified on the grounds that at least if *he* were in charge, they would be humanely treated. As always, adventure followed him, and he was torpedoed and shipwrecked twice. Although he found the New World greatly changed, with the advent of progress, civilisation and the abhorrent commerce, it did provide him with material for future sketches and more histories of Latin America.

With the end of the war, a last half-hearted political fling saw him defeated as the Independent Liberal candidate for West Stirlingshire in 1918. Times had changed, the people had already realised many of Graham's ideas of the 1880s, and there was no place for an old Don Quixote in the post-war years. Now in his seventies, he witnessed the death of his friends Conrad and Hudson, and finally in

1925, his mother, Mrs. Bontine, a constant companion, inspiration and moral supporter, died at the age of ninety-seven, after an active life devoted to literature, culture, and, not least, charity. An old man with no ties, he set out to visit scenes of his youthful triumphs. In 1925, on a sentimental journey to Venezuela, he went six hundred miles up the Orinoco in an old ship, then returned to explore the llanos on horseback.

The last decade of his life Don Roberto spent mostly at Ardoch, devoting himself to the great passions of his life, writing and riding, with much time and energy spent in the cause of Scottish nationalism. Even in his last years he was producing a book a year, often histories of South America, though *Doughty Deeds* (1925), the biography of his famous eighteenth-century ancestor, Sir Robert Graham, and several of his sketches were emotional and literary expressions of his sense of Scottishness, which was often more sentimental than political. Long interested in nationalism (cf. his efforts for Irish Home Rule on Bloody Sunday and other occasions),[6] which he considered the first step towards internationalism, he did not deem his views contrary to the socialist doctrines which he expounded in the 1880s and 1890s. In fact, he was a member of the Home Rule Association as early as 1886, and was the first president of the Scottish Labour Party in 1888, before becoming disillusioned with official socialism. In 1928, named the first president of the Nationalist Party of Scotland, founded in Glasgow, he addressed the inauguration demonstration in King's Park, Stirling on 23 June, the anniversary of Bannockburn, in eloquent and patriotic terms. Although he was narrowly defeated by Prime Minister Baldwin for the Lord Rectorship of Glasgow University in October 1928, his defeat was regarded as a personal and nationalist victory. With associates like Compton Mackenzie, Neil Gunn, Hugh MacDiarmid and others, he dedicated himself unsparingly with his great oratory, extravagant style and picturesque speech to the cause of Scottish nationalism at meetings in Stirling, Elderslie, Bannockburn and elsewhere in those halcyon days of the early 1930s. It has been suggested that Graham was exploited, even betrayed, by many of the nationalist advocates. One wonders as to his reaction at today's new wave of nationalism, fortified by an economic and commercial lever, symptomatic of industrial progress and creeping civilisation, creatures he berated all his life.

Graham was no narrow nationalist, and though preoccupied with the affairs of Scotland and its independence, he took trips in the last years of his life to Ceylon and South Africa, extending his field of travel. Then, finally, the master of life, having partaken to the full, decided in 1936, at the age of eighty-three, to make the final pilgrimage to the scene of his first adventures, Argentina. Although obviously unwell, he set out on 18 January 1936. By March he had contracted a serious attack of bronchitis, and he died of pneumonia in Buenos Aires on 20 March 1936.

After a countrywide tribute by the people of Argentina, where he is still revered for his contribution to their national literature, his body was shipped home to Scotland. On Saturday 18 April 1936 mourners came from all over

Britain to attend the simple, dignified funeral service, and to pay tribute with speech, music and silence to the "Scottish Arthur of our day," to the "noblest Scotsman of them all," as William Power described him in his funeral oration. From the Duke of Montrose, the chief of the clan Graham, to the village black-smith of Gartmore, the people paid tribute to a great Scotsman. The strains of "The Floo'ers o' the Forest" and "Lochaber No More" underlined the poignant sense of loss as he was buried beside his wife in the ruined Augustinian priory on the island of Inchmahome, on the Lake of Menteith.

The following year, June 1937, a monument to Don Roberto was unveiled at Castlehill, Dumbarton, on ground that he had given to the National Trust for Scotland, with representatives from Argentina and Uruguay, and the Duke of Montrose, for Scotland, performing the unveiling ceremony. To commemorate "Scotland's outstanding citizen," as the *Scots Independent* called him, there was a fine medallion by Alexander Proudfoot, with an epitaph (that only *just* survived the ravages of vandalism) bearing these words which will transcend the bricks and mortar in their homage to the spirit of

ROBERT BONTINE

CUNNINGHAME GRAHAM

1852-1936

FAMOUS AUTHOR

TRAVELLER AND HORSEMAN

PATRIOTIC SCOT

AND CITIZEN OF THE WORLD

AS BETOKENED

BY THE STONES ABOVE

DIED IN ARGENTINA

INTERRED IN INCHMAHOME

HE WAS A MASTER OF LIFE

A KING AMONG MEN

THE WRITER

Robert Bontine Cunninghame Graham's literary career began, in a sense, in his childhood. Because of his varied life and his many travels, he was an inveterate letter-writer from the earliest days. Even as a boy, when living far from home in Harrow and Brussels, and on his visits to his Spanish relatives, young Robert wrote letters to his mother, Mrs. Bontine. The countless bundles of letters long preserved in the family home at Ardoch and now at Harden, the National Library of Scotland in Edinburgh, and wherever there exist collections of Graham material,[7] attest to the habit that was to stay with him till his last days.

Even when he was not physically able to write, especially in the later years, he dictated to a friend.

In his youth he took himself to Argentina after his schooldays. His experiences on the pampas with the gauchos provided him with both the material and the opportunity to describe his adventures. His letters to his mother, his family and his friends reveal the man of action and the nascent writer. His participation in the gaucho wars of the 1870s left him with a wealth of memories which were to be the stuff of his South American sketches written thirty years later. These same experiences were to inculcate in him the radical spirit that was to motivate his "socialist" writings of the 1880s and 1890s, when he devoted himself to the cause of the workers in publications like *The Social-Democrat, Justice, The Labour Leader* and *The Labour Elector*,[8] into which he poured articles, reports, news items, letters, etc. Though apparently of a specialist nature, they provided him with an opportunity to exercise his trade, and served as a basis for later sketches whose mood conveyed his philosophical, if not his political, preoccupations of this period.

His trip to Mexico, Texas and the South-West U.S.A. with his new bride in the early 1880s had not only underlined his concern with the oppressed— whether it be Mexican Indians, Argentine gauchos, Scottish miners, Zulus or Turks—but helped him to formulate his views and his fears about a possible literary career: "I have tried two or three times to make a magazine article out of the Mexican journey, but I find I have no talent whatever in that line . . . I think I have no literary ability whatever."[9] Sketches like "Un pelado" and "A Hegira," written as a result of his Mexican adventures, belie the poor opinion he held of his own literary ability. Some thirty books, not counting translations, prefaces, pamphlets, etc. indicate that his fears had little basis.

His youthful travels over, and his political career terminated by his disenchantment with the "official" labour movement, Graham was now free to fulfil his duties as a Scottish laird and to pursue the literary career already hinted at in his Latin American letters and his socialist journalism. When he did come to write his first book, he treated of matters close to home, the region that he knew so well. *Notes on the District of Menteith* (1895), which purports to be a travel guide "for tourists and others," is still a valuable aid to visitors to that beautiful, misty area. However, Graham's pithy remarks on the Scottish character, customs, history and a host of other topics which he was eminently qualified to treat, enable the book to transcend the merely regional, factual and descriptive. It is significant that he chose the area he knew best, the region of Menteith, which was to be the source of so many of the sketches gathered in this collection. Scotland, its past and future, were all the stuff of his work.

It is not surprising that he described what he knew intimately, for his whole literary credo was based on such personal manifestation of one's own experiences and one's own vital sensibility. Though it plays down Graham's own status as a writer, and underestimates the aesthetic qualities which were so obviously an integral part of his work, his Apologia in *His People* (1906) is a true expression of his feelings towards his craft: "Still I believe, that be it bad or good, all that a writer does is to dress up what he has seen, or felt, and nothing real is evolved from his own brain, except the words he uses, and the way in which he uses them. Therefore it follows that in writing he sets down (perhaps unwittingly) the story of his life" (p. x). In the Preface to *Faith* he reiterates this view of the writer's trade: "All that we write is but a bringing forth again of something we have seen or heard about. What makes it art is but the handling of it, and the imagination that is brought to bear upon the theme out of the writer's brain" (p. xii).

This attitude towards his art, coupled with his cavalier approach to the business of correction and proof-reading of manuscripts, has earned him the label "amateur of genius." His tendency to mock his readers in his very personal prefaces, and his oft-stated affirmation that he wrote to please himself and not the many-headed public, whom he variously called "incurious," "disingenuous" and the like, have not helped his reputation as a serious or "lovable" writer. Critics have preferred to heed the idle threats—for example, that *Brought Forward* (1916) was his swan song—or be offended by the "ice of his disdain" or what Conrad called his "philosophy of unutterable scorn," rather than admit the evidence of forty years of writing. Others have seen fit to admire the man, the politician, the traveller, the horseman, but have failed to recognise the solid corpus of writing that bears witness to the serious author.

One of the tragedies of Graham's literary career is that he is often recognised and appreciated abroad, especially in Argentina, but neglected at home. Graham helped to foster this neglect by underestimating his own skills, whilst praising and actively supporting the work of literary friends and contemporaries like Hudson and Conrad, as well as others less talented than himself. This lack of appreciation has been particularly manifest in Scotland where but a few critics and kindred spirits have seen beyond the self-denigratory observations of his literary credo. Although W. M. Parker, as early as 1917, was impressed by the "Scottish Maupassant," his virile style, his sense of colour and his love of Scottish worthies, he felt that Graham's fame rested on his gaucho sketches and his description of prairie, pampa and sierra life.[10] The same ambivalence can be seen in one description of Graham as another Sir Walter Scott—of South America!

One of the few Scottish writers to appreciate Graham, in the 1920s and 1930s and also after his death, was Hugh MacDiarmid. MacDiarmid saw Graham not only as a great Scottish nationalist but also potentially as the greatest Scotsman of his generation and the only one to "win the second rank as an imaginative artist." He was shrewd enough to perceive Graham's status as both a first-rate writer and a Scottish writer *hasta los tuétanos*, or to the marrow, as Graham might have said in another setting: "Cunninghame Graham possesses to a higher degree than any Scot of his generation those vital qualities of the Scottish genius."[11]

Though Graham was perhaps more appreciated in the thirties, one cannot help but feel that two events helped to nurture this interest in him—his association with the nationalist movement, and his death in 1936. To be fair, however, writers like Frederick Niven, another neglected Scots-Canadian novelist, though not afraid to criticise his defects, and appreciative of his humanitarian and quixotic qualities, still recognised Graham's unique style of writing.[12]

Few writers are as eulogistic as William Power, who considered Graham to be the doyen of Scottish literature and "perhaps the finest literary artist alive in Europe today"—quite an extravagant claim in 1935.[13] Whilst identifying with the political activities of Graham on behalf of the nationalist cause, Power was astute enough to recognise the value of his Scottish sketches as crystallisations of his actual experiences and observations—as Graham had always maintained. Like MacDiarmid, Power saw the special literary product that emerged out of the cosmopolitanism of the wandering Scot—but which was no less Scottish in its essence. It often takes the writer to go on his travels to appreciate and keenly observe the foibles, virtues and, in general, the character of his own race. Power was also able to distinguish, as I shall demonstrate later, Graham's efforts to rid Scottish literature of the "insular sentiments of the kailyards," who preferred to bury their heads in the "cabbage patch" of the past rather than face the historic reality of late nineteenth-century Scotland, and his attempts to describe in his later sketches a "twilight Scotland, ennobled by tragedy and defeat," whilst the Scotland of his dreams is "nobly self-reliant and bravely idealistic."[14]

Compton Mackenzie, whose multi-volumed memoirs, *My Life and Times*, contain many references to Cunninghame Graham, was a youthful admirer of Don Roberto, or Don Quixote as he liked to call him, but, one has to concede, mostly for his efforts on behalf of Scottish nationalism, which movement received a mortal blow with the death in 1936 of its most eminent figure(-head?). Though his obituary list was supplemented by writers sympathetic to nationalism, like George Scott Moncrieff and Henry Nevinson, and although Scottish writers over the years, like Neil Munro and Nigel Tranter, have made the odd reference to Graham, none has consistently praised the man and appreciated the writer like Hugh MacDiarmid.

Naturally sympathetic to Graham in the halcyon days of nationalism in the late 1920s and early 1930s, MacDiarmid's attitude to the man and writer never changed. Writing thirty years later in a centenary study, he still praised his spirit and achievements, though Graham was one of those "damned aristos." His saving grace was that he did not suffer fools gladly, especially those of bourgeois outlook. With all his attributes, however, Graham today, as in 1952, is unknown, therefore unappreciated in Scotland. If he tended to travel, and was thus absent from Scotland for long periods, his fervent Scottish nationalism counterbalanced the tradition of the wandering Scot. MacDiarmid, not given to extravagant eulogies, is one of the few to recognise in Graham the rare phenomenon—a Scottish writer who is also an international figure. His familiarity with the literature of Spain and Latin America in no way diminished his love for, and knowledge of, Henryson, Dunbar, Burns, Scott, Smollett and other masters of Scottish letters, whose names are scattered profusely throughout his sketches. When one weighs the many fine funeral orations given on Graham's death, and the obituary notices lauding "the noblest Scotsman of them all," "the peer of the greatest," "the most outstanding citizen"—all sincere but emotional homages at the time —the tribute of Hugh MacDiarmid, no flatterer of men, several decades later, rings out magnificently: "He was indeed a prince and paladin of our people. . . . There is no finer figure in all the millenary pageant of Scotland's writers."[15]

Since *Notes on the District of Menteith* was the only book devoted *exclusively* to Scotland, and was deemed by Graham a mere travel guide for tourists, his reputation as a Scottish writer rests largely on his Scottish sketches. I use these literary terms advisedly, since this division too is false, for it is difficult to differentiate amongst the genres in Cunninghame Graham's writing. His travel books contain beautiful sketches whilst his biographies and his histories spill over into each other and also into the travel story, and so on. All of his books contain much that is political, philosophical, literary, biographical, and, not least, autobiographical. It has been said that no biography of Graham is necessary, since he writes his own, putting so much of himself into all his work. However, given his versatility and his fecundity as a writer, Graham is perhaps best known for his contribution to the sketch.

If it is difficult to distinguish between the various genres in Graham's production, it is well nigh impossible to define what constitutes a sketch. It is not really a short story, although he has been called a Scottish Maupassant, since his sketches do not depend on the development of plot, but rather evoke a scene. Nor does he rely on characterisation or trick-endings, like O. Henry, though many of his sketches have qualities that place them close to the short story.[16] In Section VI I have collected several examples of what might be called "stories"— "Beattock for Moffat," "At the Ward Toll," "Brought Forward," etc. Not really a short story, the sketch is not an essay either, *à la* Hazlett or Lamb, although some of the Latin American descriptive sketches on the gaucho life of the pampas might approximate to that genre, for example, "The Horses of the Pampas," "The Lazo," "The Bolas," etc.[17] Thus, it is easier to state what this particular form of writing is *not*, rather than what it is. However, given the period in which he lived, his close association with Impressionism, his temperament, and literary credo, it is not surprising that he considered himself an impressionist.[18] What he produced, then, was mostly the impressionistic sketch, in which he evoked a scene or situation, mostly taken from his own experience or occasionally from his imagination. As a writer, he has a genius for what Frederick Watson called the "phrase that bites into the mind and haunts the memory."[19] His use of casual reminiscence, interpolations and indirections are typically impressionist. It is this mixture of fiction and autobiography that gives Graham's sketches that special flavour and renders difficult any precise attempt to identify or define.

Graham tended to underplay his aesthetic qualities, but he was esteemed by writers like Conrad, Hudson, Ford Madox Ford and others, who saw in his work much of the "art behind the artlessness," and explained Graham's lack of success on the stupidity of the public and the jealousy and ignorance of other writers.[20] Although conscious of aesthetic problems, and appreciative of the artistic worth of others, Graham was not a sophisticated or experimentalist author, when it came to techniques. If his aim in the impressionistic sketch is basically to evoke a scene, all he has to do is to dig down into his wealth of experience and his treasure-house of memories. One of his favourite techniques is to have a group gathered together—in a camp, a ship, a hotel, a drawing-room (as in "M'Kechnie v. Scaramanga")—and in order to while away the hours one, or several, will tell a tale, usually based on his own experiences. These story-tellers are often Scottish exiles in Africa, Mexico, Argentina, Europe, New Zealand, or sometimes Graham himself, or a laird ("Fidelity"). Often Graham does not need the stimulus of the group, and will simply go off in search of lost time by means of a memory, flashback, triggered off by a sight, a smell, a chance remark, or simply in his imagination. Another favourite technique is his "conjecture" approach. Encountering a death, for example, sets the mind working as to who the person might have been, how he came to be in this situation, what his youth might have been like, what his family might have felt, and so on.

The sketches are salted with interjections and asides on life, death, religion, politics, and often civilisation, progress and commerce, which were the main objects of his barbs. Though he would have rejected the moralist label, and would have shrunk modestly from the tag of philosopher, Graham's biting and perceptive comments on, and humane treatment of, the victims of time, fame, failure and success, bring to his sketches a timeless quality that helps them to transcend mere contemporary observation, the essay of manners and the "twist-ending" type of short story. His use of proverbs, popular sayings, the vernacular of whichever country he was describing, lends a certain verisimilitude. The subtle, and often ironic, use of footnotes and parentheses gives a unique flavour to the pieces, as well as illuminating and illustrating the effect intended.

All his collections of sketches are introduced by penetrating prefaces which are more than mere forewords to his books. Termed the prince of preface-writers, his skill in this particular area was so great that he was constantly sought, producing prefaces for the works of Hudson, Conrad, Tschiffely and other well-known contemporaries. Not only did he use his prefaces to affirm his views on the role of the writer, burning political problems like colonialism and imperialism, and philosophical questions upon the essence of life, but also occasionally he used the preface itself to paint a sketch, for example, the Preface to *Hope*. This tendency to overlap the genres, characteristic of all his work, which was first manifest in *Notes on the District of Menteith*, reveals itself clearly in the Scottish sketches.

If *Notes on the District of Menteith* is the first *concrete* reflection of Graham's Scottishness as a writer, every collection of his sketches from *Father Archangel of Scotland* (1896) to *Mirages*, published in the year of his death (1936), provides samples of his Scottish sketches. In fact, it is possible to see a certain evolution during these forty years in his Scottish sketches. From the first decade of his literary life, especially in the Scottish sketches of *The Ipané* (1899), "Salvagia," "Heather Jock" and "A Survival,"[21] he devoted himself to correcting the excessive sentimentality of the Kailyard school as exemplified in the romantic, escapist fiction of "Ian Maclaren" [John Watson] (1850–1907), S. R. Crockett (1860–1914), and J. M. Barrie (1860-1937). Works like Maclaren's *Beside the Bonnie Brier Bush* (1894), Crockett's *The Lilac Sunbonnet* (1894), and Barrie's *Auld Licht Idylls* (1888), set against an artificially rustic background, are characterised by trite domestic conversation in the vernacular, stereotyped Scottish figures, and a tendency to wallow in emotionalism that easily degenerates to bathos. The result in Graham's early sketches is a bitter portrayal of the defects of the Scottish character, somewhat in the naturalistic manner of George Douglas Brown's *The House with the Green Shutters* (1901). The next two decades up to 1916 (*Brought Forward*), or his middle period, saw the bulk of his work. During this stage, having purged himself of the early virulence, he settled down to a more realistic portrayal of places and people, of death and parting, of types and characters, of customs and events, of funerals and cemeteries, with *occasional* flights latterly into the dream world of mythology and sentimentality, which were to be the characteristics of the third and last period. This third epoch, which took up the last decade of his life, coincided with his identification with the cause of Scottish nationalism. During this period, especially in *Redeemed* (1927), his political nationalism is reflected in his literary nostalgia and melancholy, his longing for a past Scotland, a land of islands and fairies, of myths and dreams, a noble Caledonia to which one can escape, if only in one's reverie. Though not a return to the excesses of the Kailyard school against which he had reacted so vehemently in the 1890s, there is a softness of touch, a yearning for a happiness long disappeared in the distant mists of Celtic Scotland—the dreams and wishes of an old man who loves his country.

Within the framework of the development of his sketches, there is, however, a constant. In all of Graham's work, one finds an acute sense of melancholy, reflected in his preoccupation with parting and grief, with exile and death—especially death. In his description of landscapes and scenes, in which he has been compared favourably with Robert Louis Stevenson, he has a penchant for grave-yards, monuments and tombs. His portrayal of situations and scenes ends inevitably with death, funeral, and burial. Even the character sketches of types and figures conclude with a detailed description of their demise. The Scots leave Scotland, many never to return. Those who come back do so to die—as do even the foreigners who come to visit. Despite his quick wit and his sharp tongue, despite his aggressive political stand both at the beginning of his career (socialism) and at the end (Scottish nationalism), there is in Graham, as in all Scots, he seems to imply, from the Norse invaders, up through the Wallace and Bruce epoch, Culloden, the Highland Clearances, a certain character trait, rooted in "oppression's woes and pains," which is a historical reflection of the Scots' acceptance of grief and death. In this sense, Graham is the typical Scot—some would say the quintessential Scot. Thus, in spite of all his travels, as Amy Wellington and others have pointed out, Cunninghame Graham remained a Scot, and it is when he writes of Scotland that he shows most emotion.

Emotion by itself, however, is not the essence of good writing. In his literary treatment of Scotland Graham fuses sentimental involvement, an easy familiarity with, and a shrewd appreciation of, the region described, an intense identification with the life and character depicted, and a skilful handling of his material. To render in aesthetic terms the life-style, nature and metaphysical concerns of a people is no mean achievement. Through his Scottish sketches Graham has performed this feat admirably for his country. Scotland should surely, and finally, recognise and be grateful to Robert Bontine Cunninghame Graham, a great man, a true Scot, and a sadly neglected writer.

THE TEXT

Though one would prefer to have all of Graham's Scottish sketches between the covers of this book, it is not possible for reasons of volume. It has been my pleasant, though difficult task, to choose which of the sketches are best representative of Graham's art. The selection, then, is mine—as are the organisation and division of the pieces into the order of the various groups.

Graham, as Conrad and others, not least his editors and publishers, have complained, was little concerned with the formal preparation and revision of his manuscripts.[22] This laxity, which stems from his view of the role of the artist (already quoted), manifests itself clearly not only in the original volumes of sketches, but also in the reprinted collections which were selected and compiled rather than edited by Tschiffely (*Rodeo*), Edward Garnett (*Thirty Tales and Sketches*) and Paul Bloomfield (*The Essential R. B. Cunninghame Graham*).

In general, Cunninghame Graham showed scant respect for the niceties of manuscript preparation, and little concern for uniformity in formal, grammatical details with regard to quotation marks, parentheses, capitalisation, etc. Also, mainly because he wrote his fifty Scottish sketches over a period of forty years from 1896 to 1936, there is a lack of consistency in his use of proper names, Scottish and foreign words. Part of my editorial duties has been to impose an overall style in the sketches selected, with regard to italicisation, capitalisation and other such matters. Obvious orthographical and typographical errors have been corrected. As Graham tends at times to spell phonetically a Scottish or a foreign word—sometimes differently in different sketches over his four decades of literary production—I have tried to remedy this abuse also.

Graham, although he had a wonderful feeling for descriptive prose and impressionistic language, in his enthusiasm sometimes creates problems of punctuation. Whenever necessary, I have judiciously inserted, or discreetly removed, a comma, semi-colon, or full stop, in the interests of clarity—for example, in a long intricate sentence, complicated by parenthetical insertions. However, my editorial touch has been light, since I would not presume to correct the art of Graham by interfering too much with the text. Such intervention would be to tamper with his evocative, creative prose which requires but token assistance to remove the minor blemishes of form and to restore the sketches to their full beauty.

Since these are Scottish sketches, there are, of course, many allusions to Scottish history, literature and language. Graham often uses Scottish words peculiar to the settings and characters depicted in his stories. Because he had absorbed these expressions—Gaelic and Lowland Scots—over the years, he tends to use them loosely. Whenever possible, I have tightened up his handling, corrected the spelling, and generally rendered consistent his deployment of Scottish vernacular. With regard to literary and historical, as well as linguistic, matters, I have supplied explanatory footnotes for the benefit of the general reader and non-Scots.[23]

Some of the words may be unfamiliar to the non-Scots who read Graham, and the Glossary should provide a useful aid to a fuller enjoyment and appreciation of the sketches. This is not an exhaustive list, nor is it intended to be a specialist or technical catalogue of words and expressions. Rather than an expert in the Scottish language, I am a Scot interested in the writings of Cunninghame Graham.

For other interested readers who may wish to compare this edition with the original pieces, I have supplied a Bibliography. A selected bibliography of books and articles on Graham also suggests further reading. This present selection of Scottish sketches is intended to offset, to a certain extent, the lack of available material by, and the appreciation of, this forgotten Scottish artist.

NOTES

1. *Doughty Deeds*, London, Heinemann, 1925.
2. See my article "Voices of Socialism: R. B. Cunninghame Graham," *Tribune*, Vol. 30, No. 17, 29 April 1966, 14.
3. In his Notes to the play Shaw confesses to having stolen the scenery, surroundings and atmosphere from Graham's book. See my article "Bernard Shaw and Don Roberto," *The Shaw Review*, xv, No. 3, Sept. 1972, 94-103.
4. She was an author in her own right, apart from contributing several sketches to Graham's first collection, *Father Archangel of Scotland* (1896). She is best known for her 2-volume *Santa Teresa: Her Life and Times*, London, A. & C. Black, 1894, and *The Christ of Toro*, London, Eveleigh Nash, 1908, mostly sketches and stories set in Spain.
5. Mary Queen of Scots is reported to have spent her happiest days here.
6. See my article "Don Roberto and Bloody Sunday," *Irish News*, 7 Sept. 1967, 4.
7. Especially in the H. F. West Collection, Baker Library, Dartmouth College, Hanover, New Hampshire (where Herbert West gathered many valuable papers and documents), and the University of Texas. Published collections of letters *to* Graham include the excellent, scholarly work of Cedric T. Watts, *Joseph Conrad's Letters to R. B. Cunninghame*

Graham, London, Cambridge University Press, 1969, and the earlier
W. H. Hudson's *Letters to R. B. Cunninghame Graham*, edited by
Richard Curle, London, Cockerel Press, 1941.

8. See my article "R. B. Cunningham Graham and *The Labour Elector*," *The
    Bibliotheck*, VII, No. 3, 1974, 72-5.

9. In a letter to his mother from San Antonio (3 July 1880).

10. *Modern Scottish Writers*, Edinburgh & Glasgow, William Hodge, 1917, 195-219.

11. In *Contemporary Scottish Studies*, First Series, London, Leonard Parsons, 1926,
    49-57.

12. In "Cunninghame Graham," *Library Review*, III, Winter 1932, 376-81; reprinted
    in *Coloured Spectacles*, London, Collins, 1938, 133-41.

13. In *Literature and Oatmeal*, London, George Routledge, 1935, 168-9.

14. *ibid.*, 169.

15. *Cunninghame Graham: A Centenary Study*, Glasgow, Caledonian Press, 1952, 40.

16. See James Steel Smith, "R. B. Cunningham Graham as a Writer of Short
    Fiction," *English Literature in Transition*, XII, No. 2, 1969, 61-75; and Sarah
    Stambaugh, "Towards the Short Story," Ph.D. Thesis, University of
    Minnesota, 1969, 118-19.

17. Sarah Sims Way, in "R. B. Cunninghame Graham and his Portraits of the
    Countries of the River Plate," M.A. Thesis, University of Georgia,
    1958, describes him as an "essayist with a genius for artfully retelling
    travel experiences."

18. See Laurence Davies, "R. B. Cunninghame Graham and the Concept of
    Impressionism," D.Phil. Thesis, University of Sussex, 1972.

19. In "R. B. Cunninghame Graham," *The Bookman*, London, XLIX, No. 294,
    March 1916, 174-6.

20. Several anecdotes bear retelling. The one that Frank Harris narrates in his
    biography *Bernard Shaw* (London, Victor Gollancz, 1931, 126, 129)
    shows Shaw's reaction to a piece Graham had written on the funeral
    of William Morris: "... a little masterpiece, a gem of restrained yet
    passionate feeling; absolute realistic description lifted to greatness by
    profound poetry. Shaw too was overwhelmed with admiration of
    Graham's story." Uttering the usual cliché about Graham's being an
    "amateur of genius," Harris goes on to comment: "It's a pity he hasn't
    to earn his living by his pen." "A good thing for us," cried Shaw; "he'd
    wipe the floor with us all if he often wrote like that."
        In the Introduction to *Rodeo* (p. xi), Tschiffely tells how he and
    some colleagues were discussing Graham's lack of popularity. Accord-
    ing to one cynical friend, it was because "he writes too well." This
    feeling is echoed by Ford Madox Ford in "Literary Portraits: R. B.
    Cunninghame Graham and *A Hatchment*," *Outlook*, XXXII, 20
    December 1913, 859-60. Madox Ford complains that *A Hatchment* will
    not be a success because "the public is too stupid and we writers are
    too jealous and ignorant."

21. In fact, these sketches were originally published in periodical form as early as
    1896 in *Saturday Review*.

22. Conrad chides him thus in a letter dated 9 December 1898: "You haven't
    been careful in correcting your proofs. Are you too *grand seigneur* for
    that infect labour? Surely I, twenty others, would be only too proud
    to do it for you" (*Joseph Conrad's Letters to R. B. Cunninghame Graham*,
    III).

23. In general, I have not tampered with Graham's (phonetic? careless?) efforts to

transcribe Gaelic words and names, although they are usually irregular. However, since Gaelic spelling has never been standardised, and given the lack of agreement and uniformity as to the rendering of Gaelic forms, I have on the whole left them as Graham wrote them. I am grateful to Nancy Curme for her advice on matters relating to the Gaelic language.

Section I

LANDSCAPES AND PLACES

EDITOR'S PREFACE

Cunninghame Graham embarked on his literary career by writing some notes as a guide for travellers and tourists in the district of Menteith. Many of the sketches in this section are about that area where the Graham estate at Gartmore was situated near the family burial ground on the island of Inchmahome in the Lake of Menteith.

I have included first *general* descriptive essays of the region he knew best, depicted in its various states, depending on the seasons and the weather. Then, in narrowing fashion, there are *particular* sketches about a loch, a road, a kirk, a house, a well, returning in cyclical fashion to an island (The Island of the Nuns) shrouded in the mist, the resting-place of the warrior clans of old—ready to rise again. Graham's sentimental moralising on the fate of the Scots, a people re-nowned for its fighting qualities, is a product of his late association with the Scottish nationalist movement in the last decade of his life ("Inch Cailleach" was written in 1927). Nostalgia for a return to a past and glorious Scotland, steeped in myth and legend, peopled by fairies (cf. "Tobar na Réil") and heroes, is, of course, the old man's longing for a Golden Age of Scotia, more spiritual than political. It is a fact that Scots are notoriously nostalgic, as witnessed by the annual gatherings of patriotic exiles throughout the world on Hogmanay, Burns' Night and St. Andrew's Day.

Graham's preoccupation with melancholy and death, which runs like a leit-motiv throughout his sketches, as we see in the many deathbed, funeral and graveyard scenes, may be more than a personal obsession. He would appear to suggest that it is common to a nation whose people are products of their geography and their history,[1] which in turn help to form the character of the Scottish people.

NOTES

1. On his tombstone is inscribed the Spanish proverb: "Los muertos abren los ojos a los que viven" ("The dead open the eyes of the living").

POLLYBAGLAN

Alone it stood, outside the world, remote and desolate, washed by a sea of heather, just where the sluggish Forth, meandering slowly like a stream of oil through Flanders Moss, had formed a grassy link, but not of those which, as the saying went, were worth a knight's fee in the north

In times gone by, the moss, which in most places marches with the Forth, leaving a narrow ribbon of green turf, had been drained off and floated down the stream, exposing in its place some acres of stiff clay and a dull, whitish scaur. In these the steading stood like some lacustrine dwelling on the river's edge, shut from the world by moss. Moss, moss, and still more moss, which rose piled like a snow-wreath to the west, and south, and east whilst on the north the high clay bank sank steep into the flood.

The drumly water flowed between banks of peat, through which at intervals a whitish clay peeped out, like strata in a mine. Slowly it flowed in many windings towards the sea, cutting the Flanders Moss across, receiving as it went the streams which gurgled deep below the surface of the ground, forming canyons in miniature, and issuing out to join the river through a dense growth of bulrushes, rank-growing coltsfoot, and low alder bushes. The deep black pools, on which the foam brought by the current slowly whirled round and round before it took its course down stream, were menacing in their intensity of gloom. Rarely the sun fell right upon them, and when it did its light never appeared to pierce the water, which seemed to turn it back again, as if the bottom held some mystery down in its amber depths. Perhaps in ages past some Celtic fishers, paddling their coracles, had chosen out the place to build their cottary, remote from all mankind and inaccessible. But having chosen, with the instinct of their race, they gave a name to it which, strange and incoherent to the Saxon ear, to them was typical of the chief feature of the place. Stream of the ragweed it was dubbed by the rude settlers, perhaps when all Moss Flanders was a forest stretching to the sea. And still the ragweed grew luxuriantly in the stiff soil, commemorating the keen eyes of the first settlers, although the meaning of the name had been long lost and twisted by the Anglo-Saxon tongue past recognition by the Celt.

The road, which wound about in the white clayey soil between the banks of moss which shut out the horizon, was laid on faggots, and in places drew so near the river's bank that a cart's body passing seemed to overhang the stream. Such as it was, this track was the sole link with the unquiet world which had its being on the far side of the great moss. But that the quiet of the mossland farm should not too easily be broken by swift contact with mankind, the path ran up and down to every house upon the moss, making strange zigzags and parabolas, till it emerged at last on the high road. Carts in the winter time sunk to their axles, whilst in summer horses' feet stuck in the cracks formed in the sun-baked earth.

But though the road was bad, to make communication still more difficult, at intervals rough farm gates barred the way. Hung loosely, and secured by rusty back-band chains of carts, or formed of barked and crooked oak poles stuck into horseshoes in a ragged post, they either forced you to dismount and pull laboriously each bar from its confining horseshoe, or tempted you to open them on horseback, when their schauchlin hinges and bad balance usually drove them on your horse's hocks as you essayed to pass.

When all the obstacles were overcome and you had reached your goal and slithered through the clay which formed the fields between the river and the moss, the world seemed leagues away. That is, the ancient world, in which men plough and reap and sow, watching the weather as a fisherman watches the shaking of his sail, possessed one, and real things resumed their sway, whilst agiotage and politics, with arts and sciences, fell to their proper value in the great scheme of life. The scanty crop of oats, growing like rice, in water which seemed to lie eternally in the depressions of the clay, although the dwellers in the farm averred that it "seeped bonnily awa' at the back en'," became as all-important as the Stock Exchange. The meagre turnips and potatoes, drooping and blackening with disease, between whose furrows persicaria and fumitory grew, moved one's compassion, and excited admiration for the men who, in the fight with Nature, wrung a livelihood from such unfruitful soil. Fences there naturally were none, but piles of brushwood fastened with rusty wire to crooked posts did duty for them, whilst broken ploughs and carts, which had seen weary service on the clayey roads, stood in the gaps and did as well as gates.

Some scattered drain-pipes lying in the fields looked like the relics of a battlefield of agriculture, in which the forces of the modern world had been defeated in the contest with the moss.

But road and drain-pipes, thatched farmhouse and broken fences, the stunted crop and wind-hacked ash tree growing by the farm, were but the outward signs, whilst the interior significance lay in the billowing moss, the sluggish river, and in the background of the lumpy hills, which from the steading seemed to rise sheer from the heathy sea.

Vaguely the steading and the cultivated land stood out for progress; the broken carts and twisted ploughs seemed to stretch out their hands to Charing Cross; but moss and mountain, river flowing deep, the Equisetum growing on its banks, and the sweet-gale, its leaves all wet with mist, reminded one that the forgotten past still lived in spite of us.

Deep in the soughing of the wind, waving the heath with furrows and shaking out its dry brown seeds on the black soil, came the sighs of a race whose joys were tinged with melancholy, and in the mists which crept along the faces of the hills its spirit seemed to brood, making the dwellers in the land appear as out of place as a poor Indian, dressed in a torn frock coat and with an eagle's feather stuck in a hard felt hat, looks in a frontier town.

The tussocks of the heather were not made for boots to tread upon, nor the few acres of poor soil, redeemed at many times their worth fee-simple, to be sown in a fourfold rotation, or to have top dressing and bone manure shot from an agricultural machine upon their clay. A pair of Highland garrons ought to have scratched the surface of the ground, yoked to some pristine plough by ropes which cut into their chests, or harrowed with a thorn bush, and the broken implements which lay about but seemed to accentuate the undying presence of an older world. But as the place in which a man is set to live always proves stronger than his race or creed, the dweller in the farm, though not a Highlander, had put on all the exterior and not a few of the interior graces of the Celt.

Tall and shock-headed, and freckled on the red patches of the skin which a rough crop of beard and whiskers left exposed, his eyes looked out upon the world as if he had a sort of second sight begot of whisky and of loneliness. His monstrous hands hung almost to his knees, which in their turn stuck forward in the way a horse's hock sticks back; but for all that he crossed the moss as lightly as a mountain hare springs through the snow before a collie dog. Although his feet encased in heavy boots, looked more adapted for the muddy roads which wound through his domain than for the heather, he seemed to have become, during his lifelong sojourn in the place, as light of foot as any clansman on whose feet in the old times the dun deer's hide was tied to form a moccasin. The country people said that he was "awfu' soople for his years," which may have been some five-and-forty, or, on the other hand, threescore, for nothing told his age, that he was a "lightsome traveller"—not that his travels ever carried him more than ten miles from Pollybaglan; but then with us to travel is to walk. Withal, a swimmer, an unusual thing amongst the older generation in Menteith.

"Ye ken, man laird, whiles I just dive richt to the bottom o' a linn, and set doon there; ye'd think it was the inside o' the Fairy Hill. Trooties, ye ken, and saumon, and they awfu' pike, a' comin' round ye, and they bits o' water weeds, wagging aboot like lairch trees in the blast. I mind ae time I stoppit doon nigh aboot half an hour. Maybe no just sae much, ye ken, but time gaes awfu' quick when ye're at the bottom o' a linn."

These talents and his skill in walking on the moss, together with his love of broken carts for gates, did not perhaps go far towards making him an agriculturist such as a landlord loves. But looking back into the past, although his rent was often in arrear, he laid up, so to speak, and quite unconsciously, a real treasure for his laird, which, though moth may corrupt, no thief would waste his time by breaking through to steal, as it lies gathering dust on the top shelf of some one's library.

And as the older life had entered into the body of the Lowland *bodach*,[1] making him seem a Highlander in all but speech, so had it filled the air of the oasis in the peaty moss, that the dry reeds upon the river-banks were turned to chanters, and gave out their laments for the forgotten namers of the land.

Well did they call it by the name Menteith, "the district of the moss," for moss invaded the whole strath, filling the space which once had been a sea with waves of heather and bog asphodel.[2] Stretching from Meiklewood, it kissed the Clach-nan-Lung. Lapping the edges of the hills upon the north and south shores of the heathy sea, it put a peaty bridle on the Forth, and from its depths at evening and at morn rose a white vapour which transformed it into a misty archipelago, upon whose waves the lonely steading rode, like the enchanted islands which old mariners described, only to lose again into the fog at the first shift of wind. Birch trees and firs reflected on the mirage of the mist floated like parachutes, and heath and sky were joined together by the vapoury pall which brooded on the moss, billowing and boiling as if some cauldron in the bowels of the earth was belching forth its steam. Fences were blotted out, roads disappeared, and from the moss strange noises rose, as Forth lapped sullenly up against the banks where Pollybaglan stood.

(From *Progress,* 1905)

NOTES

1. *bodach*, old man, "body"; often with vague otherworld connotations, i.e. the devil.
2. This whole area of Menteith, in which the family home of Gartmore was situated, was described by Graham in his first published book, *Notes on the District of Menteith* (1895).

MIST IN MENTEITH

Some say the name Menteith meant a peat moss in Gaelic, and certainly peat mosses fill a third of the whole vale. However that may be, its chiefest attribute is mist. Shadows in summer play on the faces of the hills, and snow in winter spreads a cold carpet over the brown moss. But the mist stays the longest with us, and under it the semi-Highland, semi-Lowland valley puts on its most familiar air.

When billowing waves wreathe round the hills, and by degrees encroach upon the low, flat moors, they shroud the district from the world, as if they wished to keep it from all prying eyes, safe and inviolate. Summer and spring and winter all have their charms, either when the faint green of the baulked vegetation of the north breaks out, tender yet vivid, or when the bees buzz in the heather in the long days of the short, nightless summer, or when the streams run noiselessly under their shroud of ice in a hard frost. The autumn brings the rain, soaking and blurring everything. Leaves blotch and blacken, then fall swirling down on to the sodden earth.

On trees and stones, from fences, from the feals upon the tops of dykes, a beady moisture oozes, making them look as if they had been frosted. When all is ready for them, the mists sweep down and cover everything. From the interior of the darkness come the cries of wild ducks, of herons as they sit upon the trees, and of geese passing overhead. Inside the wreaths of mist another world seems to have come into existence, something distinct from, and antagonistic to, mankind. When the mist once descends, blotting out the familiar features of the landscape, leaving perhaps the Rock of Stirling floating in the air, the three black trees upon the bare rock of the Fairy Hill growing from nothing, or the peak of the Cobbler, seeming to peer above enormous mountain ranges, though in reality nothing more vast than the long shoulder of Ben Lomond intervenes, the change has come that gives Menteith its special character.

There are mists all the world over, and in Scotland in particular; mists circling round the Western Islands, filling the glens and boiling in the corries of the hills; mists that creep out to sea or in towards the land from seawards, threatening and dreadful-looking; but none like ours, so impalpable and strange, and yet so fitting to our low, flat mosses with our encircling hills. In older days they sheltered the marauders from the north, who in their gloom fell on the valley as if they had sprung from the night, plundered and burned and harried, and then retreated under cover of the mist, back to their fastnesses.

As they came through the Glen of Glenny, or the old road behind Ben Dhu, which comes out just a little east of Invertrossachs, when the wind blew aside the sheltering wreaths of steam, and the rare gleams of sun fell on the shaggy band, striking upon the heads of their Lochaber axes, and again shifted and covered them from sight, they must have seemed a phantom army, seen in a dream, just between consciousness and sleep.

The lake, with its three islands, its giant chestnuts, now stag-headed and about to fall, the mouldering priory,[1] the long church with its built-up, five-light window, the castle, overgrown with brushwood, and with a tree springing up from the middle hall, the heronry, the rope of sand the fairies twisted, which would have made a causeway to the island had they not stopped just in the nick of time, the single tree that marks the gallows, and the old churchyard of the Port, all these the mist invests with a peculiar charm that they lack when the sun shines and shows them merely mouldering ruins and decaying trees.

So with the Flanders Moss. It, too, in mist seems to roll on for miles; its heathy surface turns to long waves that play against the foot of the low range of hills, and beat upon Craigforth as if it were an island in the sea. Through wreaths of steam, the sullen Forth winds in and out between the peat hags, and when a slant of wind leaves it clear for an instant it looks mysterious and dark, as might a stream of quick-silver running down from a mine. When a fish leaps, the sound re-echoes like a bell, as it falls back into the water, and rings spread out till they are lost beneath the banks.

After a day or two of gloom, life begins somehow or another to be charged with mystery; and, walking through the woods, instinctively you look about half in alarm as a roe bounds away, or from a fir-tree a capercailzie drums or flies off with a noise as if a moose was bursting through the trees.

Peat smoke floats through the air from cottages a mile away, acrid and penetrating, and fills the nostrils with its scent. The little streams run with a muffled tinkle as if they wished to hide away from sight. Rank, yellow ragweeds on their banks, bowed down with the thick moisture, all hang their heads as if they mourned for the lost sunshine and the day. Now and then leaves flutter down slowly to the ground like dying butterflies. Over the whole earth hangs, as it were, a sounding-board, intensifying everything, making the senses more acute, and carrying voices from a distance, focussed to the ear.

So through our mists a shepherd's dog barking a mile off is heard as loudly as if it were a yard or two away, although the sound comes slowly to the hearing, as when old-fashioned guns hung fire and the report appeared to reach one through a veil. Thus does the past, with its wild legends, the raiders from the north, the Broken Men, the Saxon's Leap, the battles of the Grahams and the McGregors, come down to us veiled by the mist of time. In the lone church-yards, whose grass is always damp the whole year round, whose earth, when a new grave is dug, is always wet, so wet that not a stone rolls from it to the grass. The tombstones, with the lettering overgrown with lichens, only preserve the names of the old enemies who now lie side by side, in a faint shadowy way. The sword that marks the resting-place of the men of the most turbulent of all the races of that borderland is usually only the shadow of a sword, so well the mist has done its work, rounding off edges and obliterating chisel marks.

Boats on the Loch o' the Port, with oars muffled by the cloud of vapour that broods upon the lake, glide in and out of the thick curtain spread between the earth and sky, the figure of the standing fisher in the stern looming gigantic as he wields his rod in vain; for, in the calm, even the water-spiders leave a ripple as they run. In the low, mossy "parks" that lose themselves in beds of bulrushes before they join the lake, the Highland cattle stand at gaze, the damp congealing on their coats in whitish beadlets, and horses hang their heads disconsolately, for no matter in what climate they are born, horses are creatures of the sun. Under the shroud of gloom it seems that something strange is going on, something impalpable that gives the valley of Menteith its own peculiar air of sadness, as if no summer sun, no winter frost, no fierce March winds, or the chill cold of April, could ever really dry the tears of moisture that it lays up under the autumn mist. So all our walls are decked with a thick coating of grey lichen on the weather side that looks like flakes of leather, and on the lee side with a covering of bright, green moss.

Thatch moulders, and from it springs a growth of vegetation; a perpetual dripping from the eaves opens a little rill below it, in which the pebbles glisten as in a mountain stream.

Along the roads the scanty traffic rumbles fitfully, and on the Sabbath, down the steep path towards the little church, knots of fantastic figures seem to stalk like threatening phantoms. When they draw near, one sees that they were but the familiar faces of McKerrochar of Cullamoon, Graham of Tombreak, Campbell of Rinaclach, and Finlay Mitchell, dressed in their Sunday clothes. They pass the time of day, daunder a little in the damp kirkyard, so heaped with graves they have to pick their way between them just as sheep pick their way and follow one another on a steep mountain path, or when they cross a burn.

Although their talk runs on their daily life—the price of beasts at the last market or the tryst, upon bad seasons and the crops, all in the compassed and depreciatory vein characteristic of their calling and their race, they once have been fantastic figures towering above the dry-stone dykes that edge the road. That glory nothing can take away from them, or from the valley where they dwell.

Nothing is stable. Snows melt and rain gives place to sun, and sun to rain again; spring melts into summer, then autumn blends insensibly with winter, and the year is out. Men come and go, the Saxon speech replaces Gaelic; even traditions insensibly are lost.

The trees decay and fall, then they lie prone like the great hollow chestnut trunks, blackened by tourists' fires, in Inchmahome. Our hills and valleys all have changed their shapes under the action either of fire or ice. Life, faiths, ideals, all have changed. The Flanders Moss that was a sea is now crossed by a railway and by innumerable roads. What, then, shall we, who have seen mists rising up all our lives, feared them as children, loved them in riper years, cling to, but mist?

Refuge of our wild ancestors, moulder of character, inspirer of the love of mystery, chief characteristic of Celtic mind, spirit that watches over hills and valleys, lochs, clachans, *bealachs* and shaggy baadans, essence compounded of the water of the sky and earth, impalpable, dark and threatening, Fingal and Bran and Ossian, and he who in outstretching Ardnamurchan strung his harp to bless the birlinn of Clanranald, all have disappeared in thy grey folds.[2]

Whether thou art death stealing amongst us, veiled, or life concealed behind a curtain, or but an emanation from the ground, which the poor student, studying in Aberdeen, working by day upon the wharves and poring over books at night, can explain as easily as he can solve all other mysteries, with his science primer, who shall say?

All that I know is that when the mantle of the damp rolls down upon us, battling with the rough oak copse upon Ben Dearch or Craigmore till all is swallowed up and a smooth surface stretches out over what, but half an hour before, was a thick wood of gnarled and secular trees that stood like piles stand up in an embankment, eaten by the sea, the mist has conquered.

Somehow, I think, its victory brings a sense of rest.

(From *A Hatchment*, 1913)

NOTES

1. Graham is referring here to the Lake of Menteith, in which is situated the island of Inchmahome where Graham and his wife Gabriela are buried in the ruined Augustinian priory.
2. Fingal is the hero of the poem of the same name in the spurious *Works of Ossian* by James MacPherson, published in 1760 and 1762. Fingal is based on the legendary Celtic hero Fionn mac Cumhail, the poet Ossian was supposedly his son, and Bran was Fionn's dog.

SNOW IN MENTEITH

All the familiar landmarks were obliterated. The Grampians and the Campsies had taken on new shapes. Woods had turned into masses of raw cotton, and trees to pyramids of wool, with diamonds here and there stuck in the fleece. The trunks of beeches stood out black upon the lee, and on the weather side were coated thick with snow as hard as sugar on a cake. The boughs of firs and spruces swayed gently up and down under the weight of snow, which bent them towards the ground.

Birches were covered to their slenderest twigs with icicles. Only the larches, graceful and erect, were red, for on their feathery branches snow could find no resting-place. On the rough bark and knotted trunks of oak trees feathery humps bulged out, through which protruded shoots with sere brown leaves still clinging to them, and on them ruffled birds sat moping, twittering in the cold.

A new and silent world, born in a night, had come into existence, and over it brooded a hush, broken but by the cawing of the crows, which fabulated as they flew, perhaps upon the strangeness of the pervading white.

Even in Eden, in the days before man's fall and woman's motherhood, all was not purer than the fields and moors under their burden of the carpet formed of the myriad scintillating flakes.

But in the copses and the shaws of oak and birch a change had come, more wondrous even than the transformation of a piece of rough grey coral, as it sinks prismatic and transfigured by the waves, dropped gently from a boat upon the beach of a sunlit lagoon.

The trees, congealed and tense, stood silent, quivering and eager for the embrace of the keen frost, their boughs all clad first with a thistle-down of cold, and then towards the tips with diamonds fashioned to their shape through which the shadow of their bark just faintly gleamed, whilst, here and there, there sparkled facets rarer and brighter than the gems of the Apocalypse. A murmur born of stillness lost itself against the blackness of a clump of firs, and yet was all apparent and persisting, as if the spirit of the frost, looking out from the north, was murmuring a self-approving blessing on his work. The sharp air hung the breath in a grey cloud against the sky. Nature was silent, and a rabbit, loping through the bush, stirred the soft echoes of the frost-nipped weeds, leaving behind a trail which seemed gigantic, with its brown markings made by the impress of his furry feet melting the new-fallen snow. In the dark woodland burns the wreaths blocked all the streams, and in the silent pools, congealed and swept clean by the wind, the little trout loomed twice their natural size in the refracted light which penetrated through the ice. The roe-deer and the hares, and

the great capercailzies, sending a shower of sparkling particles from the dark fir
trees when they took their flight, seemed to have come into their own inheritance; and woodmen, plodding heavily, their axes thrust beneath their armpits,
their hands deep buried in their pockets, looked like interlopers strayed from a
pantomine into the transformation scene of frost. The wind amongst the sedges
of the shallow pool in the sequestered clearing, where the rabbit-eaten ash copse
straggled close to the water's edge, discoursed the only music of the spheres to
which our ears are tuned, and whistled in the rowans, swinging their hanging
spathes of bark against their boles for its accompaniment.

Out on the hummocks of the withered grass it caught the frosted bracken,
twirling it round and round upon itself, and leaving at the roots a circle in the
snow which seemed the footprint of some strange new northern animal,
brought by the magic of the night from the far realms of frost.

And as the hills and woods had all become unrecognisable, the mantle of
pure white spread on the earth formed a blank page on which nothing could stir
without a record of its passage being writ at least as permanently as was the
passage of its life.

Badgers, who had adventured out for food, left their strange, bear-like
tracks in woods where no one had suspected that they lived. Roe, plunging
through the crisp white snow, made a round hole marked at the bottom with
their cloven feet, and leaving at the edge a faint red trace of blood.

The birds, in their degree, imprinted traces clear and distinct as those their
ancestors have left in rocks from the time when the world was all a snowfield or
all tropics, or all something different from what it is, as wise geologists, quarrel-
ling with each other as if they were theologians, write in ponderous tomes.

Even the fieldmice, pattering along, left tiny trails like little railways as they
journeyed from their warm nests to visit one another and interchange opinions
on the strange new scene.

Round holly-trunks sat rabbits, mere brown balls of fur, eating the bark and
scuffling to and fro, leaving well-beaten paths towards their burrows, at whose
mouth some sat and washed their faces in the snow.

Across the frozen pond, upon whose surface lay a thin rime of frost, a fox
had left his footsteps, frozen hard, mysterious as fresh Indian signs found by some
solitary hunter on the head waters of the Río Gila, and as ominous. Birds as they
flew threw shadows deeper than at noonday on the sand, so deep they seemed to
bite into the snow, as if it were determined that no living thing should pass above
it and not leave its mark.

But as the desert is an open book to the Indian tracker, who remarks the
passage of each living thing in the faint marks it leaves upon the grass, so did the
snow reveal all secrets to the most inexperienced eye.

Even when it had cleared away, the grass remained black and downtrodden,
and looked burned by every footstep that had passed.

But if it changed the woods to palaces of silver and of diamonds, the hills to
Alpine ranges, and the fields to vast white chessboards, blotting out the roads,

which it filled solid to the hedges, what a change it wrought upon the moss! The Flanders Moss that once had been a sea became an ocean, for as the peat-hags and the heather turned to waves, and as the sun lit up their tips with pink, they seemed to roll as if they wished once more to wash the skirts of the low foothills of the carse. Foaming and billowing along, they turned the brown peat moss, set with its bushes of bog-myrtle and lean, wiry-growing heather, into an Arctic sea—a waste of desolation, brilliant and desolate, and upon which the sun reflected with a violet tinge. As the waves seemed to surge around the stunted pines and birches, all looked dead, extinct, and as remote from man as when the Roman legions camping on the edge of the great moss constructed their lone camp, last outpost of the world on this side of the Thule of the frowning Grampians to the north. As night fell slowly on the drear expanse of white, Ben Lomond, catching the last reflection of the setting sun, turned to a cone of fire, and at its foot the pine woods of Drummore stood out intense and dark as if cut out of blackened cardboard, and by degrees the hills and woods melted away into a vapoury mist.

Then from the bosom of the moss came a hoarse croaking, as a heron, rising slowly into the keen night air, after his day of unproductive fishing by the black frozen pools of the slow Forth, flapped heavily away.

(From *Progress*, 1905)

LOCHAN FALLOCH

Brown billowing woods spring from the rising ground beyond the lake. The lake itself is set in fir woods on three sides, and on the other bounded by a wild moor.

Almost all round it stretches a pebbly beach, broken by beds of bulrushes, which now and then rise from a mossy patch between the stones. Islands with ruins of the past stud its smooth surface, and are reflected upside down, as in a looking-glass reversed. The woods, chiefly of beech, appear like outworks thrown before the hills to guard their mysteries. Rough, roaring burns here and there cut a passage to the lake and brawl between banks fringed with rowan trees and ash. After the woods are passed, a further outwork of wet boggy ground, in which grow willows and sweet-gale, extends.

This by degrees melts into a dull waste of ling, strewed with great boulders of rough pudding-stone. The heath grows sparser higher up, where the wind sweeps upon it all the year. Then it gives place to tracts of stones. Lastly, the hill rising up steep from the last slope is reached, and following a burn until it issues from a green mossy "well," you stand upon the ridge.

There, a panorama stretches out, studded with lakes, with woods, and interspersed with farms towards the west. Towards the east lies the brown Flanders Moss, an ancient sea, which even yet appears to roll in the white mist of evening. The whole is framed in ranges of long undulating hills, which guard the south.

Northwards, the Grampians, still mysterious and wild, tower up, in peaks, in castles, and in serrated ridges, through which the passes, now disused, formerly penetrated.

Standing upon the topmost ridge, and quite invisible from any other point, quite unsuspected, lost, almost forgotten by the outer world, is hid a little lake.

It is indeed a little hidden loch, lying so deep and unsuspected in its hollow between hills that the first Celt or Pict who came upon it, ages ago, must straight have hit upon the name it bears. Nature seems, now and then, to have suspected that a time would come when all her secrets would lie bare and open to the prying eye of vulgar curiosity, and to have hid away some of her chiefest beauties in places where they are in sanctuary, hallowed from human gaze, which at the same time worships and violates them. So, she set this her little gem, remote, hiding it as a hind conceals her young, deep in the heather, underneath the tallest bracken, and in a wilderness of hills. They tower on every side, bare, bald, and wind-swept, whilst in a corrie nestles the little lake, upon whose surface the wind scarcely or never preys, leaving it calm, mysterious, and unruffled, as if it held some secret, too natural for us to understand. If fairies still exist, they come, no doubt, from the Sith Bruach[1] which guards the Avon Dhu at Aberfoyle, and sail their boats of acorn-cups and leaves on the black lakelet. Upon the little beach they run their craft ashore and dance on the broad ribbon of smooth sand which rings the lake, as a black mezzotint is edged around with white. But if the fairies come, they come unseen, leaving no token of their passage but a few turned-up leaves which they have used for boats, and the mysterious circlet of white foam they churn, which hangs between the fringe of bulrushes and the mimic surf in which float flies that have ventured further than their wings can bear them, and now wash up and down, as in some distant island of the South Seas drowned mariners may drift upon the beach. Sunk in its hollow far from the world, the tarn seems to have been left adrift, a derelict floated down to us from some older age, and with one's eyes closed one can see strange animals of monstrous size come down the steep hillsides and drink and play, throwing about the water as they stand knee-deep. Around its banks grows Equisetum, as if to point back to a time when different vegetation, gigantic and distorted, towered by its edge, and in which harboured the strange beasts that must have been familiar to its shores.

Light-footed tribesmen, as they drove the *creagh*[2] from the fat Lowlands to their hungry hills, must have stopped by the lake to slake their thirst, prone on their breasts their rough red beards floating like seaweed on the water as they drank. Even in summer, when bees hum in the heather, and the scent of peat fresh cast and left to dry perfumes the air, and little moss-trout bask in the tiny stream that issues from the lake, or dart amongst its stones, there broods an air as of aloofness from mankind. Over the corrie which the water fills, leaving but little ground between it and the hills except at one end, where a long-forgotten, perhaps Fingalian, mountain trail is still half visible on the stones which lie amongst the ling, the wind sweeps softly, and the water-spiders, with greater faith than Peter's, walk on the surface of the lake so lightly that they hardly leave a shadow as they pass.

In winter, when the wind laments aloud for the lost sun, and the dark water of the lochan turns to black ice, whilst the white foam congealed clings round the stalks of the dead bulrushes, and all the heather droops in the keen frost, the scene is wild and threatening, as if the spirits of the past kept watch over the last of their possessions that had remained untouched. Then, in spite of the keen cold, the birds and animals all venture out, certain that they are safe, at least from man, and leave strange tracks amongst the snow, which form a chart of them and of their habits, readable but to those whose eyes have not been rendered dim by poring upon print.

Even in snow and cold, and when the wind drives all the grass and heather crouching to the ground, and when the little fish rise to the air-holes in the trans-lucent ice to breathe, and nature seems to wither in the frost, there yet remains over the *lochan dhu* an air as of content, amidst the desolation of the hills.

Whether the breeze just curls the water, or drives a dust of particles of frozen snow along the surface of the ice; whether the cotton-grass waves silkily and the bog-asphodels spring from the peat and the green "wells" are bright with mosses, or the fieldmice play hide-and-seek between the stalks of the stiff frozen grasses, the lochlet seems to smile as enigmatically as does the Sphinx, showing itself in full communion with the past. It smiles, like a fair woman who hides a guilty secret—for knowledge, especially of happiness that is not shared with others, must be guilt, and to withhold it from us, who seek it all our lives, is surely criminal—that is, if the lake's secret were not beyond our reach, removed out of our ken, by its sheer innocence. As you look down from the ridge, watching the black tarn sleeping in the heather, you see that what it holds is not for us, and that the sighing of the wind, which to it is a language comprehended, clear and sympathetic to its soul, to us serves but to stir the senses, and you turn away despairing, watching a heron or a gull enter at once into the fellowship, outside of which we stand.

It might be that at night, when the moon silvers all the waters, and mist enshrouds the hills, calling out from the grass and mosses their secret perfume; when roe steal from the copses browsing so timidly about the open patches of green herbage, scattered like islands through the heath; when dark grey moths flutter about the edges of the lake, that if a child dared venture up to the lone tarn, its eyes might open and behold a wondrous world of fairies, and it would understand all that the rustling of the wind amongst the heather really means. But if it did so, either it would turn rank poet and be damned amongst its fellows, or be snatched away to dwell for ever in some fairy hill, remote from man, seeing the world as in a *camera obscura*, with people running to and fro like ants in a perpetual gloom. No child will venture; the spell will not be broken, and the black, little loch will remain hidden from men's hearts, lost in forgetfulness, just as it was intended that it should be lost by Nature, when she hid it in the hills.

(From *Faith,* 1909)

NOTES

1. Or *Sith Bruach* or *Sith-Bhrugh*, the Fairy Hill, to which he refers also in *Notes on the District of Menteith*.
2. *creagh*, booty or plunder. Closely connected is a similar word *creaght*, i.e. nomadic cattle, which is what Graham means here. The implication, however, is that the cattle, in many cases, were stolen anyway.

THE CRAW ROAD*

All roads are said to lead to Rome. This may be so, of course, if a man follows them right round the world. Some, though, lead you to realms in which the materialism of the City of the Seven Hills has not and never had a place.

Upon them no legionary in his *caligulae*[1] and with his conquering spade upon his back has ever marched. The roads he traversed led straight to some place or another, over the tops of hills, across the rivers, passing morasses, cutting the valleys, and right across the plain, just as the state that paid him made its way to fame regardless of the feelings of the world. My road was traced originally by homing crows. Men saw them fly, and thought that where they came from there must be something worth their while to see. That was before the coming of the legionaries. The world was full of interest in those days, for fairies played upon the heathery knolls, elves sat upon the toadstools, and the white Caledonian cattle roamed the woods. The spirit of adventure was at least as strong as now, for anyone who left his home to travel, even a little way, where he had never been before, plunged into the unknown. To-day the difficulty is not that there is not a sufficiency of roads, but that there are too many Romes. This difficulty did not beset the builders of the road I write about.

Following the flight of crows across the hills, they first of all laid a few faggots in the miry places, secured a coracle or two by streams too deep to cross, and, taking in their hands a club or a stone battle-axe, set out across the hills. Thus the road they traced in times gone by is made on other principles than those in use to-day. Twisting round obstacles and in and out between the moors, skirting the base of hills, and now and then coming back upon itself in places where the first road-makers no doubt sat down to rest, it winds upon its way.

Campseyan chiefs, and then Fingalians, have passed along it in their light deerskin brogues. In places, short cuts, now long disused, still shine amongst the heath, showing stones polished by the feet of ancient forayers. Into recesses of green hills, now out again and then running along the sides of streams, it winds and penetrates. No road I know, not even that between Mendoza and San Felipe de los Andes across the stony slopes of Uspallata, where in the tempests stones roll along like leaves, is lonelier, more desolate, or looks more hostile to mankind than this wild Scottish Trail.

By rights the road should lead to nowhere in particular, but finish off in some impenetrable morass or in some corrie of the hills. That would indeed be a

* The name was originally the Cró Road, Cró in Gaelic meaning cattle. It was
corrupted into "Craw," in the Lowland speech (Graham's footnote).

crows' road, and far more interesting than the majority of roads that lead to places no one has any wish to go to, except the people who are born there and cannot get away.

This is what the Craw Road should really be if it were perfect. But, as it is, it winds about the mist-filled hollows and wild hills, on which feed black-faced sheep, and passes now and then a lone farmhouse, white and four-square, with purple slates, its stack of peats at one end, cheese-stone before the door, its fank for sheep-washing, and with a woman in a short striped petticoat vigorously thumping the blankets in the burn, and crooning out a song. It leads through realms of heath and grass unchanged, save for a sheep-drain here and there, since the beginning of the world, until it reaches one of the rare, old Scottish mansion-houses, left from an older age.

Miles from a railway station and jammed against the flank of a steep range of hills, between a melancholy little tarn, in which feed tench, and a thick wood, it stands alone and solitary. The grey peel-tower, with battlements either for defence or else to show its owner was a gentleman, stands sentinel beside a square, grey house, with steep-pitched roof and corbie steps, and with a low front door set in a roll-and-fillet moulding, opening upon the road.

The stone above the door sets forth the year of grace in which the builders rested from their task. The narrow ribbon of grey flags in front is mossed and honeycombed by time. The grass which surges up, close to the avenue, leaving a narrow space in which to turn a carriage, right before the door, has that peculiar sour and scanty look of an old pasture when only grazed by sheep. In the dank fields, which we in Scotland dignify as "parks," the trees are mostly all stag-headed, and the tall spruces on the weather side hold out bare arms, not dead, but stripped and polished by the blast like ancient ivory. Moss has spread out over the avenue, not like a carpet, but with the look of a disease, and in a corner of the grounds the ribs and trucks of an old cotton mill, built as a speculation a hundred years ago, add to the loneliness, by giving, as it were, an air of having perished in the fight with time and destiny.

The long, dank mill-lead which once set the machinery astir is silted up, in places fallen in, and, though long years have passed since it did anything but breed innumerable frogs, is still an eyesore, Nature having steadfastly refused to take it to herself and veil its ugliness.

Smoke curls unwillingly from the chimneys of the house, to be so soon absorbed in mist it leaves one doubtful whether it is smoke, or but damp floating from the trees. Squirrels and rabbits have come into their own, and look at you as on a trespasser, and from the woods even at midday roe venture forth and play. The heron's cry sounds lively, and the tinkling of the burn hidden beneath the bushes of the shrubbery almost oppressive in the deep solitude. All must look magical in the silence of the stars, when the moon ghostens in the trees, and owls float noiselessly about or pass the time of night in their long melody, from holly-bush to old Scotch fir, their cries re-echoing from the turrets of the house and sounding on the lake.

Then the tall pine trees, which throng about the little urn bearing the inscription "Haec loca cum peregrinis pinis exornavit, A.G.S.,"[2] and the date 1845, compare their notes about the flight of time, whispering uncannily. Hemlocks and Douglasses must then vie with one another, and the sequoias vaunt their stature, whilst trembling deodaras shyly claim the palm of grace from all the fellowship. Long, tapering branches, looking fingerlike and human, must be agitated, waking the birds and squirrels by their movement. And if the raiser of the urn could see the trees he planted so many years ago, now grown majestic in their age, he would indeed plume himself on his Latin and his faith, in having planted them.

Martial and angular, his frosty whiskers curling round his chin, his silver snuff-box in his hand, it is not likely that the planter of the trees ever went out at night to hear them whispering, or watch the moonbeams playing on their boughs, silent and silvery. But had he done so, standing by his urn, he would have looked as much in keeping with the scene as any one of them.

Time had been impotent to bow or mellow him; so he stood still defiant, like an old ash grown on stony ground that stretches out its boughs to meet the elements. The suns of the Peninsula, in whose wars he passed his youth, the storms of politics and of religious controversy of his middle age, had but intensified his proud, unyielding soul, and made him bitter. Perhaps the one soft corner in his heart was to the trees, now grown so beautiful and so luxuriant (after he was dead), to whom, in sure and certain hope that Nature would perform her unconscious miracle, he raised his little urn. One fain would hope that when at night, released from the presence of mankind, they whisper in the breeze, his memory is cherished, and that these foreign pines, which do indeed adorn the spot on which they grow, say now and then to one another, "Do you remember that day, long ago, when we all lay together on a cart, and the stern, white-haired, eagle-eyed old man who set us in the ground?" Meanwhile they wave and whisper, tall and beautiful, their branches covering the little burn which I remember in my youth running through a grass slope on which stood some young trees at varying intervals.

The hand that planted them is long decayed, and the old place sleeps in its corrie with something ghostly hanging over it, even in midday.

Through the rough hills, across the moors, passing the isolated white farmhouses, winds the way that leads to it; and overhead the crows caw hoarsely, and seem to say to one another when a rare traveller passes by, "There goes a man upon our road."

(From *Charity*. 1912)

NOTES

1. *caligulae*, small military boots worn by Roman soldiers.
2. "He adorned this place with foreign pines." A.G.S. could be an abbreviation of
   Ad Gloriam Suam—To his (own) honour and glory. It could also be
   the initials of an older cousin, Alexander G. Speirs of Culcreuch, by
   Fintry. (See "The Colonel" [*Charity*] for a portrait of him.) Annie
   Speirs, a dear cousin, was a great comfort to Mrs. Bontine and her
   three sons, when Major Bontine was confined to Eccles House in
   Dumfriesshire as a result of a mental breakdown due to an old military
   head injury. Aunt Annie (of Culcreuch) also owned a home in Moffat
   where the boys stayed occasionally to be close to their father. (See
   "Beattock for Moffat" [*Success*] in Section VI of this volume.)

THE GREY KIRK

In a grey valley between hills, shut out from all the world by mist and moors, there lies a village with a little church.

The ruined castle in the reedy loch, by which stand herons fishing in the rank growth of flags, of bulrush and hemp-agrimony which fringes it, is scarcely greyer than the hills. The outcrop of the stone is grey, the louring clouds, the slated roofs, the shingly river's bed and the clear water of the stream. The very trout that dart between the stones, or hang suspended where the current joins the linn, look grey as eels.

Green markings on the moors show where once paths, which the border prickers followed on their wiry nags, led towards the south, the land of fatted beeves and well-stored larders, clearly designed by Providence or fate to be the jackman's prey, but long disused, forgotten and grassed over, though with the ineffaceable imprint of immemorial use still clear.

Dark, geometrical plantations of black fir and spruce deface the hills, which nature evidently made to bear a coat of scrubby oak and birch. Wire fences gird them round, the posts well tarred against the weather, and the barbed wire so taut that the fierce winds might use them as Aeolian harps, could they but lend themselves to song.

A district which the wildness of the past has so impressed, that the main line of railway steals through its corries and across its moors as it were under protest, and where the curlew mocks the engine's whistle with his wilder cry.

The village clusters round the kirk, as bees crowd round their queen, the older houses thatched. Their coping-stones carved with a rope, remain to show how, in the older world, their rustic architects secured their roofs against the blast.

No doubt the hamlet grew between the castle and the church—the jackman of the chief, the sacristan and kindly tenants of the church, ready and near at hand to put on splent and spur, and able to take lance or spring of hyssop in their hand at the first tinkle of the bell or rout of horn.

The castle in the loch has dwindled to a pile of stones, from which spring alders, birches and sycamores, whose keys hang yellow in the wind, unlocking nothing but the sadness of the heart, which marks their growth, from the decay of the abandoned keep.

A modern mansion set with its shrubberies and paltry planted woods, where once the Caledonian forest sheltered the wild white cattle in its glades, seems out of place in the surrounding grey. Its lodge, with trim-cut laurels and with aucubas and iron gate, run in a foundry from a mould, is trivial, comfortable and modern. And the low sullen hills appear to scorn it in their fight with time, for they remain unchanged from the bold time of rugging and of rieving, when spearsmen, not a pensioned butler, kept the gate.

The crumbling and decayed stone wall, secluding jealously the boggy meadows of the park, shuts off the modern mansion with its electric light, its motor-cars, its liveried servants and its air of castellated meanness, from the old houses huddling in the wynd. They look towards the chapel with its high-pitched roof, its squat round tower with crenellated top and its sharp windows pointed like a lance. It seems to gaze at them, as if it felt they were the only links that time has left it with its old own world. The eye avoids the modern buildings in the town, the parish church, four-square and hideous, with windows like a house, and from the hills falls on the chapel and is satisfied. Only in some old missal, with the illustrations by some monk adscribed to his small round of daily cares, can you behold its equal, as it stands desolate and grey.

The chapel of a race of warriors, men dark and grey as is the stone of which its walls are built, once a lone outpost of the great mother fort in Rome, it lingers after them, sheltering their tombs and speaking of their fame. Instinctively one feels that once its doors stood open, just as it were a mosque or church in lands where faith continues the whole week, and men pray as they eat or sleep, just when they feel inclined, and naturally as birds.

In the green churchyard, whose grassy hillocks wave it like a sea, the long grey tombstones of the undistinguished dead appear like boats that make towards some haven, laying their courses by the beacon of the tower.

The church itself floats like a ship turned bottom upwards on the grassy sea. Its voyage is ended, and the men who once clattered in armour in its aisles and through its nave now sleep below its flags. A maimed ritual and a sterner creed prevail, and those who worship in the church have shown their faith by laying down encaustic tiles over the spur-marked stones on which their forebears jingled in their mail. A fair communion table of hewn stone, smug and well-finished and with the wounds upon the bleeding heart all stanched (as one would think), stands where the altar stood, cold and uninteresting, a symbol of the age. *Non ragioniam*;[1] on every side, lie those who, in their time, carried their wars across the border, and on the bridge at Rome charged on the people who pressed round them, just as they would have charged in Edinburgh, had any other clan presumed to take the croon of the old causeway of the High Street, and brought upon themselves an excommunication from the Pope.

Stretched under canopies of stone they lie, looking so grim and so impenitent, that one is sure they must be satisfied with their presentments, if looking down on their old haunts, they see their images. Many are absent who would have filled a niche right worthily, Tineman[2] and the Black Knight of Jedburgh[3] and others of the house, who, in their time, shook Scotland to the core. But in the middle of the aisle, in leaden caskets hooped with iron and padlocked, lie two hearts. One, that of Archibald who belled the cat,[4] the other heart has travelled much, and in its life beat higher with all generous thoughts than any of its race.[5]

He who possessed it (or was possessed by it), liked ever better, as he said, to hear the laverocks' singing than the cheeping of the mouse. His hands were able, all his adventurous life, to keep his cheeks from scars, as he averred in Seville to the Spanish knight, who wondered at their absence from his face. Carrying a heart to Palestine, he fell, not in the Holy Land, but on the frontiers of Granada, that last outpost of the Eastern world.[6] The heart he carried lies at Melrose, and his own, sealed fast in lead, soldered perhaps in some wild camp lost in the *ajarafe* of Sevilla,[7] is the chief ornament of the grey chapel of his race.

Set like a ship, the chapel lies in the long waves of sullen hill and moor that roll away towards the south.

In its long voyage through the sea of time, crews of wild warriors have clung to it, as their one refuge from the spear of life. Each in their turn have fallen away, leaving it lonely, but still weather-tight and taut—a monument of faith, as some may think, or of good masonry and well-slaked lime, as the profane may say, still sailing on the billowy moors which stretch towards Muirkirk—so little altered that any one of those who in the past have prayed within its walls, if he returned to a changed world, would cling to it as the one thing he knew.

So it drifts on upon its voyage through time, bearing its freight of warriors to their port.

(From *His People,* 1906)

NOTES

1. Or *non ragioniamo.* "We do not reason or discuss."
2. Archibald Douglas ("Tineman") who died in the terrible defeat of the Scots by Edward III at Halidon Hill (1333).
3. Sir James Douglas, "the Good," sometimes known by the family name as the Black Douglas, immortalised in verse and legend for his punitive expeditions.
4. Archibald, the 5th Earl of Angus, who imprisoned James III in Edinburgh Castle (1482).
5. Sir James Douglas was asked by Bruce to take his heart to the Holy Land, in fulfilment of a vow that Bruce was never able to keep, i.e. to go on a crusade.
6. Douglas was killed not in the Holy Land but in Spain.
7. *ajarafe,* an expanse of high land.

THE LAROCH

The grass-grown-over "founds" and the grey crumbling dry-stone walls of what had been a house stood in an island of bright, close-grown grass. About the walls sprang nettles and burdocks, and in the chinks mulleins stood out like torches, veritable hag-tapers to light the desolation of the scene. Herb robin, and wild pelargonium, with pink mallows, straggled about the ruined garden walls. A currant bush, all run to wood, with grozets and wild rasps, still strove against neglect. In the deserted long-kail patch, heather and bilberries had resumed their sway. Under the stunted ash, a broken quern and a corn-beetling stone, grown green with moss, spoke of a time of life and animation, simple and primitive, but fitting to the place. On every side the stone-strewn moor stretched to the waters of the loch, leaving a ridge of shingle on the edge. The hills were capped with mist that lifted rarely, and only in the summer evenings or in the winter frosts were clear and visible. Firs, remnants of the Caledonian forest, sprang from the rocky soil and stood out stark, retiring sentinels of the old world—the world in which they, the white cattle, the wild boar and wolf, were fellow-dwellers, and from which they lingered to remind one of the others who had disappeared. The birch trees rustled their laments, sadder than those of earthly chanters, or of the strains of a scarce-heard strathspey coming down through the glens with the west wind. The rowans on the little stony tumuli showed reddening berries, as they turned their silvery leaves towards Loch Shiel. All was sad, wild, and desolate, the soft warm rain drawing up from the ground a mist, which met the mist descending from the sky, and hung a curtain over the rocks, the strath, the loch, and everything, and glistened greyly on the wet leaves of trees. A leaden sky, seen vaguely through the rain, and broken to the west by "windows," seemed to shut out the narrow glen from all the world, confining it in plates of lead—lead in the skies, and in the waters of the loch.

Desolation reigned where once was life, and where along the loch smoke had ascended, curling to heaven humbly from the shielings thatched with reeds, with heather, and with whins, the thatch kept down with birchen poles fastened with stones, and on whose roofs the corydalis and the house-leek sprang from the flauchter feals. But now no acrid peat reek made the eyes water, or pervaded heart and soul, with the nostalgia of the North—that North ungrateful, hard, and whimsical, but lovable and leal, where man grows like the sapucaia nut, hard rinded, rough, and angular, but tender at the core. All, all were gone—gone to far Canada, or to the swamps and the pine-barrens of the Carolinas, to Georgia, to New Zealand; nothing but Prionsa Tearleach's monument, set like a lighthouse on the shores of a dead sea, the sea of failure, seemed to remind one that the pibroch once resounded through the glens. Heather and tormentil, with cotton-grass, that seemed to have preserved the feather of some bird extinct for ages, eye-bright and knapweed, hare-bells and golden rod, Prunella, meadow-sweet, with the bog-asphodel on the green springy turf near swamps, and foxgloves in the woods, all bloomed, and thought not on the departed children who had plucked them when the strath held men. It may be that the plants regretted the lost children's hands that gathered them, and were their only mourners, for thought must linger somewhere, if only amongst flowers.

In the old plough-marked ridges of the forsaken crofts the matted ragweed grew, to show the land had once been cultivated. Nature smiled through the middle mist, which shrouded loch and hill as in derision of the changes which mankind had suffered, and looked as tolerantly upon the tourists, water-proofed to the ears, as she had gazed upon the clansmen, who must have seemed as much a part of her as were the roe who peeped out timidly from the birch thickets to watch the steamboat puffing on the lake. Yet still about the laroch a hum of voices hung, or seemed to hang, to any one who listened with ears undeadened by the steamhooter's bray—voices whose guttural accents seemed more attuned to the long swish of waves and moaning of the wind than those which, in their throaty tone, mingle with nothing but the jangle of a street. Voices there were that spoke of the dead past, when laughter echoed through the glens—the low-tuned laughter of a silent race. Voices that last had sounded in their grief and tears, as the rough roof-tree fell, or worse, was left intact, as the owners of the house turned for a last look at their shielings on the solitary strath.

An air of sadness and of failure, as if the very power which placed the ancient owners on the soil had not proved strong enough to keep them there, hung on the hills and brooded on the lake—a Celtic sadness, bred in the bone of an old race, which could not hope to strive with new surroundings, and which the stranger has supplanted, just as the Hanoverian rat drove out his British cousin and usurped his place. Land, sky, and loch spoke of the vanished people and their last enterprise—their first and last, when far Lochaber almost imposed a king on England; pushed on his fortunes, shed its blood for him, and when, beaten and desperate, he fled for life, sheltered him in the greyness of its mists. But in the soul-pervading, futile beauty which hung over all, the laroch gave as it were a keynote, as the tired, vapour-ridden sun at times blinked on it and shone upon its ruined walls. It seemed to speak of mournful happiness and of the humble joys of those who felt the storm, the sunshine, and the rain as their own trees and rocks had felt them, dumbly but cheerfully, and who, departing, had left no record of themselves but the poor rickle of grey stones, or the faint echo of their hearts heard in the notes of a lament quavering down through the glens and mingling with the south-east gale. The silence of an empty land, from which the people had been driven sore against their will, and had departed to make their fortunes, and to mourn their stony pastures to the third generation and the fourth, oppressed one, whilst the winds echoed through the corries as if seeking some one to talk with about days gone by.

On the peat hags the struggling sunbeams glinted, lighting them up for a brief moment, as the flaming chimney of an ironwork in a manufacturing town breaks through the vapour of the slums and lights the waters of some dank canal, giving an air as of an opening of the mouth of hell, black and unfathomable. The stunted willow and dwarf alder fringed the margin of the rushy streams, which gurgled in deep channel, forming small linns on which the white foam flecked the tawny peat water, or, breaking into little rapids, brattled amongst round pebbles, or again sank out of sight amongst the sedge of flags. Their tinkling music was unheard, except perhaps in ears which had grown blunted with the roar of cabs. Perchance it was remembered as a legend heard in childhood is remembered faintly in old age. Straggling across the hills, the footpaths, long disused, lay white amongst the heather, the stones retaining still a smoothness made by the feet of those who, in their deer-skin moccasins, had journeyed in the past from the lone laroch to other larochs, which once had all been homesteads dear to the dwellers in them, and to-day were silent and forgotten as the half-subterranean dwellings of the Picts.

Still the sweet-gale gave out its aromatic scent, the feathery bracken waved, the hills towered up into the sky, flecked here and there with snow, and nature seemed to call to the departed people, telling them to return and find their land unchanged. She called to ears long deaf, or rendered unresponsive in their new homes, for nothing broke the silence of the glens but the harsh cry of the wild geese, flying unseen amongst the middle region of the mist, calling on high the coronach of the departed and the dead.

(From *Progress,* 1905)

TOBAR NA RÉIL[1]

Right at the summit of the pass it lies, nothing above it but the sky. On every side the billowing heath-clad hills engirdle it about. Flat stones encircle it, and on its surface water-spiders walk. Red persicaria, with wax-like stalks and ragged leaves, grows by its edge. Below it stretches out a vast brown moss, honeycombed here and there with black peat hags, and a dark lake spreads out, ringed on one side with moss, and on the other set like a jewel in a pine wood, with a white stretch of intervening sand. On it are islands with great sycamores and chestnuts, stag-headed but still vigorous, and round their shores the bulrushes keep watch like sentinels. Mists rise from moss and lake and creep about the corries of the hills, blending the woods and rocks into a steamy chaos, vast and unfathomable, through which a little burn unseen, but musical, runs tinkling through the stones. So at the little *bealach* the well lies open to the sky, too high for the lake mists to touch it, as it looks up at the stars.

They say that on a certain day in midsummer, a star when at its zenith shines into the well. Which the star is, if Rigel or Algol or Aldebaran[2] with his russet fire, is clean forgotten, for nowadays tradition has scant place in men's imagining. He who looks on the water at the fateful hour, and sees the star reflected in the well, acquires again the ancient universal tongue, by which in ages past men and the animals held speech. For him the language of the birds becomes intelligible. The trees that groan or whisper in the breeze divulge their lore, and disclose all that they have seen in their long peaceful lives. Fish in the rivers and the lakes have no more dread of him, and, rising to the surface of the linns, tell him the marvels of the deep, whilst snakes and lizards, with newts, the moles and bats, impart their troubles or their joys, making their little secrets plain, by the strange virtues of the mystic star transmitted through the well.

There is no record of any one who, having drunk, obtained the power and straightway got into communication with all animals and things. No doubt, if at the appointed hour the fountain had turned all to gold, a town would have arisen on the pass, and Baal's priesthood or an aristocracy would have reserved the right to drink and gaze upon the well, and temples of Algol or Aldebaran would have sprung up as if by magic from the hill. But man, who lives an outcast from all living things, cut off by pride and want of sympathy from beasts and birds, and careless of his own connection with the world except so far as it may bring him the twin curses, wealth and power, which have combined to make him vile, cared not for such a gift. So trees and animals and beasts, with stones and streams, watched vainly every recurring year throughout the centuries for some adventurer who should break through the bonds which held the self-crowned monarch of the world in silence, condemned for ever to live dumb but to his own kind's speech, whilst on all sides secrets he never dreamed of were waiting to be heard. So as a Highlander went past, driving his cattle from the low country in Menteith, or in the summer evenings a group of men wrapped in their plaids, with curly hazel shepherd's sticks, and carrying long single-barrelled Spanish guns, trotted along the steep and winding path, their deerskin shoes making no sound upon the stones, the rabbits sitting at their holes watched them expectantly. The birds upon the branches turned their round heads and looked towards the well. The trees and plants and heather on the hill seemed to sigh softly in the summer air, as if inviting them to halt until the mystic star should rise, then drink and break the spell.

But they, absorbed in the affairs of life, which lead men onward prisoners to the grave, discoursed of hogs and pownie-beasts, of trysts and markets, and of the price of hirsells and of queys. At times they stopped and drank, but never lingered, scooping the water in their palms or in their *cuachan* of birch-wood hooped with silver, drawing their hands across their mouths, and sometimes murmuring, "Aye, och aye, they say that when a body drinks here, when the stars are up, he learns a vast o' things, that's why they ca' it *Tobar na Réil*, but I mind lying here aince o' a summer's nicht, sleeping ye ken, after some awqua that I had doon by at old McKureton's, and never learned a thing."

And whilst they talked, the trees and stars, half-sleeping in the cold moon's light, listened but drowsily, and all they heard was Angus answer Finlay, "Och aye, McKureton just keeps the finest awqua that I ever drank no more, Finlay McLachlan," and his compeer and fellow-driver, looking up whilst kneeling by the spring, would answer sapiently, "And neither did I too." And so the well slept on, having for its one tragedy the fight between the Grahams of Menteith and Stuarts on a raid from Appin, whose leader's head, struck by a sword-cut from his body at a blow, rolled down the pass, calling out imprecations even after death.

With the exception of this brief tragedy, history the well has none. Its very name means nothing to the men who now inhabit where once its namers dwelt. The legend lives as a tradition, to be laughed or wondered at, according to the attitude of mind of him who hears it, for education has new superstitions of its own, which have expelled those of the older race. Who that to-day, when all flee from responsibility as from the plague, would incur the burden of the sorrow of the trees, the winds, the beasts? For man aspires not to equality but to command, by which, when he possesses it, he straightly becomes an outcast from his kind.

Yet, had it been but for the pleasure of another sorrow to his life, 'tis strange that no one quenched his thirst, for joy is transient, whilst sorrow lives for ever, and to prove sorrows yet unknown might have stirred some one with imagination, had there been any such a traveller on the road which winds by Glenny to the valley of the Teith. And yet the district set with *Sith-bhrughan*[3] and with traditions of a fairy causeway in the lake, a borderland of races in the past, a frontier where the Lowland hob and Highland pixie met on neutral ground, to dance upon the green, seemed to invite experiment, and call for its Columbus to explore a newer world than that he saw in Guanahani[4] from his caravel.

A gentle world in which no hatred reigns; where envy and all malice are unknown, where each one tells his secret to his friend unwittingly, because the speech they use is universal and without volition, and not as ours, confined to persons and articulate. The speech that lives in the clear water of the well, at the conjuncture of the star, has no vocabulary, no rules, no difficulties, but he who has it speaks as does the wind, and, saying nothing in particular, is understood of all. Thus it can never lie, or lead astray, and so is valueless to us, as valueless as gold upon a desert island, with no one to enslave.

No one has claimed it since the first framers of the legend paddled their coracles upon the lake. No one will claim it, or ever think but for an instant of the treasure waiting to be grasped. Red-deer and roe and kyloes on the hills are all born free of it, and swallows from the south need no interpreter, but straightway tell their travels to the birds who but a week ago have left the pole, or to the weasels and the wrens who never wandered more than a mile or two from where they saw the light. They find themselves as much at home amongst the scrubby copse, as they were, only a month ago, in cane brakes and in palms.

But if the birds and beasts, the trees and grasses and the stones, mourn the estrangement and the want of faith of man, so does mankind feel vaguely its own loneliness amongst created things with which it cannot have communication, and before which it always must be dumb. What tender idylls moss and lichens could unfold, if only some one of the passers-by throughout the centuries had learned their speech, and taught his children, taking them, as the most sacred duty in his power, upon the star's appearance in its round, to drink and learn, and thus transmit their knowledge to their children, making them all hereditary drago-men by right divine, betwixt their race and the creation of the beasts.

Drink and admire, the motto says upon the well in far Marrakesh set among its palms. Above the fountain, built by some pious pilgrim, who perhaps had felt the desert's thirst and reared this monument to the one God—He who alone brings comfort in the sands—the horseshoe arch is blue with pottery. Intricate patterns marked in lustrous tiles cross and recross each other, and arabesques repeat some pious saw or play upon God's name. Over the humble fountain on the pass unknown to fame, the skies are canopy, and the stars set in them, celestial glow-worms of the firmament, which mark the hours the passers-by neglect. No pious pilgrim there has hedged about the spring with masonry. No sculptured stone relates its virtues, for it serves but as a drinking-place for roe, who, as they drink, admire and give their thanks instinctively, wiser by far than man. No one remembers the lone well among the heath or cares for it, but to smile scornfully at the old simple legend of the past. In all the district where it lies, few know its bearings, and, for the name, refer to it "as a sort o' Gaelic fash aboot a star; I mind my feyther kent the meaning o' it," dismissing it at once as "juist a haver, auncient but fair redeekllous, an auld wife's clishmaclaver," beneath the notice of an "eddi-cated man."

So it sleeps quietly upon the pass just where the road descends to Vennachar and rises from Menteith. Winds sweep the bents and rustle in the ling, setting the cotton-grass a-quivering, bowing the heads of the bog-asphodel, and carrying with them the sharp perfume of the gale, sweeter and homelier than the spice of Araby.

In the dark mirror of the lake below, the priory and the castle hang head downwards, and on the bulrushed shore the wavelets break amongst the stones. The earl's old pleasance, now neglected, is a park for cows, its few surviving syca-mores have withered at the top, and soon will follow those who planted them into the misty region of the past.

The well, the star, the scrubby oak copse on the hill, the old Fingalian road, distinct in moonlight, or in the morning after frost, for time itself appears unable to efface the taint man's footsteps leave upon the ground, remain and call to the chance passer-by to stop and drink at the conjunction of the star. They call in vain, and nature in the breeze still raises its lament, uncomprehended by the ears of man, who, in his self-forged fetters, fails to understand.

(From *His People,* 1906)

NOTES

1. *Tobar Na Réil*, Well of the Star.
2. Rigel is a star of the first magnitude in the constellation of Orion. Algol is in the constellation Perseus, and Aldebaran is a star of the first magnitude in the constellation of Taurus.
3. *Sith-bhrughan*, Fairy hills.
4. *Guanahani*, Island in the Caribbean, one of the Bahamas, discovered by Columbus on 12 October 1492, on his first voyage of discovery.

INCH CAILLEACH

The Island of the Nuns lies like a stranded whale upon the waters of the loch, with its head pointing towards the red rocks of Balmaha. Tradition tells of a nunnery on the island in times gone by, and certainly it must have been a fitting place to build a convent on. A deep, dark strait cuts it off from the world. No spot in the whole earth could be more fitted for a conventual life of meditation, or for the simple duties performed in simple faith, such as string out a life like beads upon a rosary, till the last prayer is said.

Fell opportunity, that has so often turned saints into sinners, could have had no place upon the rocky islet in the lake. The voices of the sisters singing in the choir must have been scarce distinguishable from the lapping of the wavelets on the beach, or, blending with them, made up a harmony, as if nature and men were joining in a pantheistic hymn. Nuns may have lived upon the island with, or without, vocation, have eaten out their hearts with longing for their lost world, or, like the Saint of Ávila, in mystic ecstasy have striven to be one with the celestial spouse. All this may well have been, but the dim sisterhood has left no record of its passage upon earth except the name Inch Cailleach, beautiful in its liquid likeness to the sound of the murmuring waves, and the wind sighing in the brackens and the bents.

Ben Lomond towers above the wooded island, with its outcrop of grey rocks, and in the distance Ben Vorlich, Meall nan Caora and Bein Chabhair seem to protect it from all modern influence by their grim aspect and aloofness, for even their rare smiles, when the sun hunts the shadows across their rocky faces, still are stern. If the lone, wooded inchlet once sheltered nuns, or if the name was merely given it to commemorate some ancient Highland *cailleach*, who had retired there to gaze into the mists upon the hills, or dream of Fingal and Cuchullin as she sat nodding over a fire of peat, certain it is that nature must have put forth her best creative power to form so fitting a last resting-place for the wild clan, whose bones are laid beneath the mossy turf round the great sculptured stones.

Right on the top of a long shoulder of the island, within the ruined walls of the old chapel whose broken pillars, moss-grown finials and grooved door-jambs lie in a growth of bilberries among the invading copse, the Gregarach for centuries have interred their dead. They and the wild McFarlanes—was not the moon known as McFarlanes' Bowat?[1]—rest from their labour at the sword. Quietly they lie, they who knew never a quiet hour in life. Equal in death and equal in misfortune when they lived, had they consulted all the heralds and their pursuivants they could not have hit upon a device more fitting than the cross-handled sword that is cut roughly on so many of their tombs. Bitterly they paid for the slaughter of Glenfruin, with two hundred years of outlawry, and with the hand of every man against them. Well did they deserve the title of the "Clan Na Cheò,"[2] for the mist rolling through the corries was their best hiding-place, the natural smoke-screen that protected all the Clan Gregor from their enemies. On the leafy island in the great lake alone they found a resting-place, and though the long grey stones by which they swore are few in number, the grassy hillocks that dot the burial-ground encircled by the ruined walls are numberless. Nowhere could men have found a spot so fitting for a long sleep after their foray in the world. The soughing wind among the thickets of scrub-oak, of hazel and of birch, the fresh, damp scent of the sweet-gale and staghorn moss, the belling of the roe at evening, the strange, sweet wildness of the steep, isolated island with its two headlands and its little plain, now buried deep in wood, must lull the resting children of the mist.

A steep and winding path leads from the pebbly beach, and crosses and re-crosses a little rill, brown but transparent, as it wends its way towards the lake in miniature cascades and tiny linns, in which play minnows. It makes a tinkling music for the sleepers among the ruins of what was once Inch Cailleach parish church. It passes now and then a fir, whose bright red trunk stands out aflame among the copse, and bears the cones from which Clan Alpine took its badge. Here and there clumps of scarlet dockens mark the way, like Stations of the Cross upon a Calvary. Hardly a footstep has beaten down the grass, for up above, in the lone circle of grey stones, lie men whose names were written in characters as evanescent as the smoke-scrolls an aeroplane traces upon the sky. Clearly imprinted on the peaty soil, roe tracks call up the memory of men who passed the best part of their lives in following the deer. The silence of the woods is only broken by the flight of some great capercailzie, as its wings beat against the leaves when it first launches into flight, or by the cushats cooing, deep and full-throated as the bell-bird's call in the Brazilian wilds.

The loneliness, the sense of isolation, although the world is just at hand, and tourist-laden steamers ply upon the loch, passing but a few hundred yards away and breaking up the picture of the wooded island reflected in the lake, as in a mirage, with their paddles, are as absolute as if the islet was situated in the Outer Hebrides.

The very scent of the lush grass, set about thickly with the yellow tormen-tils, with scabious and bog-asphodel, strikes on the nostrils as from an older world, in which the reek of petrol and the noise of factories were unknown. Many a procession of ragged warriors, in the past, their deerskin buskins making scarce a sound upon the stones, must have toiled up the winding path to lay their dead within the little burial-ground, and then, the ceremony over, stepped noise-lessly away into the sheltering mist. The nuns, McGregors, and McFarlanes all have passed away, and are as if they never had been, yet they have left an aura that still pervades the leafy isle. Nothing is left of them but the vaguest memory, and yet they seem to live in every thicket, every copse, and as the burn runs brattling to the lake it sings their threnody. When all is hushed at night and owls fly noiselessly, their flight hardly disturbing the still air, and the rare nocturnal animals that all-destroying progress (or what you call the thing) has left alive, surely the spirits of the nameless sleepers under the mossy turf rise like a vapour from their graves, commune with Cuchullin and with Fingal, pat Bran's rough head, and fight old battles once again; until at the first streak of dawn they glide back to their places under the sculptured stones.

Let them sleep on. They have had their foray, they have chased the roe and followed the red-deer. The very mists upon the mountains are far more tangible than they are now. Let them rest within the ruined walls of the dismantled chapel buried in the copse, that has shown itself more durable than the stone walls that lie about its roots. Bracken and heather, bog-myrtle, blaeberry and moss exhale their odours, sweeter than incense, over the graves where sleep the nameless men. The waves still murmur on the beach, the tiny burnlet whispers its coronach. Under their rude tombstones men whose feet, shod in their deerskin brogues, were once as light as fawns, are waiting till the shrill skirl of the Piob Mor[3] shall call them to the great gathering of the clans.

(From *Redeemed,* 1927)

NOTES

1. *bouet* or *bowet,* i.e. a hand lantern.
2. *Clan Na Cheò,* Clan of the Mist.
3. *Piob Mor* or *Piob-Mhor,* the great Highland bagpipe.

Section II

THE SCOTTISH CHARACTER

EDITOR'S PREFACE

In the last two sketches of the previous section Graham's descriptions of the Well of the Star and the Island of the Nuns highlight an interest in the mythical, legendary past, and a sentimental longing for a ressurection of the fallen dead, who would, somehow or other, emerge from the mist and lead Scotland into a glorious future. "A Vigia" (1910), the island of dreams, is, as it were, a stopping-off place, spiritual and geographical, a misty island of the mind that links the present with the past.

This sentimental view of the past, however, does not exclude a bitter indictment of the present. Whatever notions he may have had about the Scottish character of old did not prevent him from launching a bitter attack on the failings of the Scottish temperament, as reflected in an early collection of sketches, *The Ipané* (1899). Graham's scathing assault on the laziness, coarseness, drunkenness and general viciousness of the Scottish race reaches its peak of naturalism in "Salvagia" and "A Survival," which in their "exaggerated realism" emulate the work of the contemporary master, Zola. In Scottish literary terms, of course, they represent an attempt to counter the excessive sentimentalism of the Kailyard, even before the appearance of Brown's *The House with the Green Shutters*. In the confrontation with death, however, in "Salvagia," the predominant reaction is stoicism.

Thirty years later, mellowed by his own approaching death and an emotional relationship with Scottish nationalism, in "Euphrasia" (1927) he goes full circle, returning, if not quite in cheerfulness at least in reconciliation, to the dreamy memories of the past Ossianic heroes, sparked off by the sight of a Gaelic war memorial. Graham's ambivalent attitude to death, which projects him variously into the past and into the future, is equalled only by the ambivalence of his race, which ranges from coarse materialism and heartlessness to the dreamy nostalgic sentimentality so characteristic of the Scot, long conditioned by departure scenes, not least by death, the final farewell.

A VIGIA

When the old Spanish navigators, sailing in virgin seas, uncharted, undeflowered by keels, passed by some islet about which they were doubtful, seeing it dimly as the mist lifted for a moment, or in the uncertain light of the false dawn, they called it a vigia, a place to be looked out for, and their old charts are dotted here and there with the Vigia of the Holy Spirit, the Trinity, the Immaculate Conception, or the Exaltation of the Cross.

Their followers, sailing with ampler knowledge, but less faith, kept a look out for the mysterious shoals or islets, not often finding them, unless they chanced to run upon them in the dark and perish with all hands. These were vigias of the seas, but there exist vigias of the mind, as shadowy and as illusive, to the full, as any that Magellan, Juan de la Cosa, or Sebastian Cabot marked upon their charts. We all know of such islands, low-lying, almost awash, as it were, in the currents of the mind. On them we make our land-fall when we choose, without a pilot, except memory, to guide us in the darkest night. We land and roam about alone, always alone, for those who once inhabited them, and welcomed us whenever we sailed in, are now all harboured. Commonly we stay but little there, for though the men we knew are dead, their ghosts so jostle us that we are glad once more to re-embark and sail again into a world of noise, that modern anaesthetic of the mind, still knowing that one day we must return and swell the shadowy procession that walks along the shores of their dead, saltless seas. There is an island, whose whereabouts I do not care precisely to reveal, although only a little strait divides it from a land of mist, of money-making, a land of faiths harder by far than facts, yet there it rides swaying on the sea like some great prehistoric ship, looking out westward in the flesh, and with the interior vision straining its eyes to keep its recollection of the past, fresh and undimmed. Green grass, white sands, limpid blue seas, with windows here and there of palest green in them, through which you look into the depths and count the stones, watch sea anemones unfold like flowers, and follow the minutest fish at play fathoms below your boat; these keep it fresh, old, and uncontaminated. One likes to think of virgin souls, and so I like to think of this oasis in the desert of the sea as virgin, in spite of tourists, steamboats, and the stream of those who go to worship and defile. They have the power to trample down the grass, to leave their sandwich papers and their broken bottles in the ling, but the fresh wind coming across a thousand leagues of sea eludes them. That they can never trample down. So may a woman in a brothel be the mattress of the vilest of mankind and keep some corner of the soul still pure; for it is dull, befitting only to the spirit of the so-called wise, to say the age of miracles is dead. Those who have kept their minds unclogged with knowledge know that they never cease.

So old my island is that it seems young—that is, it still preserves an air as of an older world, in which men laboured naturally just as a bee makes honey; a world where the chief occupation of mankind was to look round them, as the Creator did in Eden, and to find all things good. So they pass all the morning, meeting their fellows and saluting them, and in the afternoon repass and resalute, then work a little in the fields, lifting up hay upon a fork with as much effort as an athlete in a circus raises a cannon in his teeth, till it is time to sit down on a stone and watch the fishing-boats return upon the tides, the steersman sitting on the gunwale with his knee jammed against the tiller, and the sheet firmly knotted round a thwart. Just as of Ávila, it might be said of my vigia that it is all made up of saints and stones, for not a stone is without its corresponding saint or saint without his stone. Thus in both places does the past so dwarf the present that things which happened when the world was young seem just as probable as the incredible events we see before our eyes.

Upon a mound that looks out on a sand-locked bay the heathen crucified some of the new faith a thousand years ago, bringing, as we might think, their crosses with them ready made, or rigging up a jury cross, fashioned from spars and oars, for not a tree grows, or has ever grown, upon the island where now the sheep feed peacefully on the short, wiry grass broken with clumps of flags. A little further on fairies appeared the other day, not to a man herding his sheep and dazed with solitude, but to a company of men who all declare they saw the "little people" seated upon a mound. Fairies and martyrs both seem as natural as does the steamer landing its daily batch of tourists to hurry through the street where the kings sleep under their sculptured stones, gaze at the Celtic crosses and the grey, time-swept church which lies a little listed, as it were, to starboard, upon the grassy slope where once there stood the wattled temple of the Apostle of the Isles. The mud-built church, where the Apostle chanted his last Mass, is nearer to us than the cathedral, now being killed with care. We see the saint lie dying, and his white, faithful horse approach and make its moan and, bowing down its head, ask for his blessing, as is recorded by the chronicler, with that old, cheerful faith in the impossible that kept his world so young.

So standing on the Capitol, the Church, popes, cardinals, and saints, the glory of the Middle Ages, the empire, the republic, and the kings, melt into mist and leave us, still holding, as our one sure possession, to the two children suckled by the wolf. Some men, like Ponce de León, have sailed to find the fountain of eternal youth, landed upon some flowery land, left it, and died still searching,[1] all unaware the object of their quest, had it been found, would have left paradise a waste. There in my island, whose longitude and latitude, for reasons of my own, I keep a secret, there is, I think, some fountain in which those who bathe recover, not their youth, but the world's youth, and ever afterwards have their ears opened to the voices of the dead.

So, seated on the ground amongst the flowers that grow in miniature amongst the grass, bedstraw, and tormentil, upon the cairn-topped hill from which the saint of Gartan saw his vision,[2] they see the history of the isle acted before them, as in an optic mirror of the mind. The setting still remains just as it was when the "summer sailors" from the north fell on the peaceful monks one day in June, twelve hundred years ago, and sacrificed them and their prior to their offended gods. The thin, white road which cuts the level machar into two has probably replaced an earlier sheep-track or a footpath of the monks. The dazzling white houses, with their thatched roofs secured against the wind by stones slung in a rope, only require a little more neglect to fall again into the low, black Pictish huts. The swarthy people, courteous and suave, in whom you see a vein of subcutaneous sarcasm as they lean up against a house, sizing the passing stranger up to the last tittle at a glance, would all look natural enough with glibs of matted hair, long saffron Celtic shirts, and the Isles kilt, made out of a long web of cloth, leaving the right arm bare.

Still in the Isle of Dreams remains the primitive familiarity between the animals and man, which only lingers on in islands or in the regions where no breath of modern life has set a bar between two branches of the same creation with talk about the soul. The still, soft rain yet blots the island from the world, just as it did of yore, and through its pall the mysterious voices of the sea sound just as menacing and hostile to mankind as they did when the saint preached to the seals upon the reef. Perhaps—who knows?—he preaches yet to those who have the gift of a right hearing of the soft, grating noise the pebbles make in a receding wave upon the beach. The wind continues its perpetual monsoon, blowing across the unpolluted ocean for a thousand leagues. In the white coves, the black sea-purses, which the tide throws up like necklaces of an antique and prehistoric pattern, are spread upon the sands, waiting the evening, when the mermaids issue from the waves and clasp them round their necks. Soft wind and purple sea, red cliffs and greenest grass, the echoing caves and mouldering ruins, with the air of peace, all make the islet dreamlike, sweet, and satisfying.

To have seen it once is to have seen it to the last day of one's life. The horses waiting at the rough pierhead to swim a mile of channel with its fierce, sweeping tide, the little street in which the houses spring from the living rock which crops up here and there and forms a reef right in the middle of the road, are not a memory, but a possession, as real as if you held the title-deeds duly engrossed and sealed. When all is said and done, the one secure and lasting property a man can own is an enchanted city such as one sees loom in the sky above the desert sands. That, when you once have seen it, is yours for ever, and next comes a Vigia, which but appears for a brief moment in the mind, as you sail past on some imaginary sea.

(From *Hope,* 1910)

NOTES

1. Juan Ponce de León (*c.* 1460-1521), Spanish conquistador, first governor of the
      newly discovered Puerto Rico (1509) and discoverer of Florida (1513).
2. Gartan is reputedly the Irish birthplace of St. Columba.

SALVAGIA

Almost the most horrible doctrine ever enunciated by theologians is, in my opinion, the attribution of our misfortunes to Providence. An all-wise power, all-merciful and omnipresent, enthroned somewhere in omnipotence, having power over man and beast, over earth and sky, on sea and land, able (if usually unwilling) to suspend all natural laws, seated above the firmament of heaven, beholding both the evil and the good—discerning, we may suppose, the former without much difficulty, and the latter by the aid of some spectroscope at present not revealed to men of science—sees two trains approaching on one line, and yet does nothing to avert the catastrophe or save the victims. Withal, nothing consoles humanity for their misfortunes like the presence of this unseen power, which might do so much good, but which serenely contemplates so many evils.

I have often thought that, after all, there is but one idea at the bottom of all faiths, and that, no matter if the divinity be called Jehovah, Allah, Moloch, Dagon, or the Neo-Pauline Providence of the North Britons, the worshippers seem to esteem their deity in proportion as he disregards their welfare.

Some have maintained that the one common ground of all the sects was in the offertory; but more recent reflection has convinced me that the impassibility of Providence provides a spiritual, if unconscious, nexus which unites in one common bond Jews, Christians (whether Coptic, Abyssinian, Greek, or Roman), Mohammedans, Buddhists, the Church of England, with that of Scotland, and the multitudinous sects of Nonconformists, who, scattered over two hemispheres, yet hate one another with enough intensity to enable mankind to perceive that they have comprehended to the full the doctrines of the New Testament.

I know a little village in the country generally described in old Italian maps under the title of "Salvagia," where the providential scheme is held in its entirety. Nothing, at first sight, proclaims the fact why a great power should specially concern itself about the place. Still, is it not the case that, as a rule, blear-eyed, knock-kneed young men imagine that they touch the heart of every woman who pities their infirmities? Do not red-haired and freckled, cow-houghed maidens usually attend a fancy ball attired as Mary Queen of Scots, and think their fatal beauty deals destruction on the sons of men, unconscious that their lack of charms preserves them safe from those temptations by means of which alone virtue can manifest itself? That which holds good of individuals often applies to people in the bulk. So of my village in Salvagia. A straggling street, looking upon a moor, bordered by slated living boxes, each with its jaw-box at the door and midden at the back, its ugly strip of garden without flowers, in which grew currants, gooseberries, with nettles, docks, potatoes, and the other fruits known to the tender North.

In every house a picture of Dr. Chalmers flanked by one of Bunyan, and a Bible ever ready on a table for advertisement, as when a minister or charitable lady calls, and the cry is heard of "Jeanie, rax the Bible doon, and pit the whisky-bottle in the aumrie." Two churches and two public-houses, and a feud between the congregations of each church as bitter as that between the clients of the rival inns. No whisky or no doctrine from the opposing tavern or conventicle could possibly be sound. No trees, no flowers, no industry, except the one of keeping idiots sent from Glasgow, and known to the people as the "silly bodies." Much faith and little charity, the tongue of every man wagging against his neighbour like a bell-buoy on a shoal. At the street corner groups of men stand spitting. Expectoration is a national sport throughout Salvagia. Women and children are afraid to pass them by. Not quite civilised, nor yet quite savages, a set of demi-brutes, exclaiming, if a woman in a decent gown goes past, "There goes a bitch."

A school, of course, wherein the necessary means of getting on in life is taught. O education, how a people may be rendered brutish in thy name! Behold Salvagia! In every town, in every hamlet, even in the crofting communities upon the coast, where women till the fields and men stand idle prating of natural rights, the poorest man can read and write, knows history and geography, arithmetic up to the Rule of Three—in fact, sufficiently to overreach his neighbour in the affairs of life.

Still, in the social scale of human intercourse the bovine dweller in East Anglia is a prince compared to him. How the heart shrinks, in travelling from London, when, the Border passed, the Scottish porter with a howl sticks his head into the carriage and bellows, "Tackets—are ye gaeing North?" No doubt the man is better educated than his southern colleague, but as you see him once, and have no time to learn his inward grace, his lack of outward polish jars upon you. After the porter comes the group of aged men at Lockerbie, all seated in the rain, precisely as their forbears sat when Carlyle lived at his lone farm upon the moor. Then come barefooted boys selling the *Daily Mail*, the *Herald*, and *Review*, till Glasgow in its horror and its gloom receives you, and you lose all hope.

Throughout Salvagia "Thank you" and "If you please" are terms unknown. In railway trains we spit upon the floor and wipe our boots upon the cushions, just to show our independence; in cars and omnibuses take the best seats, driving the weaker to the wall like cattle in a pen. In streets we push the women into the gutters, "It's only just a woman" being our excuse. Our hearts we wear so distant from our sleeves that the rough frieze of which our coats are made abrades the cuticle of every one it rubs.

Back to our village—"Gart-na-cloich," I think the name, meaning the enclosure of the stones. Stony indeed the country, stony the folks, the language, manners, and all else pertaining to it. Even the *parameras*[1] outside Ávila, where every boulder is a tear that Jesus wept, is not more sterile. Not that Jesus had ever aught to do with Gart-na-cloich. The deity worshipped there is Dagon, or some superfetated Moloch born in Geneva.

In no Salvagian village is there any room for a gentle God. "Nane of your Peters; gie me Paul," is constantly in everybody's mouth, for every dweller in Salvagia studies theology. Faith is our touchstone, and good works are generally damned throughout the land as rank Erastianism.[2] Only believe, that is sufficient. "Show me your moral man," exclaims the preacher, "and I will straight demolish him." The congregation nod assent, being convinced "your moral man" is not a dweller in Salvagia, or, if he was, that the profession of a "cold morality" on earth must lead to everlasting fire in the only other world they hear of in the kirk.

Our sexual immorality, and the high rate of illegitimacy, we explain thus. No thrifty man would buy a barren beast. Therefore, as we cannot buy our wives and sell them if they prove unprofitable, 'tis well to try them in advance, and as our law follows the Pandects of Justinian,[3] being more merciful to those who come into a hard world through no fault of their own than that of England, the matter is put right after a year or so, and all are pleased. That which a thing is worth is what it brings, we teach our children from their earliest days. We inculcate it in our schools, at mart and fair, in church, at bed and board, and that accounts for the hide-bound view we take of everything. Anger and love move us not much. We seldom come to blows after the fashion of the people in the mysterious region that we call "up about England." A stand-up fight with knock-down blows is not our way, not for the lack of courage but from excess of caution and the knowledge that we have intuitively that calumny kills further off than blows. How we get married is a mystery I have never solved, for no Salvagian ever seems heartily to wish for anything, or, if he does, is far too cautious to make his wishes known. Perhaps that is the reason why the Germans drive us out from business as easily as the Norwegian rat expels the original black rat, or the European extirpates the natives of Australia.

Withal, we have our qualities, but well concealed, and only to be found after a residence of fifty years within our gates. In spite of kailyard tales, we snivel little, and cant not much more than our neighbours do; and we have humour, though the kailyarders record it not, for fear of troubling the Great Heart which only likes "a joke," and is impervious either to humour or to wit. Sometimes we have a touch of pathos in our composition which startles, coming as it does from an unlikely source.

In Gart-na-cloich there dwelt one Mistress Campbell, a widow and the mother of four sons, all what we call "weel-doing" lads—that is, not given to drink, good workers, attenders at the church, not of those who pass their "Sawbath" lounging about and spitting as they criticise mankind.

Going to church with us replaces charity—that is, it covers an infinity of things. A man may cheat and drink, be cruel to animals, avaricious, anything you please, but if he goes to church he still remains a Christian and enters heaven by his faith alone. Our faith we take from Paul, our doctrine from Hippo,[4] so that we need do nought but bow the knee to our own virtues, and be sure that we are saved.

No one could say that Mistress Campbell's cottage was neat or picturesque. No roses climbed the walls, nor did the honeysuckle twine round the eaves. For flowers a ragged mullein growing in a wall, a plant of rue, one of "old man," with camomile and gillyflowers, did duty. Apple and damson trees grew round the "toon," the fruit of which was bitter as a sloe. Beside the door the cheesestone with its iron ring, a stoup for water shaped like a little barrel, a feal spade, and a rusty sickle lying in the mud, gave promise of the interior graces of the house.

Inside the acrid smell of peat, with rancid butter, and the national smell of whisky spilt and left to dry, assailed your nose.

All round the kitchen stood press beds in which the children slept. Before the fire grey woollen stockings dried whilst scones were baking, and underneath the table lay a collie dog or two snapping at flies.

The inner chamber had the peculiar musty smell of rarely opened rooms. Upon the walls a picture of Jerusalem, set forth in a kind of uphill view, was balanced by a sampler which may have been the Ten Commandments, the Maze at Hampton Court, the Fountains at Versailles, or almost anything you chose, according to your view. Not tidy or convenient was the house, but still a home of the peculiar kind that race and climate has made acceptable.

The widow's faith was great, her household linen clean, and her chief pride, after her sons, was centred in her cows, called in Salvagia kye. She liked to sit in church and fall asleep, as pious people do during the sermon. Seated between her sons, her Bible in a handkerchief scented with lavender, she had the faith not merely able to move mountains, but with her Bible for a lever, had she but got a fulcrum, to move the world itself. She knew her Church was right, the others wrong, and that sufficed her; and, for the rest, she did her duty to her sons and cows and to her neighbours.

Years passed by, the world wagged pretty much as usual in Gart-na-cloich; sometimes a neighbour died, and we enjoyed his funeral in the way we love, whilst listening in the house of woe to the set phrases of the minister, which use has constituted a sort of liturgy.

Winter succeeded summer, and day night, without a thing to break the dreary life we think the best of lives because we know none else.

Years sat but lightly upon Mistress Campbell, for she had reached the time of life when countrywomen in Salvagia seem to mummify and time does nothing on them. Her sons grew up, her cows continued to give milk, the rent was paid in season. Nothing disturbed her life, and folk began almost to murmur against Providence for His neglect to visit her.

Then came a season with the short, fierce spell of heat which goes before the thunderstorm, and constitutes our summer. In every burn the children paddled, trout gasped, and cattle sought a refuge from the midges in the stream.

A little river, in which, before the days of knowledge, kelpies were wont to live, flows past the town.

Its glory is a pool (we call it linn) known as the Linn-a-Hamish. Here the stream spreads out and babbling in its course wears the stones flat as proverbs in the current of men's speech get broadened out. The boys delight to throw these flat stones edgeways in the air, to hear the curious muffled sound they make when falling in the water, which they call a "dead man's bell." Alders fringe the bank, and in the middle of the pool a little grassy promontory juts out, on which cows stand swinging their tails, and meditate, to at least as good a purpose as philosophers. The linn lies dark and sullen, and a line of bubbles rising to the top shows where the under-current runs below the stream. In a lagoon a pike has basked for the last thirty years. In our mythology, one Hamish met his death in the dark water, but why or wherefore no one seems to know. Tradition says the place is dangerous, and the country people count it a daring feat to swim across.

There the four sons of Mistress Campbell went to bathe, and all were drowned. Passing the village, I heard the Celtic Coronach, which lingers to show us how our savage ancestors wailed for their dead, and to remind us that the step which separates us from the other animals is short. I asked a woman for whom the cry was raised. She answered, "For the four sons of Lilias Campbell." In the dull way one asks a question in the face of any shock, I said, "What did she say or do when they were brought home dead?"

"Say?" said the woman; "nothing; n'er a word. She just gaed out and milked the kye."

(From The Ipané, 1899)

NOTES

1. The bare Castilian moorlands.
2. The doctrine attributed, perhaps unjustly, to the German physician-theologian Thomas Erastus (1524-83), which maintains the supremacy of the state in ecclesiastical matters.
3. Part of the compilations of Roman law made by command of Justinian, Emperor of the East (527-65).
4. i.e. St. Augustine of Hippo.

A SURVIVAL

To be a Scotchman nowadays is to fill a position of some difficulty and trust.

It is expected that when he takes pen in hand that he must write, no matter what his predilections, antecedents, or education may have been, a language which no Englishman can understand. It is in vain to plead that all our greatest writers in the past have written in what they hoped was English.

Hume, Smollett, Thomson, and Sir Walter Scott, with Dugald Stuart and Adam Smith, endeavoured to make themselves intelligible, even to Englishmen.

Dunbar,[1] the greatest poet that Scotland has produced, wrote in a language but little differing from that of Chaucer, who, by the way, he styled his master, acknowledging him to be of "Makkaris Flowir."[2]

Bishop Douglas did not translate Virgil into the rough jargon of the peasants of his day.

Master Robert Henryson,[3] the author of "Robene and Makyne," one of the few pastorals tolerable to those who do not live in towns, is almost as easy of comprehension as is Spenser.

Drummond, of Hawthornden, rarely uses a Scottish word. Carlyle, it is true, made himself a language after his own image in which to express his philosophy, but neither language nor philosophy seem likely to endure, and future generations may yet remember him but as a humourist.

Burns occasionally "attempted the English," but his success in that language was not striking, and a man of genius is neither subject to rules, nor can he usually found a school to carry on his work.

Be all that as it may, the fact remains that the modern Scottish writer, to be popular in England, must write a dialect which his reader cannot understand. If novelists north of Tweed must live (and write), they must perforce adopt the ruling fashion, if possible be clergymen and treat entirely of weavers, idiots, elders of churches, and of all those without whose aid, as Jesus, son of Sirach,[4] says, no state can stand.

Now, though I have but little skill of the jargon which these Levites have invented, let no Southron think that I depreciate the worthy folk of whom they write. They are all honourable men (I mean the Levites), and if it please them to represent that half the population of their native land is imbecile, the fault is theirs. But for the idiots, the precentors, elders of churches, the "select men," and those land-ward folk who have been dragged of late into publicity, I compassionate them, knowing their language has been so distorted, and they themselves been rendered such abject snivellers, that not a henwife, shepherd, ploughman, or any one who thinks in "guid braid Scots," would recognise himself dressed in the motley which it has been the pride of kailyard writers to bestow. Neither would I have Englishmen believe that the entire Scotch nation is composed of ministers, elders, and maudlin whiskified physicians, nor even of precentors who, as we know, are men employed in Scotland to put the congregation out by starting hymns on the wrong note, or in a key impossible for any but themselves to compass.

England to-day looks at a native of North Britain from a different standpoint from that of half a century ago. In the blithe times of clans and mosstroopers, when Jardines rode and Johnstones raised, when Grahams stole, McGregors plundered, and Campbells prayed themselves into fat sinecures, we were your enemies. In stricken fields you southern folks used to discomfit us by reason of your archers and your riders sheathed in steel. We on the borders had the vantage of you, as you had cattle for us to steal, houses to burn, money and valuables for us to carry off. We having none, you were not in a state to push retaliation in an effective way.

Later, we sent an impecunious king to govern you, and with him went a train of ragged courtiers all with authentic pedigrees but light of purse. From this time date the Sawneys and the Sandies, the calumnies about our cuticle, and those which stated that we were so tender-hearted that we scrupled to deprive of life the smallest insect which we had about our clothes. You found our cheek-bones out, saw our red hair, and noted that we blew our noses without a pocket-handkerchief to save undue expense. You marked the exiguity of our "Pund Scots," our love of sixpences (which we called saxpence) and you learned the word "bawbee." So far so good, but still you pushed discovery to whisky, haggis, sneeshin, predestination, and all the other mysteries both of our cookery and faith. The bagpipes burst upon you (with a skirl), and even Shakespeare set down things about them which I refrain from quoting, only because I do not wish to frighten gentlewomen. Then came the road to England that we chiefly used, all others in our country being but fit for partridges, but that well worn and beaten down, just like the path to hell. King George came in, in pudding-time, and all was changed, and a new race of Scotsmen dawned on the English view. The '15 and the '45 sent out the Highlanders, rough-footed and with deer-skinned thongs tied round their heads, dressed in short petticoats and claymores in their hands, they marched and conquered and made England reel, retreated, lost Culloden, and the mist received them back. But their brief passage altered your view again, and you perceived that Scotland was not all bailie, prayer-monger, merchant, and sanctimonious cheat. By slow degrees we rose from moss-trooper and thief to impecunious courtier, then became known as pious business-men, ready to cheat and pray on all occasions, but still ridiculous, as those who have no money must of necessity appear to richer men. Our want of wit amazed you, for you did not know we wondered at your want of humour, and so both of us were pleased.

Then Scott arose and threw a glamour over Scotland which was nearly all his own. True we were poor, but then our poverty was so romantic, and we appeared fighting for home and haggis, for foolish native kings, for hills, for heather, freedom, and for all those things which Englishmen enjoy to read about, but which in actual life they take good care only themselves shall share. The pale-faced Master and the Highland chief, the ruined gentleman, the smuggler, swash-buckler, soldier, faithful servant, and the rest, he marked and made his own, but then he looked about to find his counterfoils, the low comedians, without whose presence every tragedy must halt.

Then came the Kailyarders and said that Scott was Tory, Jacobite, unpatri-otic, un-presbyterian, and that they alone could draw the Scottish type. England believed them, and their large sale and cheap editions clinched it, and to-day a Scotchman stands confessed a sentimental fool, a canting cheat, a grave, senten-tious man, dressed in a "stan o' black," oppressed with the tremendous difficulties of the jargon he is bound to speak, and above all weighed down with the re-sponsibility of being Scotch. I know he prays to Gladstone and to Jehovah turn about, finds his amusement in comparing preachers, can read and write and cypher, buys newspapers, tells stories about ministers, drinks whisky, fornicates gravely but without conviction, and generally disports himself after a fashion which would land a more imaginative and less practically constituted man within the precincts of a lunatic asylum before a week was out.

All this I know, and I know virtue which has long left London and the South still lingers about Ecclefechan, hangs about Kirriemuir, is found at Bridge of Weir, and may yet save us when England is consumed with brimstone, as were the Cities of the Plain. But I object to the assumption that the douce, pawky, three per-centling of the kailyard has quite eclipsed the pre-Culloden type. In remote places it still remains in spite of education, kodak, bicycle, cheap knowledge and excursion trains; it lingers furtively without a reason, but perhaps that of disproving Darwinism. The men who named the hills, the streams, the stones, who hunted, fished, and fought, who came out of the mist, who followed, like dumb, faithful dogs, the foolish Stuarts, and fought against the brutal Hanoverians to their own undoing, have now and then a type lingering pathetically and ghost-like from the dim regions of a pre-commercial age.

All that still lingers from another age is what we call a ghost—a ghost per-haps of happier freer times, when men were less tormented about little things than we who live to-day. Even in Scotland there still exist some few remains of the pre-Knoxian and pre-bawbee days, though fallen into decay.

Not far from where I live there dwells a worthy man, *Scottissimus Scotorum*, a Scot of Scots, enriched by sweating of some sort, but still a kindly soul; kindly, of course, in everything but trade, which is a thing apart and sacred, semi-divine, sent straight from God, and like divinity, the teinds, baptismal regeneration, and hell-fire, quite beyond argument; a Liberal, of course—that is, a Liberal wishing to drag down all men over him—a Tory of the Tories to all below him, but yet a kindly, worthy, wealthy, and not intolerable man; a moralist, if such a thing there be, thinking all sins but fornication venial; a teetotaler—that is for others—but himself taking at times his glass of whisky for the reasons which have been so cogently set forth by St. Paul the Apostle to the Caledonians. My friend lives in a house to which is joined a small estate called Inverquharity. Now, though a Radical, nothing rejoices him so much as to be designated territorially as Inverquharity, and to give out he is third cousin to the Earl of Bishopbriggs. These inconsistencies give zest to life and go some way towards redeeming even North Britain from the load of dreariness which Kailyarders depict. One of the themes the worthy ex-sweater, now turned bonnet-laird, delights to dwell on is that race has little influence upon a man. For take (he says) a Highlander and place him in the same conditions as a Lowland Scot, and he at once alters his mode of life, becomes industrious, and soon assimilates himself to those with whom he dwells. Nothing so difficult as to discuss such questions with my worthy friend. What the true Scotsman wants is argument, and it angers him as much if you agree with him as if you argue and confute his argument. If you agree you are a hypocrite, and arguing shows your narrow-mindedness, so that the safest is to say nothing and be thought a fool. Talking one day, he broached the theory that the crofters of the Hebrides were really fond of work, and that their idleness arose from lack of opportunity. "See," he remarked, "in Manitoba how they improve in new surroundings, and without a landlord to rack-rent and oppress." All landlords, in my friend's opinion, are rank tyrants, and though he likes to meet them individually, even to dine with them if they have titles, in the bulk they are accurst. Of course, there is no tyranny in trade, and if a strike takes place, why who so loud as he to call for extra police, to write for soldiers, and to complain that magistrates are weak, and that a whiff of melenite is needed just to clear the air?—for commerce, as all know, came down from heaven, took root in Glasgow, and never can do wrong.

Talking of earls and dukes, and of the shameless immorality of countesses, the iniquity of game laws (though he himself preserves), stakes in the country and the state of trade, the villainy of servants, the rate of illegitimate births and other things on which men, placed as he is placed, delight to dwell, he asked me if I knew a farm known as the Offerance. I knew the spot, a little croft with hideous little house, four windows and a door, with slated roof, and with two spruces ragged with the wind which sweeps across our favoured land on either side the "toun." A little garden, in which grew "berries," as we style gooseberries and currants, and those sub-acid apples and plums which flourish in the north. A barn, a byre, and a horse mill, with its mushroom-looking top and four wide openings, contrived on purpose to give the horses cold when resting from their work; and over all that air of desolation which the lack of flowers and neatness with the excess of wind and rain impart to Scottish farms—withal, not illappointed, the fields well drained and top-dressed, the fences in repair, the gates well painted, and the whole place a thrifty, ugly, wire-fenced, and necessary blot upon the land. Though a small holding, nothing was done by hand, crops were scientifically dropped from machines into the ground, and then the harvest ready, as artfully manoeuvred out, so that the acme of rural dullness and town desolation was attained.

The tenant of this paradise was just about to leave, and Inverquharity

announced that he was going to put his theory of environment into immediate
execution, to get a crofter family down from the Hebrides to occupy the place. It
seemed to me that if he must have islanders, he might as well have got them
from Tahiti as the Hebrides, but still I held my peace.

Time passed, and Inverquharity and I drifted apart, and Offerance, crofters,
and theories of rent escaped my mind. Riding one day to visit a hill farm, I passed
the Offerance. It looked a little unfamiliar, and seemed to have passed into a
different state. Outside the door a fire of peats was burning, on which a kettle,
hung to three birchen poles, essayed to boil. Before the fire two ragged children
sat, searching each other's heads as diligently as if they had both been scriptures. A
different air of desolation brooded on the place. The fences were all broken,
ground untilled, and little zig-zag paths traversed the fields where short cuts had
been made. The gates were off their hinges, lay on the ground or had been burnt,
and in a gap a broken cart stood jammed into the hedge. The stock was not
extensive, and reminded one of that one sees outside an Arab's tent or Indian
wigwam, mangy and full of ticks, and with the bones protruding through the
hidebound skin. Two skinny ponies, with their feet hoppled with withy ropes
which left the flesh all raw, were feeding on the weeds. Some Highland cattle and
a goat or two, some scabby sheep, a pack of sheep dogs and a lean, miserable cow,
comprised the lot, and left me wondering if the owner ever expected to pay rent,
or looked upon the Offerance as a fee simple given to him by Providence on
which to put out all his agricultural lore, and teach the natives the Ossianic mode
of carrying on a croft. Close to the house a tall, athletic man, half drunk (but not
so drunk as to have lost his wits), wrapped in a plaid and leaning on a stick, his fell
of rough black hair descending to his small grey eyes, stood looking at a woman
and a girl planting potatoes after the method known in the Highlands as the "lazy
bed." That is, instead of ploughing, you dig lightly with a spade, turning the turf a
little over on one side, then put in the potatoes and rearrange the turf. The plan is
excellent, and saves much work, manure is not required, or sweat of brow, and
the soil is exhausted almost as quickly as a crofter can desire.

To see and understand took me but little time, and mentally I said, "This is
the crofter family which my worthy friend has brought." On my horse fidgeting,
the man looked up, came to the road unsteadily, and tried to seize my reins, then,
taking off his hat, poured out a flood of compliments, all in the Gaelic tongue. I
on my part caught a word here and there, learned he was glad to see me, and
understood nothing particular, except the word "Tighearnas," which he repeated
at the end of every phrase. It means a chief, and is used by Highlanders as gipsies
use "captain" on a racecourse when they wish to flatter or delude. The rain
poured down, and he stood there bareheaded, talking and talking till I thought I
should go mad. In a mixed jargon of broken Gaelic, and that sort of idiot English
that we use to make our meaning clear to foreigners, I asked him to put on his
hat and not to be a fool. He answered, "Neffa," and though I found that he knew
English pretty well, he beckoned to his wife to act as his interpreter.

"Donald," she said, "is out of Wester Ross, he does not like the digging, but

Inverquharity is pleased with him, for he puts up such a bonny prayer." This with the sing-song accent which all Highlanders affect.

Knowing the species, I was sure digging and ploughing, and every form of man-ennobling work, was not his style, and asked why he stood bareheaded, and if he liked the place.

"Och, aye," he said, "Offerance of Inverquharity is a pretty place, and a vera pretty name it has itself whatever."

Strange as it may appear, the uncouth syllables sounded quite different when pronounced by him. His wife, continuing, informed me that Donald never put on his hat when talking to one he thought a "chentleman," and though he cared but little for hard work, he was a "pretty gamekeeper," and a first-rate man to beat.

The semi-sacrament of whisky-money having duly passed, I rode away amongst a shower of what I took for blessings in the Ossianic tongue.

Turning I saw the Offerance through the rain, black but uncomely, ragged and wind-swept—a picture of the old-world Scotland which has almost disappeared. Sloth was not altogether lovely, but prating progress worse.

I might have left the place quite discontented even with mankind, had I not recollected that the world is to the young, and noted that the children's diligence had been rewarded, and that one was handing something to the other with quite an air of pride.

(From *The Ipané*, 1899)

NOTES

1. William Dunbar (1465?-1530?), Franciscan friar, diplomat of James IV, and satirical poet, author of the "Thrissill and the Rois," a political allegory, and the elegy "Lament for the Makaris."
2. "The Flower of the Poets."
3. Robert Henryson (1430?-1506), probably a clerical schoolmaster, was of the poetry school of Chaucer, and author of "Tale of Orpheus."
4. The name of the author of a well-known and oft-cited Jewish apocryphal work, commonly known as *Ecclesiasticus* but often quoted by the author's name, belonging to Jewish Wisdom Literature.

EUPHRASIA[1]

On a mound in an upland field, right in the middle of a waste of ragwort, black knapweed, and a sea of myriads of eyebright, looking like stars upon a winter's night, there stands a War Memorial. The poorly carved Iona cross and cast-iron railings, with their gate looking as if bought at an ill country iron-monger's, serve but to render its loneliness still more pathetic, contrasted with the over-whelming landscape. "Agus Bheannaich an Sluagh no Daoine Uile a Therig iad Fein gu Toileach (Nehemiah, xi. 2)" runs the Gaelic text upon the plinth. Rendered in English it states: the men whose names are cut upon the stone gave their lives willingly. I do not doubt it, for they were born and passed their youth on the same soil and in the self-same atmosphere, sharp and invigorating, tempered with the acrid reek of peat, that nurtured Fingal, Cuchullin, Fergus and the heroes that the Celtic Homer sang.

At the foot of the lean field where stands the cross, there winds a long sea-loch with nothing on its shores except a ruined castle to show that man has sailed its waters since King Haco's fleet visited it six hundred years ago.[2] As it was when he saw it from his rude birlinn, with his oarsmen bending to their task, their shields ranged on the galley's sides, their swords bestowed beneath their feet upon the vessel's floor, so it remains to-day. The tide still leaves great fringes of brown kelp and yellow dulse upon its slippery rocks; seals still bask on the islands; the dogfish hunts the shoals of herrings, and the Atlantic clean, snell air comes up between South Uist and Benbecula, just as the "summer sailors" felt it on their tanned cheeks, stirring their yellow hair, in the days when in their long ships they scourged the Hebrides.

Green, flat-topped mountains tower up on the far side of the loch; great moors, on which grow nothing but the cotton grass, sweet gale and asphodel, stretch towards the fantastic range of the dark, purple mountains to the east. Jagged and serrated, unearthly looking, shrouded in mists that boil and curl about their sides, they rise, looking as if they had something ominous about them, hostile to mankind.

The Ossianic heroes still seem to stalk about their corries and peep out from the mists approvingly at their descendants, whose names are cut upon the little, lonely monument, set in its sea of wild flowers, opposite the loch. Far off Quir-aing, Blaaven and Bein a Cailleach; the unquiet tide rip opposite Kyle Rhea, Coruisk and Sligachan; all the wild myrtle-scented moors, the black peat haggs, the air of wildness and remoteness from the world that even motors hooting on the road, and charabancs with loads of tourists, four-beplussed, shingled, and bur-berried to the eyes, cannot dispel entirely, make a fit setting for a memorial to men bred and begotten in the isle. Most of them served in Scottish regiments, MacAskill, Royal Scots; MacMillan, London Scottish; McAlister, Scottish South Africans; Galbraith, New Zealand Infantry; MacPhee, Black Watch; McKinnes, Scots Guards; McDonald of the Rhodesian Rifles, and many more, all Skye men, whose bones moulder in battle-fields far from the Winged Isle.

That nothing should be wanting to connect the warriors with their sea-roving ancestors, Captain McFarlane and Angus Cumming of the Mercantile Marine sleep with their slumbers soothed by the murmur of the waves above their heads, a fitting resting-place for men born in an island into which the sea-lochs bore to its very heart. Out of what shielings, with their little fields of oats and of potatoes that stretch like chess-boards on the hill-sides, won from the uncongenial soil by the sweat of centuries of work, the humble warriors came, only their families can tell.

It matters little, reared as they were with one foot in the past, one hand on the *caschrom*, the other on the handle of some up-to-date reaping machine from Birmingham. Those only who had gone out to the Colonies could have known much about the outside world, until the breaking out of the Great War, in which they lost their lives. For them no placards, with their loud appeals to patriotism, could have been necessary. For a thousand years their ancestors had all been warriors, thronging to enlist in the Napoleonic Wars, eager to join Montrose and Claverhouse, and fighting desperately among themselves when there was peace abroad. They fought their fight, giving up all that most of them possessed, their lives. And now, although their bodies are disintegrated in the four quarters of the globe, it well may be their spirits have returned to some Valhalla in the mists that roll round Sligachan.

Seasons will come and go; the ragworts blossom in the fields where stands the monument, wither and die, and flower again next year. Time will roll on. The names carved upon the stone become forgotten. The cross may fall, and the cheap iron railings exfoliate away to nothing. The very wars, in which the Islemen fell, become but a mere legend, as has happened to all other wars.

Men's eyes will turn more rarely to the memorial in the windswept field, and they will ask what it commemorates. Still, the wild hills will not forget, as they have not forgotten the story of the wars fought by the driver of the twin thin-maned, high-mettled, swift-footed, wide-nostriled steeds of the mountains, Sithfadda and Dusrongeal. But if the eyes of men are turned no longer to the plinth, with its long list of names and Gaelic text, when the spring comes, and once again the eyebright springs in the hungry field, the west wind sweeping up the loch will turn a million little eyes towards the cross.

(From *Redeemed,* 1927)

NOTES

1. *Euphrasia*, Cheerfulness. The tone of the sketch would indicate that Graham's title is slightly ironic.
2. King Haakon of Norway who, with his invading Norsemen, was finally defeated at the Battle of Largs (1263).

Section III

SCENES AND SITUATIONS

EDITOR'S PREFACE

The tendency of the Scottish character to moralise on death and parting is consolidated in some of Graham's representative "situation" sketches. As he says in "A Braw Day" (an ironic title, since the owners are vacating their home, just as Graham and his wife had to give up Gartmore), "to bid good-bye to buildings and familiar scenes seemed natural, as life is but a long farewell."

The sketches in this section were chosen because they depict best Graham's ability to portray a scene, often past, like the description of the market in "Falkirk Tryst." The fact that they all depict a parting, funeral, or death is but a coincidence, though it could hardly be otherwise, given Graham's philosophical temperament and literary bent. The sale of the family estate at Gartmore was a tragedy surpassed only by the death of his wife in 1906. His personal situation is mirrored in the pathetic description in "Fidelity" (narrated by a Scottish laird) of a wounded curlew facing death, supported by its faithful mate. The ploughman's funeral (and the stoicism of his widow) in "At Dalmary" and Keir Hardie's in "With the North-East Wind" are but two of the many funerals that were the stuff of other sketches—the funerals of Queen Victoria, William Morris and Joseph Conrad being the best-known.

These descriptions of death and funeral scenes also tell us much about the Scottish character, as revealed in the previous section, and prepare the way for another interesting aspect of Graham's work—his immortalising of certain types who brightened the Scottish landscape, and well-known figures on the local scene.

A BRAW DAY[1]

Never before, in the long years that he had passed in the old place, had it appeared so much a part of his whole being, as on the day on which he signed the deed of sale.

Times had been bad for years, and a great load of debt had made the fight a foregone ending from the first. Still he felt like a murderer, as judges well may feel when they pronounce death sentences. Perhaps they feel it more than the prisoner, for things we do through fate, and by the virtue of the circumstances that hedge our lives about with chains, often affect us more than actions which we perform impelled by no one but ourselves.

The long, white Georgian house, with its two flanking wings, set in its wide expanse of gravel, which, like a sea, flowed to a grassy, rising slope, looked digni-fied and sad. An air, as of belonging to a family of fallen fortunes, hung about the place. The long, dark avenue of beeches, underneath one of which stood the gallows stone, looked as if no one ever used it, and on its sides the grassy edges had long ago all turned to moss, a moss so thick and velvety you might have swept it with a broom.

The beech mast crackled underneath your feet as you passed up the natural cathedral aisle, and on the tops of the old trees the wind played dirges in the cold autumn nights, and murmured softly in the glad season "when that shaws are green."

The formal terraces were roughly mown and honeycombed by rabbits, the whinstone steps were grown with moss, and here and there were forced apart by a strong growing fern that pushed out to the light.

The seats about the garden were all blistered with the sun and rain, and the old-fashioned coach-roofed greenhouse looked like a refrigerator, with its panes frosted by the damp. Under the arch, which led into the stable yard, stood two dilapidated dog kennels, disused, but with some links of rusty chain still hanging to them, as if they waited for the return of shadowy dogs, dead years ago.

The cedars on the slope below the terraces stretched out their long and human-looking branches, as they were fingers seeking to restrain and hold those whom they knew and loved.

All was serene and beautiful, with the enthralling beauty of decay. The fences were unmended, and slagging wires in places had been dragged by cattle into the middle of the fields. Most of the gates were off their hinges, and weeds had covered up the gravel of the walks.

Nettles grew rankly in the grass, and clumps of dock, with woody stems and feathery heads, stood up like bulrushes about the edges of a pond. Even at noonday, a light mist still clung about the lower fields below the house, marking out clearly where old "peat hags" had been reclaimed.

Such was the place at noonday; melancholy as regards the lack of care that want of means had brought about; but bright and sunny as it lay facing to the south, sheltered by groups of secular sycamores and beech.

At night a feeling as if one had been marooned upon some island, far away from men, grew on the inmates of the house.

Owls fabulated from the tree-tops, their long, quavering call seeming to jar the air and make it quiver, so still was everything.

The roes' metallic belling sounded below the windows, and the sharp chirping of the rabbits never ceased during summer nights, as they played in the grass.

When the long shadows, in the moonlight, crept across the lawn, it seemed as if they beckoned to the shadows of the dead, in the old eerie house. Those who had gone before had set their seal so firmly upon everything, planting the trees, and adding here a wing and there a staircase, that those who now possessed the house dwelt in it, as it were, by the permission of the dead.

One day remained to him whose ancestors had built the house; who had lived in the old ruined castle, in the grounds, and who had fought and plundered, rugged and reived after the fashion of their kind. All had been done that falls to a man's lot to do at such a time. The house stood gaunt and empty. By degrees, the familiar objects, that time and sentiment make almost sacred and as if portions of ourselves, had been packed up, and on the walls, the pictures taken down, had left the blank spaces that recalled each one as perfectly as if it had been there.

Steps sounded hollow in the emptiness and desolation on the stairs, and bits of straw and marks of hobnailed boots showed where the workmen had been busy at their task.

Here and there marks of paint and varnish on a door showed where a heavy piece of furniture had touched in passing, as sometimes after a funeral you see the dent made by the coffin in the plaster of the passage, as it was carried to the hearse.

A desolating smell of straw was everywhere. It permeated everything, even to the food, which an old servant cooked in the great, ungarnished kitchen, just as a tramp might cook his victuals at the corner of a road.

The polished staircase, which from their childhood had been a kind of fetish to the children of the house, shielded from vulgar footsteps by a thick drugget and a protecting strip of holland, but bleached a snowy white, was now all scratched and dirtied, as if it were no better than the steps which led to the backyard.

The owner and his wife, after their years of struggle, had felt at first as if their ship had got into a port; and then as days went by, and by degrees, the house, which they had cared for more than their own lives, grew empty and more empty, till it was left a shell, now found their port had vanished, and they were left without an anchorage.

Still, there was one more day to pass. What then to do with it? The house was empty, the few old servants that remained, tearful and wandering to and fro, pleased to be idle and yet not knowing what to do with unaccustomed leisure, jostled each other on the stairs.

The horses had been sold, all but one little old, black pony; the dogs all sent away to friends.

Standing at the hall door, looking out on the sweep of gravel all cut up by carts, the owners stood a little while, dazed and not able to take in that twenty years had flown. It seemed but yesterday that they had driven up to the same door, young, full of expectation and of hope.

Now they were middle-aged and grey. The fight had gone against them; but still they had the recollection of the struggle, for all except the baser sort of men fight not to win, but simply for the fight.

Some call it duty, but the fight's the thing, for those who strive to win become self-impressed, and that way lies the road to commonplace. Verily, they have their reward; but the reward soon overwhelms them, whilst the true fighters still fight on, with sinews unrelaxed.

At last, after having looked about in vain for sticks, but without finding one, for they had all been packed or given away as keepsakes, they walked out to the sundial in the great gravel sweep before the door. Though they had sat and smoked upon its steps a thousand times, watching the squirrels play at noon, the bats flit past at sundown, it yet seemed new to them, and strange. With interest they saw that it was half-past three in China, eight in the evening in New Orleans, and midnight at La Paz.

Somehow it seemed that they had never seen all this before, and that, in future, time would be all the same the whole world over, or at least that it would not be marked by little brazen gnomons on a weather-beaten slab of slate. The garden, with the gardeners gone and the gate open, seemed as strange as all the rest. The flowers that they had planted, and forgotten they had planted, in the course of time had come to be considered in the same way as the old castle just outside the garden walls, as things that had existed from the beginning of the world.

Weeds choked the gravel in the lower walk, bounded by a long hedge of laurel cut into castles at due intervals. They both agreed next week they should be hoed, and then stopped, smiled and looked away, fearing to meet each other's eyes. The sun beats on the old stone wall, ripening the *magnum bonum* plums, for it was in September, and both thought they will be ripe in a few days, but feared to tell each other what they thought.

The tangled, terraced beds, where once had stood old vineries, all had been planted with herbaceous plants, which, from the want of care, had grown into a jungle; but a jungle unutterably beautiful, in which the taller plants, the coreopsis, bocconias, Japanese anemones, and larkspurs stood up starkly, as palm trees rear themselves out of a wilderness of dwarf palmettoes and of grass.

Over the garden gate, marauding ivy had run across the stone on which the arms of the decaying family were cut in hard grey whinstone, with the date 1686 in high relief, flanked by a monogram.

Upon a bench, from which the view stretched over the great moss that marked the limits of an ancient sea, and out of which a wooded hill rose like an island, the only thing that broke the level plain between the garden and the distant hills, they sat and let the sun beat on them for the last time, as it had often done during their years of struggle and of fight.

Descending through a gate, which slagged a little on its hinges, and grated on the stone lintel as it opened after a heavy push, they passed into the narrow strip of extra garden, taken in as it were by afterthought, in the old Scottish fashion, which never seemed to have enough of garden laid about a house. They bade good-bye to the long line of *arbor vitae* clipped into cones which cast their shadows on the path so clearly that you were half inclined to lift your feet in passing, they looked so firm and round.

The curious moondial, with its niches coloured blue and red; the burial-ground hidden away amongst the trees, and with a long, grass walk, mossy and damp, leading up to its old grey walls, they visited but did not see, as they were so familiar, that they had become impossible to look at, but as parts and parcels of themselves.

The day seemed never-ending, and in the afternoon, to pass the time, seeing a water conduit underneath a road choked up with leaves, the departing owner of the place set about working hard to clear it, and, having done so, congratulated himself on a good piece of work. To bid good-bye to buildings and familiar scenes seemed natural, as life is but a long farewell; but to look for the last time on the trees—trees that his ancestors had planted, and by which he himself recognised the seasons, as for example by the turning yellow of the horse-chestnuts, which he saw from his bedroom windows, or the first pinkish blush upon the broken larch, whose broken top was cased in lead—that seemed a treason to them, for they had always been so faithful, putting out their leaves in spring, standing out stark and rigid in the winter and murmuring in the breeze.

The whispering amongst their branches and the melodious tinkle of a little burn that crossed the avenue were sounds which, on that last day, pervaded all the air and filled the soul with that deep-seated feeling of amazement that looks out, hopeless and heart-rending, from the eyes of dying animals.

The interminable day came to an end at last. The sun set, red and beautiful, over the low, flat moss, and disappeared behind the hills. The owls called shrilly from the trees, and the accustomed air of ghostliness, intensified a thousandfold by solitude, pervaded all the house.

The mysterious footstep, which in the course of years had grown familiar, even in winter nights, as it passed up the corridor and stopped with a loud knock on the end bedroom door, again grew terrifying as it had been on the first night that they had heard it years ago.

From out the spaces where the pictures once had hung, the well-known faces seemed to peer, but unfamiliar-looking, with an air as of reproach.

The smallest footfall sounded as loud as if it were the trampling of a horse; and candles, stuck in bottles here and there, gave a dim, flickering light, casting dark shadows on the floor.

Long did the owners gaze into the night, watching the stars come out in their familiar places. The Bear hung right across the cedars, almost due north, Alphecca close to the horizon, the Square of Pegasus quite horizontal, and Fomalhaut in the south-west, athwart the corner of the Easter Hill.

A light, white frost turned all to silver, and the lake in the east middle distance lay like a sheet of burnished silver under the moon, its islands mirrored dimly and as if floating in the air. No leaf was stirring, and as they sat around a fire of logs, talking of were-wolves, fairies, and superstitions of another land, with their old Spanish friend and servant,[2] the night wore on so rapidly that it was day-light almost as it appeared, before the sun went down.

Short preparations serve for those about to go, and when a few old servants and retainers took their leave, and a black pony slowly took their trunks down to the station, looking forlorn in the immensity of the beech avenue, they closed the door upon their house.

Quickly the trees rushed past, the pond with its tall island looking like a ship, the giant silver firs, the castle, which they beheld as in a dream, all floated by. Just at the cross-roads which led into the park, beside the gate, a man stood waiting for them.

He carried in his hand a hedgebill, and stood there waiting, as he had waited for the past twenty years, for orders for the day.

Now, he held out his hand, opened his mouth, but said nothing, and then, looking up with the air of one well learned in weather lore, said, "Laird, it looks like a braw day."

(From *Charity*, 1912)

NOTES

1. This sketch is clearly based on Graham's own sad experience of having to sell his Gartmore estate in 1901 because of debts incurred by his father.
2. This is obviously Peregrina, the Galician servant of Don Roberto and his wife.

FALKIRK TRYST

In these days when every vestige of old custom and old speech is being rapidly submerged in the dumb waves of progress, the word "tryst" should be preserved by Act of Parliament. How well it figures in the Border Ballads—"Atte the Reidswire, the Tryst was set," "Gailie she came to the Trysting Tree," and half a hundred other instances, show what a fine poetic word it is. None other in the language could supply its place, ... the trysting oak, at which Wallace is said to have convened his merry men in the Blane Valley, would sound poor enough, as poor as the Holy Scriptures, put into the modern vulgar tongue. Besides all this, it is a word that to Scotchmen (such as have no Gaelic) gives an air of superiority over the mere Englishman. Many years ago I crossed with a lady, who always had maintained that between English and Lowland Scotch there was no difference, from the West Ferry to Dumbarton in the ferry-boat.

It was raining cats and dogs, and, as we waited in the rain beside the rickety old pier below the castle, a cab drove slowly up. We eyed it curiously. I asked the driver to take us to the railway station. He rather surlily refused. Whereupon one of a host of long-shore youths who were standing, heedless of the rain, watching a full-rigged ship being towed down the Clyde (being moved apparently by the air of discomfort which the lady who was with me showed), remarked, "Hurl them up, Jimmy." Jimmy relaxed his features, and answered in an apologetic way, "I canna, man, I'm trysted."

We tramped up to the station in the rain, but never afterwards did my companion maintain that the two languages were identical.

During my boyhood, Falkirk Tryst was an event to be looked forward to, for droves of ponies from the Islands and the north used to be driven down the pass by an old drove road which passed Aberfoyle. Thin and wild-eyed, with ropy manes and tails that swept the ground, they strayed along.

Chestnuts and piebalds, duns with a black stripe down their back and markings like a tiger on the hocks, cream-colours with dark tails and manes, skewbalds and bays (never a single roan), they used to remind me of the troops of mustangs that I had read of in Mayne Reid.[1] Behind them on a pony, with his knees up to his mouth, a broken snaffle bridle, and in his hands a long, crooked hazel stick, the drover followed, always enveloped in his plaid. A dog or two hung at his pony's heels, and in a language that was strange to us as Telegú, he used to shout anathemas at beasts that lagged behind.

Slowly they trailed along, for time was what the driver had most at his command, stopping to crop the grass or drink at the broad, shallow crossing of the mountain burns, standing about in knots knee-deep, and swishing with their tails, just as in after life I have seen wild horses do in both Americas. Foals trotted by their mothers' sides, and the whole road was blocked between its dry-stone dykes, surmounted by their feals.

Usually these herds of ponies, collected from the far Highlands and the Islands, were the first sign of the approaching Tryst. Sometimes, however, early in the morning if we were going out to fish, at one of those broad, grassy spaces, which in those days existed at the crossing of four roads, we used to come upon men lying round a fire. Wrapped in their plaids on which the frost showed white, or the dew shone just as it does upon a spider's web, their sticks laid near their hands, they slumbered peacefully. Around them grazed West Highland cattle, black, dun, or chestnut, their peaceful disposition belied by their long, curving horns and shaggy foreheads, and as we passed, one of the men was sure to rise upon his elbow, pull his plaid off his head, and after looking around to see the cattle had not strayed, throw wood upon the fire, and then lie down to sleep again, after muttering a salutation either in Gaelic or in the singsong English which in those days men of his kidney spoke. Great flocks of blackfaced sheep were also to be met with coming southwards to the Tryst, driven by men who daundered on behind them with that peculiar trailing step that only those who passed their lives upon the road were able to acquire. Generally two or three accompanied the herd, dressed usually in homespun tweeds, which smelt of wool and peat smoke, and were so thick that those who wore them looked like bears, as they lounged heavily along.

All of them had a collie, which if he was not trained, they led tied by a cord without a collar round his neck, and fastened to a button on their coats. The dogs looked lean and wolfish, for it was long before the times when they were fashionable as pets, and at a sign, or in response to some deep guttural Gaelic order, they turned back straying sheep so dexterously, one used to wonder where the line that separated their instinct from their master's reason ended or began.

As the droves slowly took their passage through the land, the drovers often would sell a pony-beast, or a stot that had got footsore, to farmers on the way. These sales were not concluded without expenditure of time and whisky and an infinity of talk.

Then the tired colt or calf was led into the byre, and the long line of ponies or of cattle started again, filling the road from side to side and leaving as it passed a wild, warm smell of mountain animals.

Such were the outward visible signs of Falkirk Tryst as I remember them, so many years ago, before the railways and the weekly sales reduced it to a mere cattle market, shorn of importance and of historic connection with the past. The country folks in upland farms and grazing districts looked on it as one of the important functions of the year.

"So many weeks from the October Tryst." "It would be aboot the Tryst that Andra married Jean," "I canna pay ye till the Tryst," were all familiar sayings, and the date itself was as well known to all as Hallowe'en or Hogmanay, or even the New Year.

In those days Christmas was not held as a holiday except in districts such as Strathglass, Morar, or Moidart, or in the islands where the old faith prevailed, and where the phrases "if you please" and "thank you" were usual accidents of speech, which to a free and self-respecting man were not derogatory.

Mankind, however, must have festivals, and thus the Tryst had somehow crept into the Scottish Colin Clouts' Calendar.[2]

The drovers and the droves, coming as they did from the mysterious regions "above the pass," brought with them something of romance, and in fact, as they strayed along our roads they always called to my recollection etchings by Callot[3] of the Hungarian gipsies which, bound in an old crushed morocco cover, used to lie in the drawing-room and be shown to us as children on Sundays and wet afternoons.

It may be, too, that, unknown to themselves, the Lowland ploughmen working in the fields looked at the drovers as a man accustomed to office work looks on a sailor as he passes by, with feelings oscillating between contempt and envy of his adventurous life.

Certain it was that the old Highland drovers would not have changed their mode of life for anything. To wake up on a bright morning in October, and shake the hoar frost from one's clothes, collect the cattle, and having sent the whisky bottle round, once more to find oneself upon the road, with the scene changing constantly as one strolled along, must have been pleasanter by far than settled occupation with its dull daily round.

To travel round the Highlands buying a pony here, another there, three or four ewes or stots on one farm, and then setting out upon the trip to Falkirk, sleeping by the herd, and after perhaps a fortnight arriving at the Tryst, to find the booth set up, the other drovers gradually dropping in, exchanging notes on prices, and on the incidents of the march, produced a kind of [life] that Scotland knows no more.

The "parks" by Larbert, where the Tryst was held, presented on the fateful day the aspect of a fair, with the tents and the crowd of country people.

Sheep bleated and cows lowed, and, as it generally was raining, a smell of tar and wool hung in the air. Knots of men wrapped in plaids, their clothes showing the signs of having camped by the roadside, their faces tanned or reddened by the sun, their beards as shaggy as the coats of the rough kyloes that they passed their lives with, chatted with Lowland shepherds from the Cheviots.

Dealers from England, better dressed but slower in their minds and speech than any Scotsman possibly can be, surveyed the animals, poking them with their sticks, and running down their points after the fashion of the intending buyer in every country of the world. Rough-looking lads, but with that air of super-natural cunning that commerce with the horse imparts, ran ponies up and down.

Beefy-faced cattle-dealers from the Midlands roared at Highlanders whose English was defective, thinking to make them understand by noise; and Highlanders, who themselves understood English almost as well as they did, and spoke it far more purely, pretended to mistake their meaning to get more time to think what they should say.

When, after an infinity of haggling, a price was reached, to which the seller gave assent, both parties would adjourn to one of the tents, to wet the bargain, and sit down at a white, deal table, placed upon the grass, and swallow whisky in a way that no one not connected with the cattle trade could possibly achieve. On them it had no more affect than milk, unless to make the fiery faces of the Yorkshire dealers a thought redder, and set the Highlanders a-talking still more fluently than when they had gone in.

Quarrels were rare, and drunkenness not common with such seasoned vessels; but on the rare occasions when the whisky had proved stronger than the head, they lay down peacefully to sleep it off, beside their animals, with their heads buried in their plaids.

The day wore on, amidst the lowing of the beasts and noise of bargaining, and towards evening the roads were full of strings of animals being driven off, either towards the railway, or on the way to their new homes. I often wondered if they missed the rough and shaggy men, so near to them in type, or thought about the upland pastures in the glens, or the sweet, waving grass of island machars in the lush Lowland fields.

It pleases us and stills our conscience to say that animals know no such feeling, but yet "I hae my doots," and the wild whinnyings and jerks back on the halter must mean something, ... but after all they have no souls.

Not that such speculations ever entered anybody's head at Falkirk Tryst. Well, well, the Tryst, that is as I knew it in my boyhood, has slipped away into the realms of old, forgotten, far-away memories.

It formed a link between the modern world and times when kilted drovers with their targets at their backs, girt with their claymores, their feet shod in the hairy brogues by which they gained the name of the Rough-Footed Scots, drove down their kyloes and their ponies through the very *bealach* that I remember in my youth. They are all gone with the old world they lived in; but still the shadows fall upon the southern slopes and creep into the corries of the Ochils that overlook the historic parks by Larbert in which the Tryst was held. Heavy-nailed boots now press the grass that once was brushed so lightly by the Highland brogues. No one now sleeps beside the roads, nor, rising with the dawn, wrings out the dewdrops from his plaid.

The life that once was real now seems fantastic; not half so real as the shadows on the hills, and even they only endure whilst the sun shines, chasing one another up and down till it peeps in again.

(From *A Hatchment*, 1913)

NOTES

1. Thomas Mayne Reid (1818-83), novelist who wrote such works as *The Rifle Rangers* (1850), *The Scalp Hunters* (1851) and *The Headless Horseman* (1866).
2. "Colin Clout's Come Home Again" is the name of a poem written by one of Graham's favourite poets, Edmund Spenser (1552?-99), after a visit to London (1589-91). Spenser took the name from Skelton's Colyn Cloute and called himself Colin Clout in all his poetry. Part of the attraction of "Colin Clout's Come Home Again" for Graham is its praise of the simple country life, as manifest in events and festivals like the Falkirk Tryst.
3. Jacques Callot (1592-1635), French engraver and etcher, noted for his fine battle scenes and large groupings of people.

AT DALMARY

The road led out upon an open moor, on which heather and wiry grass strove for the mastery. Here and there mossy patches, on which waved cotton-grass, broke the grey surface of the stony waste, and here and there tufts of dwarf willow, showing the silvery backs of their grey leaves, rustled and bent before the wind.

The road, one of those ancient trails on which cattle and ponies were driven in old times down to the Lowland trysts, was now half covered up with grass. It struggled through the moor as if it chose to do so of its own accord, now twisting for no apparent reason, and again going straight up a hill, just as the ponies and the kyloes must have straggled before the drovers' dogs. It crossed a shallow ford, in which the dark brown moorland trout darted from stone to stone when the shadow of a passer-by startled them as they poised, their heads up stream, keeping themselves suspended as it were by an occasional wavering motion of their tails, just as a hawk hangs hovering in the air.

Beside the stream, a decaying wooden bridge, high-pitched and shaky, reminded one that in the winter the burn, now singing its metallic little song between the stones, brown and pellucid, with bubbles of white foam floating upon its tiny linns or racing down the stream, checking a little in an eddy, where a tuft of heavy ragweed dipped into the flood, was dangerous to cross.

The aromatic scent of the sweet-gale came down the breeze, mixed with the acrid smoke of peats. Hairbells danced in the gentle breeze, and bumble-bees hummed noisily as they emerged, weighed down with honey, from the ling.

Across the moor, from farms and shielings, and from the grey and straggling village built on each side of the rough street, in which the living rock cropped up and ran in reefs across the road, came groups of men dressed in black clothes, creased and ill-fitting, with hats, grown brown with years of church-going and with following funerals in the rain. They walked along as if they missed the familiar spade or plough-handle to keep them straight, just as a sailor walks uneasily ashore.

As they trudged on they looked professionally on the standing crops, or passed their criticisms on the cattle in the fields. Root crops, they thought, were back, taties not just exactly right, a thocht short in the shaws, and every cow a wee bit heigh abune the tail, for praise was just as difficult a thing for them to give as blame was easy, for they were all aware their God was jealous, and it did not befit them to appear more generous than He. Hills towered and barred the north, and to the south the moors stretched till they met another range of hills, and all the space between them was filled with a great sea of moss, eyed here and there with dark, black pools on which a growth of water-lilies floated like fairies' boats. A wooded hill, which sloped down to a brawling river, was the fairies' court. Another to the south, steep, rising from the moss, the Hill of the Crown, received its name back in the times of Fingal and of Bran. Gaps in the hills showed where, in times gone by, marauders from the north had come to harry and to slay. The names of every hill, lake, wood, or stream were Gaelic, and the whole country exhaled an air of a romantic past.

In it the dour, black-coated men, although they thought themselves as much a part and parcel of the land as the grey rocks upon the moor, were strangers; holding their property but on sufferance from the old owners, who had named every stone, and left their impress even in the air.

It seemed the actual dwellers acted as it were a play, a sort of rough and clownish interlude, upon a stage set out for actors whom the surroundings would have graced.

Still, though they shared the land, just as we all do, by favour of the dead, they had set their mark upon it, running their rough stone walls across the moors and to the topmost ridges of the hills, planting their four-square, slate-roofed houses in places where a thatched and whitewashed cottage, with red tropaeolum growing on the corner of the byre, a plant of mullein springing from a crevice in the wall, and flauchtered feals pegged to the thatch with birchen crockets,[1] or kept down with stones, would have looked just as fitting as theirs looked out of place. A land in which the older dwellers had replaced the nymphs and hama-dryads[2] by the fairies, where, in the soft and ceaseless rain, the landscape wore a look of sadness, that the mist, creeping up on the shoulders of the hills, at times turned menacing, was now delivered over to a race of men who knew no shadows, either in life or in belief. If they believed, they held each letter of "The Book" inspired, and would have burned the man who sought to change a comma to a semicolon; and if they had rejected faith as an encumbrance they could do without, denied the very possibility of any god or power but mathematics, hold-ing the world a mere gigantic counting-house in which they sat enthroned. The moaning birches and dark murmuring pines, the shaggy thickets by the streams, and the green hummocks under which tradition held Pictish or Celtic chiefs reposed, the embosomed corries over which the shadows ran, as imperceptibly as lizards run upon a wall, turning the brown hillside into gold, which melted into green as it stole on, until it faded into a pale amethyst, faint and impalpable as is a colour in a dream, seemed to demand a race of men more fitted to its moods than those who walked along the road chatting about the crops. Still it may be that though the outward visible sign was so repellent, the unexpected and interior softness of the black-clothed and tall-hatted men was bred in them by their sur-roundings, for certainly their hard, material lives, and their black, narrow, anti-human faith could not have given it.

The road led on until on the south side of it a path, worn in the heather and the wiry grass, and winding in and out between the hillocks, crossed here and there by bands of rocks, outcropping, but smoothed down on the edge by the feet of centuries, broke off, not at right angles after the fashion of a modern road, but on the slant, just as a herd of driven animals slants off, stopping at intervals to graze.

The knots of black-clothed men, some followed by their dogs, slowly converged upon the path, and stood a minute talking, passing the time of day, exchanging bits of news and gossip in subdued voices, and mopping vigorously at their brows, oppressed with the unwonted weight of their tall hats.

"We've had a braw back end, McKerrachar," Borland remarked. The worthy he addressed, a gaunt, cadaverous man, so deeply wrinkled that you could fancy in wet weather the rain [running] down the channels in his face, spat in contemplative fashion, rejoining in a non-committal way:

"No just sae bad . . . markets are back a wee." A nod of assent went round the group, and then another interjected:

"I dinna mind sae braw a back end for mony a year; aye, ou aye, I'll no deny markets are very conseederably back."

Having thus magnified his fellow, after the fashion of the stars, he looked a moment with apparent interest at his hat, which he held in his hand, and ventured the remark:

"A sair blow to the widow, Andra's death; he was a good man to her."

No one answering him, he qualified what he had said by adding:

"Aye, sort of middlin'," and glanced round warily, to see if he had overstepped the bounds by the too indiscriminating nature of his praise.

The house towards which the various knots of men were all converging stood at the foot of a green, grassy mound, which looked as if it might have been the tumulus of some prehistoric chief. On it grew several wind-bent ash trees, and within twenty yards or so of the front door of the grey cottage, with its low thatched eaves, there ran a little burn. Two or three mulleins, with flowers still clinging to their dying stalks, on which they stuck like vegetable warts, sprung from the crevices between the stones of the rough byre. A plant or two of ragweed grew on the midden on which a hen was scratching, and out of it a green and oozy rivulet of slush filtered down to the stream. On one side was a garden, without a flower, and with a growth of straggling cabbage, gooseberry bushes, and some neglected-looking raspberry canes, as the sole ornaments. In the potato patch a broken spade was stuck into the ground. All round the house some straggling plum trees, with their sour fruit half ripened and their leaves already turning brown, looking as if they had struggled hard for life against the blast, in the poor, stony soil, gave a peculiar air of desolation, imparting to the place a look as of an oasis just as unfruitful as the waste which stretched on every side. On one side of the door, but drawn a little on the grass, not to obstruct the way, there stood a cart, with a tall, white-faced and white-pasterned horse between the shafts, held by a little boy. Peat smoke curled lazily out of the barrel stuck into the thatch that served as chimney, and cocks and hens scratched in the mud before the door, bees hummed amongst the heather, and once again the groups of men in black struck a discordant note.

Inside the house, upon four wooden chairs was set the coffin of the dead ploughman, cheap and made in haste, just as his life had been lived cheaply and in haste, from the first day that he had stood between the stilts, until the evening when he had loosed his horses from the plough for the last time, his furrow finished and his cheek no more to be exposed to the November rain. Now in the roughly put together kist he lay, his toil-worn hands crossed on his breast, and with his wrinkled, weather-beaten face turned waxen and ennobled, set in its frame of wiry whisker, and his scant hair decently brushed forward on his brow. The peats burned brightly in the grate and sent out a white ash which covered everything inside the house, whitening the clothes of the black-coated men who stood about, munching great hunks of cake and slowly swallowing down the "speerits" which the afflicted widow pressed upon them, proud through her tears to say, "Tak' it up, Borland," or "It will no hurt ye, Knockinshanock; ye ken there's plenty more."

The white peat ash fell on the coffin-lid just as the summer's dust had fallen upon the hair of him who lay inside, and lay upon the polished surface of the thin brass plate, on which were superscribed the dates of the birth and of the death of the deceased, his only titles to the recollection of the race with whom his life had passed. Now and again the widow, snatching a moment from her hospitable cares, brushed off the dust abstractedly with her pocket-handkerchief, just as a man might stop upon the way to execution to put a chair straight or to do any of the trifling actions of which life is composed. As she paused by the coffin, the assembled men exchanged that furtive look of sympathy which in the North is the equivalent of the wild wailings, tears, and self-abandonment of Southern folk, and perhaps stamps on the heart of the half-shamefaced sympathiser even a deeper line.

When all had drunk their "speerits" and drawn the backs of their rough hands across their mouths and shaken off the crumbs from their black clothes, the minister stood forth. Closing his eyes, he launched into his prayer with needless repetition, but with the feeling which the poor surroundings and the brave struggle against outward grief of the woman sitting by the fire in the old high-backed chair, in which her husband had sat so long, evoked, he dwelt upon man's passage through the world.

Life was a breath, only a little dust, a shadow on the hills. It had pleased the Lord, for reasons of His own, inscrutable, but against which 'twere impious to rebel, for a brief space to breathe life into the nostrils of this our brother, and here he made a motion of his hand towards the kist, then to remove him to a better sphere after a spell of toil and trouble here on earth. Still we must not repine, as do the heathen, who gash themselves with knives, having no hope, whereas we who enjoy the blessings of being born to a sure faith in everlasting bliss should look on death as but a preparation for a better life. No doubt this hope consoled the speaker for all the ills humanity endures, for he proceeded to invoke a blessing on the widow, and as he prayed the rain beat on the narrow, bull's-eye window-panes. He called upon the Lord to bless her in her basket and her store, and to be with her in her outgoings and incomings, to strengthen her and send her resignation to His will. He finished with the defiance to humanity that must have wrung so many tears of blood from countless hearts, saying the Lord had given and that the Lord had taken, blessed be His name.

All having thus been done that all our ingenuity can think of on such occasions, four stalwart neighbours, holding their hats, which tapped upon their legs, hoisted the coffin on to their shoulders and shuffled to the door. They stooped to let their burden pass beneath the eaves which overhung the entrance, and then emerging, dazed, into the light, their black clothes dusted over with the white ashes from the fire, set down the coffin on the cart. Once more the men gathered into a circle and listened to a prayer, some with their heads bare to the rain, and others with their hats held on the slant to fend it off as it came swirling down the blast. A workman in his ordinary clothes took the tall, white-faced horse close by the bit, and, with a jolt which made the kist shift up against the backboard, the cart set out, swaying amongst the ruts, with now and then a wheel running up high upon one side and now and then a jerk upon the trace-hooks, when the horse, cold with his long wait, strained wildly on the chains. The rain had blotted out the hills, the distant village with its rival kirks had disappeared, and the grey sky appeared to touch the surface of the moor. A whitish dew hung on the grass and made the seeded plants appear gigantic in the gloom. Nothing was to be heard except the roaring of the burn and the sharp ringing of the high caulkins of the horse as he struck fire amongst the stones on the steep, rocky road.

Leaning against the doorpost, the widow stood and gazed after the vanishing procession till it had disappeared into the mist, her tears, which she had fought so bravely to keep back, now running down her face.

When the last sound of the cart-wheels and of the horse's feet amongst the stones had vanished into the thick air, she turned away and, sitting down before the fire, began mechanically to smoor the peats and tidy up the hearth.

(From *Hope*, 1910)

NOTES

1. *birchen crockets*, little ornaments usually in the shape of buds or curled leaves, made of birch, used to peg down the thatching of cut turfs.
2. *hamadryads*, wood nymphs fabled to live in trees.

FIDELITY

My tall host knocked the ashes from his pipe, and crossing one leg over the other looked into the fire.

Outside, the wind howled in the trees, and the rain beat upon the window-panes. The firelight flickered on the grate, falling upon the polished furniture of the low-roofed, old-fashioned library, with its high Georgian overmantel, where in a deep recess there stood a clock, shaped like a cross, with eighteenth-century cupids carved in ivory fluttering round the base, and Time with a long scythe standing upon one side.

In the room hung the scent of an old country-house, compounded of so many samples that it is difficult to enumerate them all. Beeswax and potpourri of roses, damp, and the scent of foreign woods in the old cabinets, tobacco and wood smoke, with the all-pervading smell of age, were some of them. The result was not unpleasant, and seemed the complement of the well-bound Georgian books standing demure upon their shelves, the blackening family portraits, and the skins of red deer and of roe scattered about the room.

The conversation languished, and we both sat listening to the storm that seemed to fill the world with noises strange and unearthly, for the house was far from railways, and the avenues that lead to it were long and dark. The solitude and the wild night seemed to have recreated the old world, long lost, and changed, but still remembered in that district just where the Highlands and the Lowlands meet.

At such times and in such houses the country really seems country once again, and not the gardened, gamekeepered mixture of shooting ground and of fat fields tilled by machinery to which men now and then resort for sport, or to gather in their rents, with which the whole world is familiar to-day.

My host seemed to be struggling with himself to tell me something, and as I looked at him, tall, strong, and upright, his face all mottled by the weather, his homespun coat, patched on the shoulders with buckskin that once had been white, but now was fawn-coloured with wet and from the chafing of his gun, I felt the parturition of his speech would probably cost him a shrewd throe. So I said nothing, and he, after having filled his pipe, ramming the tobacco down with an old silver Indian seal, made as he told me in Karachi, and brought home by a great-uncle fifty years ago, slowly began to speak, not looking at me, but as it were delivering his thoughts aloud, almost unconsciously, looking now and then at me as if he felt, rather than knew, that I was there. As he spoke, the tall, stuffed hen-harrier; the little Neapolitan shrine in tortoise-shell and coral, set thick with saints; the flying dragons from Ceylon, spread out like butterflies in a glazed case;

the "poor's-box" on the shelf above the books with its four silver sides adorned with texts; the rows of blue books, and of Scott's novels (the Roxburgh edition), together with the scent exuding from the Kingwood cabinet; the sprays of white Scotch rose, outlined against the window blinds; and the sporting prints and family tree, all neatly framed in oak, created the impression of being in a world remote, besquired and cut off from the century in which we live by more than fifty years. Upon the rug before the fire the sleeping spaniel whined uneasily, as if, though sleeping, it still scented game, and all the time the storm roared in the trees and whistled down the passages of the lone country house. One saw in fancy, deep in the recesses of the woods, the roe stand sheltering, and the caper-cailzie sitting on the branches of the firs, wet and dejected, like chickens on a roost, and little birds sent fluttering along, battling for life against the storm. Upon such nights, in districts such as that in which the gaunt old house was situated, there is a feeling of compassion for the wild things in the woods that, stealing over us, bridges the gulf between them and ourselves in a mysterious way. Their lot and sufferings, joys, loves, and the epitome of their brief lives, come home to us with something irresistible, making us feel that our superiority is an unreal thing, and that in essentials we are one.

My host went on: "Some time ago I walked up to the little moor that over-looks the Clyde, from which you see ships far off lying at the Tail of the Bank, the smoke of Greenock and Port Glasgow, the estuary itself, though miles away, looking like a sheet of frosted silver or dark-grey steel, according to the season, and in the distance the range of hills called Argyle's Bowling Green, with the deep gap that marks the entrance to the Holy Loch. Autumn had just begun to tinge the trees, birches were golden, and rowans red, the bents were brown and dry. A few bog-asphodels still showed amongst the heather, and bilberries, dark as black currants, grew here and there amongst the carpet of green sphagnum and the stag's-head moss. The heather was all rusty brown, but still there was, as it were, a recollection of the summer in the air. Just the kind of day you feel inclined to sit down on the lee side of a dry-stone dyke, and smoke and look at some familiar self-sown birch that marks the flight of time, as you remember that it was but a year or two ago that it had first shot up above the grass.[1]

"I remember two or three plants of tall hemp-agrimony still had their flower heads withered on the stalk, giving them a look of wearing wigs, and clumps of ragwort still had a few bees buzzing about them, rather faintly, with a belated air. I saw all this—not that I am a botanist, for you know I can hardly tell the difference between the Cruciferae and the Umbelliferae, but because when you live in the country some of the common plants seem to obtrude themselves upon you, and you have got to notice them in spite of you. So I walked on till I came to a wrecked plantation of spruce and of Scotch fir. A hurricane had struck it, turning it over almost in rows, as it was planted. The trees had withered in most cases, and in the open spaces round their upturned roots hundreds of rabbits burrowed, and had marked the adjoining field with little paths, just like the lines outside a railway-station.

"I saw all this, not because I looked at it, for if you look with the idea of see-

ing everything, commonly everything escapes you, but because the lovely afternoon induced a feeling of well-being and contentment, and everything seemed
to fall into its right proportion, so that you saw first the harmonious whole, and
then the salient points most worth the looking at.

"I walked along feeling exhilerated with the autumn air and the fresh breeze
that blew up from the Clyde. I remember thinking I had hardly ever felt greater
content, and as I walked it seemed impossible the world could be so full of rank
injustice, or that the lot of three-fourths of its population could really be so hard.
A pack of grouse flew past, skimming above the heather, as a shoal of flying-fish
skims just above the waves. I heard their quacking cries as they alighted on some
stooks of oats, and noticed that the last bird to settle was an old hen, and that,
even when all were down, I still could see her head, looking out warily above
the yellow grain. Beyond the ruined wood there came the barking of a
shepherd's dog, faint and subdued, and almost musical.

"I sat so long, smoking and looking at the view, that when I turned to go the
sun was sinking and our long, northern twilight almost setting in.

"You know it," said my host, and I, who often had read by its light in
summer and the early autumn, nodded assent, wondering to myself what he was
going to tell me, and he went on.

"It has the property of making all things look a little ghostly, deepening the
shadows and altering their values, so that all that you see seems to acquire an
extra significance, not so much to the eye as to the mind. Slowly I retraced my
steps, walking under the high wall of rough piled stones till it ends, at the copse
of willows, on the north side of the little moor to which I had seen the pack of
grouse fly after it had left the stooks. I crossed into it, and began to walk towards
home, knee-deep in bent grass and dwarf willows, with here and there a patch of
heather and a patch of bilberries. The softness of the ground so dulled my footsteps that I appeared to walk as lightly as a roe upon the spongy surface of the
moor.. As I passed through a slight depression in which the grass grew rankly, I
heard a wild cry coming, as it seemed, from just beneath my feet. Then came a
rustling in the grass, and a large, dark-grey bird sprang out, repeating the wild cry,
and ran off swiftly, trailing a broken wing.

"It paused upon a little hillock fifty yards away, repeating its strange note,
and looking round as if it sought for something that it was certain was at hand.
High in the air the cry, wilder and shriller, was repeated, and a great grey bird
that I saw was a whaup slowly descended in decreasing circles, and settled down
beside its mate.

"They seemed to talk, and then the wounded bird set off at a swift run, its
fellow circling above its head and uttering its cry as if it guided it. I watched them
disappear, feeling as if an iron belt was drawn tight round my heart, their cries
growing fainter as the deepening shadows slowly closed upon the moor."

My host stopped, knocked the ashes from his pipe, and turning to me,
said:—

"I watched them go to what of course must have been certain death for one of them, furious, with the feelings of a murderer towards the man whose thoughtless folly had been the cause of so much misery. Curse him! I watched them, impotent to help, for as you know the curlew is perhaps the wildest of our native birds; and even had I caught the wounded one to set its wing, it would have pined and died. One thing I could have done, had I but had a gun and had the light been better, I might have shot them both, and had I done so I would have buried them beside each other.

"That's what I had upon my mind to tell you. I think the storm and the wild noises of the struggling trees outside have brought it back to me, although it happened years ago. Sometimes, when people talk about fidelity, saying it is not to be found upon the earth, I smile, for I have seen it with my own eyes, and manifest, out on that little moor."

He filled his pipe, and sitting down in an old leather chair, much worn and rather greasy, silently gazed into the fire.

I, too, was silent, thinking upon the tragedy; then feeling that something was expected of me, looked up and murmured, "Yes."

(From *Brought Forward,* 1916)

NOTES

1. This is the description of the fields and the view above Graham's family home at Ardoch, between Dumbarton and Cardross.

WITH THE NORTH-EAST WIND

A north-east haar had hung the city with a pall of grey. It gave an air of hardness to the stone-built houses, blending them with the stone-paved streets, till you could scarce see where the houses ended and the street began. A thin grey dust hung in the air. It coloured everything, and people's faces all looked pinched with the first touch of autumn cold. The wind, boisterous and gusty, whisked the soot-grimed city leaves about in the high suburb at the foot of a long range of hills, making one think it would be easy to have done with life on such an uncongenial day. Tramways were packed with people of the working class, all of them of the alert, quick-witted type only to be seen in the great city on the Clyde, in all our Empire, and comparable alone to the dwellers in Chicago for dry vivacity.

By the air they wore of chastened pleasure, all those who knew them saw that they were intent upon a funeral. To serious-minded men such as are they, for all their quickness, nothing is so soul-filling, for it is of the nature of a fact that no one can deny. A wedding has its possibilities, for it may lead to children or divorce, but funerals are in another category. At them the Scottish people is at its best, for never more than then does the deep underlying tenderness peep through the hardness of the rind. On foot and in the tramways, but most especially on foot, converged long lines of men and women, though fewer women, for the national prejudice, that in years gone by thought it not decent for a wife to follow to the grave her husband's coffin, still holds a little in the north. Yet there was something in the crowd that showed it was to attend no common funeral that they were "stepping west." No one wore black, except a minister or two, who looked a little like the belated rook you sometimes see amongst a flock of seagulls, in that vast ocean of grey tweed.

They tramped along, the whistling north-east wind pinching their features, making their eyes run, and as they went, almost unconsciously they fell into procession, for beyond the tramway line, a country lane that had not quite put on the graces of a street, though straggling houses were dotted here and there along it, received the crowd and marshalled it, as it were mechanically, without volition of its own. Kept in between the walls, and blocked in front by the hearse and long procession of the mourning-coaches, the people slowly surged along. The greater portion of the crowd were townsmen, but there were miners washed and in their Sunday best. Their faces showed the blue marks of healed-up scars into which coal dust or gunpowder had become tattooed, scars gained in the battle of their lives down in the pits, remembrances of falls of rock or of occasions when the mine had "fired upon them."

Many had known Keir Hardie in his youth, had "wrocht wi' him out-by," at Blantyre, at Hamilton, in Ayrshire, and all of them had heard him speak a hundred times. Even to those who had not heard him, his name was as a household word. Miners predominated, but men of every trade were there. Many were members of that black-coated proletariat, whose narrow circumstances and daily struggle for appearances make their life harder to them than is the life of any working man before he has had to dye his hair. Women tramped, too, for the dead leader had been a champion of their sex. They all respected him, loving him with that half-contemptuous gratitude that women often show to men who make the "women question" the object of their lives.

After the Scottish fashion at a funeral, greetings were freely passed, and Reid, who hadna' seen his friend Mackinder since the time of the Mid-Lanark fight, greeted him with "Ye mind when first Keir Hardie was puttin' up for Parliament," and wrung his hand, hardened in the mine, with one as hardened, and instantly began to recall elections of the past.

"Ye mind yon Wishaw meeting?"

"Aye, ou aye; ye mean when a' they Irish wouldna' hear John Ferguson. Man, he almost grat after the meeting aboot it."

"Aye, but they gied Hardie himself a maist respectful hearing ... aye, ou aye."

Others remembered him as a boy, and others in his home at Cumnock, but all spoke of him with affection, holding him as something of their own, apart from other politicians, almost apart from men.

Old comrades who had been with him either at this election or that meeting, had helped or had intended to have helped at the crises of his life, fought their old battles over, as they tramped along, all shivering in the wind.

The procession reached a long dip in the road, and the head of it, full half a mile away, could be seen gathered round the hearse, outside the chapel of the crematorium, whose ominous tall chimney, through which the ashes, and perchance the souls of thousands have escaped towards some empyrean or another, towered up starkly. At last all had arrived, and the small open space was crowded, the hearse and carriages appearing stuck amongst the people, like raisins in a cake, so thick they pressed upon them. The chapel, differing from the ordinary chapel of the faiths as much as does a motor driver from a cabman, had an air as of modernity about it, which contrasted strangely with the ordinary looking crowd, the adjacent hills, the decent mourning coaches and the black-coated undertakers who bore the coffin up the steps. Outside, the wind whistled and swayed the soot-stained trees about; but inside the chapel the heat was stifling.

When all was duly done, and long exordiums passed upon the man who in his life had been the target for the abuse of press and pulpit, the coffin slid away to its appointed place. One thought one heard the roaring of the flames, and somehow missed the familiar lowering of the body ... earth to earth ... to which the centuries of use and wont have made us all familiar, though dust to dust in this case was the more appropriate.

In either case, the book is closed for ever, and the familiar face is seen no more.

So, standing just outside the chapel in the cold, waiting till all the usual greetings had been exchanged, I fell a-musing on the man whom I had known so well. I saw him as he was thirty years ago, outlined against a bing or standing in a quarry in some mining village, and heard his once familiar address of "Men." He used no other in those days, to the immense disgust of legislators and other worthy but unimaginative men whom he might chance to meet. About him seemed to stand a shadowy band, most of whom now are dead or lost to view, or have gone under in the fight.

John Ferguson was there, the old-time Irish leader, the friend of Davitt and of Butt. Tall and erect he stood, dressed in his long frock-coat, his roll of papers in one hand, and with the other stuck into his breast, with all the air of being the last Roman left alive; Tom Mann, with his black hair, his flashing eyes, and his tumultuous speech peppered with expletives; beside him, Sandy Haddow, of Parkhead, massive and Doric in his speech, with a grey woollen comforter rolled round his neck, and hands like panels of a door; Champion, pale, slight, and interesting, still the artillery officer, in spite of Socialism; John Burns; and Small, the miners' agent, with his close brown beard and taste for literature. Smillie stood near, he of the seven elections, and then check-weigher at a pit, either at Cadzow or Larkhall. There, too, was silver-tongued Shaw Maxwell and Chisholm Robertson, looking out darkly on the world through tinted spectacles; with him Bruce Glasier, girt with a red sash and with an aureole of fair curly hair around his head, half poet and half revolutionary.[1]

They were all young and ardent, and as I mused upon them and their fate, and upon those of them who have gone down into the oblivion that waits for those who live before their time, I shivered in the wind.

Had he, too, lived in vain, he whose scant ashes were no doubt by this time all collected in an urn, and did they really represent all that remained of him?

Standing amongst the band of shadowy comrades I had known, I saw him, simple and yet with something of the prophet in his air, and something of the seer. Effective and yet ineffectual, something there was about him that attracted little children to him, and I should think lost dogs. He made mistakes, but then those who make no mistakes seldom make anything. His life was one long battle, so it seemed to me that it was fitting that at his funeral the north-east wind should howl amongst the trees, tossing and twisting them as he himself was twisted and storm-tossed in his tempestuous passage through the world.

As the crowd moved away, and in the hearse and mourning-coaches the spavined horses limped slowly down the road, a gleam of sunshine, such as had shone too little in his life, lighted up everything.

The swaying trees and dark, grey houses of the ugly suburb of the town were all transfigured for a moment. The chapel door was closed, and from the chimney of the crematorium a faint blue smoke was issuing, which, by degrees, faded into the atmosphere, just as the soul, for all I know, may melt into the air.

When the last stragglers had gone, and bits of paper scurried uneasily along before the wind, the world seemed empty, with nothing friendly in it but the shoulder of Ben Lomond peeping out shyly over the Kilpatrick Hills.

(From *Brought Forward*, 1916)

NOTES

1. Graham, of course, could have included himself in this group. He was a close associate of Keir Hardie, with whom he founded the Scottish Labour Party in 1886. See my articles in *Tribune* and *The Bibliotheck* already mentioned in the Introduction.

Section IV

TYPES AND FIGURES

EDITOR'S PREFACE

Though Cunninghame Graham consorted with many notable personalities in his political and literary activities (John Burns, Parnell, Prince Kropotkin, on one hand, and George Bernard Shaw, Hudson, Oscar Wilde, on the other) and wrote sketches about Keir Hardie and Joseph Conrad, most of the types and figures he describes were less than celebrities.

Some of his "characters" had gained local fame (like Heather Jock) or were relatives (like Miss Christian Jean and the Beggar Earl), but others were merely a fisherman he met casually on a boat trip, a traveller and a retainer he encountered in his daily life. Other notable members of his family on whom he wrote sketches were his Aunt Eleanor, his uncle, the colonel, the admiral, all of whom, although fascinating character studies, are only marginally connected with the Scottish sketches.

One quality they had in common was that they were all interesting, all "characters," even eccentrics, as some people were wont to classify Graham himself.[1] Don Roberto had a great affection for the worthies of this world, even those who were obviously of unbalanced mind, like Heather Jock. His North African sketches abound with references to the high esteem in which the "mad" of that region were held. Linked with this trait is Graham's admiration for the greatest madman of all, Don Quixote, with whom he has often been compared physically and spiritually—for the knight's idealism and tilting at windmills.[2] What emerges from Graham's treatment of these figures is his appreciation of their innocence and childlike attributes, and also his regret for a simple way of life now gone and the disappearance of old values.

"Heather Jock" and "Miss Christian Jean" provide Graham with an opportunity to lament the passing of customs and types, and, extending the quixotic image, to tilt a lance against the triple evil of Commerce, Civilisation and Progress, which he saw ruining not only the "barbaric" regions of South America and North Africa but also Scotland. His depiction of "down-and-outs," odd types and social pariahs sets him off on one of his favourite topics, success, which gave its name to a sketch and a collection: "For those who fail, for those who have sunk still battling beneath the muddy waves of life, we keep our love, and that curiosity about their lives which makes their memories green when the cheap gold is dusted over, which once we gave success."[3] To achieve this "success" many pawky and ambitious Scotsmen took themselves to foreign climes in search of fame, fortune and whatever the new lands might provide.

NOTES

1. Because of escapades like his fruitless gold hunt in Spain, and his attempt to reach Tarudant, the Forbidden City of Morocco.
2. See my article "Don Roberto and Cervantes," *Anales Cervantinos* (Madrid), XI, 1972, 129-37.
3. *Success*, London, Duckworth, 1902, 2.

HEATHER JOCK

To differ from the crowd, whether as a genius, an idiot, a politician, or simply to have a differently shaped beard from other men, will shortly be a crime. At present, out of pure philanthropy for ourselves, we seclude our madmen in prisons euphemistically called lunatic asylums. In the East the madman still walks the streets, as free as any other man, and gives his judgment on things he does not understand, like any other citizen. True, in the East there generally is sun, and every evil with the sun is less.

There is no sun in Scotland, but not so long ago our semi-madmen and our idiots philosophised about the world, taking the bitter and the sweet of life in public, just like the rest of us. The custom had its inconveniences; but, on the other hand, perhaps, was just as merciful as that which to-day shuts up all harmless, foolish creatures within four walls to save the sane the pain of seeing them.

What reasons influenced William Brodie, bred a weaver at the Bridge of Weir in Refrewshire, to first turn pedlar, or, as we say (*Scotice*),[1] "travelling merchant," and from that to transmigrate himself into a wandering singer and buffoon under the name of Heather Jock, are quite unknown. The status of a Scotch Autolycus has, no doubt, charms. We do not look on pedlars with the disdain with which in England the trading class is viewed. Rather, we honour them for the use we have of them, knowing the Lord created them for some wise purpose of his own not yet made plain. Hucksters and merchants both are prone to sin, and as a nail sticks fast between the joinings of the stones, so sin sticks close between selling and buying; at least so Jesus, son of Sirach,[2] tells us, and though not quite canonical himself, his works are much esteemed in Scotland for their "pawkiness." But, being practical, we see as little honour in higgling for thousands as for halfpennies, and call men "merchants" whether they carry packs upon their backs or send out ships freighted with shoddy goods to sell to niggers.

So no one asked his reasons, but accepted him just as he was, with head-dress like an Inca of Peru stuck all about with pheasants' and peacocks' feathers, bits of looking-glass, adorned with heather, and fastened underneath his jaws with a black ribbon; with moleskin waistcoat; bee in his bonnet; humour in his brain; with short plaid trousers, duffel coat, and in his hand a rude caduceus made of a hazel stick, and in the centre a flat tin heart, set round with jingling bells, and terminating in a tuft of ling; in figure not unlike a stunted oak of the kind depicted in the arms of Glasgow, or such as those which grow in Cadzow Forest, and under which the white wild cattle feed, as they have done since Malcolm Fleeming[3] slew one with his spear and saved the king.

The minstrel's features of the Western Scottish type, hard as flint, yet kindly, his eyes like dullish marbles made of glass, such as the children in Bridge of Weir call "bools," his hair like wire, his mouth worn open and his nose merely a trap for snuff, hands out of all proportion large, and feet like planks, his knees inclining to be what the Scotch call "schauchlin,"[4] and imparting to his walk that skipping action which age sometimes bestows on those who in their youth have passed a sedentary life; a true *faux bossu*,[5] and though without a hump, having acquired the carriage of a hunchback by diligence or sloth. In fact, he seemed a sort of cross between a low-class Indian, such as one sees about a town in South Dakota, and an orang-outang which had somehow got itself baptised.

From Kilmacolm to Mauchline, from Dalry to Ayr, at a Kilwinning Papingo,[6] at races, meets, fairs, trysts, at country house or moorland farm, to each and all he wandered and was welcome.

His minstrelsy, if I remember right, was not extensive as to repertory, being comprised of but one dreary song about a certain "Annie Laurie," originally of a sentimental cast, but which he sang with humoursome effects of face, at breakneck speed, jangling his bells and jumping about from side to side just like a Texan cowboy in Sherman, Dallas, or some Pan Handle town during the process of a barroom fight, to dodge the bullets. At the end he signified his wish to lay him down to die for the object of his song, and did so, elevating, after the fashion of expiring folk, his feet into the air and wagging to and fro his boots adorned with what the Scotch call tackets.

Perhaps it was the dispiriting nature of the performance which drew sympathy from men whose lives were uninspired. They might have thought a livelier buffoon untrue to nature from his unlikeness to themselves. What he had seen during his wandering life he treasured up, relating it (on invitation) to his hearers in the same way an Arab or a Spaniard quotes a proverb as if it was a personal experience of his own. Once in his youth "west by Dalry" he chanced to see a panorama of the chief incidents of Scottish history. What specially attracted his attention (so he said) was when the lecturer enlarged upon the fate of Rizzio: "Man, he just depicted it so graphically ye fancied ye could hear the head gae dunt, dunt, dunting, as they pulled the body doon the stairs."[7]

Our northern wit runs ghastly and dwells on funerals; on men at drinking parties, dead but quite the gentleman still sitting at the board; sometimes on people drunk in churchyards; but always alternating, according to the fancy of the humorist, from one to the other of our staple subjects for jesting, whisky or death. But Heather Jock, like other memories of youth, faded away, and the constant spectacle of much superior buffoonery in parliaments, in marts, at scientific lectures, literary clubs, and other walks of life, bore in upon me that all the world is but a pantomine, badly put on the stage by an incompetent stage manager, ourselves the mummers, and each man, according to the estimation he is held in by his fellows, a pantaloon or clown.

One day in Tucumán, amongst the orange gardens, mounting my horse, which for my personal safety I had to do with a bandage over his eyes and foot tied to the girth, and thinking that the business of my life, which then consisted chiefly in going out by break of day to round my cattle up (*parar rodeo*, as the gauchos say), was not inferior after all to that passed in a European office—where men begin at twenty to enter nothings in a ledger, and old age creeps on them finding them bald-headed at the same task—I chanced to get some letters.

The messenger who brought them slowly got off his horse; his iron spurs, like fetters on his naked feet, clanked on the bricks of the verandah; he seemed perturbed—that is, as much perturbed as it is possible to be upon the frontiers— his hat was gone, around his head he wore a handkerchief which had been white when it left Manchester some years ago; his horse was blown and wounded, but still he stood impassively handing me the bag and asking after the condition of my health with some minuteness. Was he tired? "No, señor, not over-tired." Would he take a drink? "Yes, to the health of all good Christians." Where was his brother who used to ride with him? "Dead, *patroncito*, and I hope in glory, for he died like a Christian, killed at the crossing of the Guaviyú by the infidel who came on us as we were crossing with the water to our saddle skirts." This with a smile to make the unpleasant news more palatable in the delivery. Christian, I may explain, upon those frontiers is rather a racial than a religious status. All white men are *ex officio* Christians, with the possible exception of the English, who, as they listen to their mass mumbled in English, not in Latin, are less authentic. However, said the gaucho (always with my permission), he would saddle a fresh horse and with some friends go out to fetch the body.

Whilst he caught a horse—a lengthy operation when the horses have to be driven first to a corral and then caught with the *lazo*—I took the bag with the feeling, firstly, that it had cost a man his life, and then with the instinctive dread which, when in distant lands always attends home news, that some one would be dead or married, or that at least the trusted family solicitor had made off with the money entrusted to him to invest.

Nothing of this was in the letters, only, as per usual in such cases, accounts of deaths and marriages of folk I did not know; of fortunes come to those I most dislike, and other matter of the regulation kind with which people at home are apt to stuff their letters to their distant friends.

One of the letters had a scrap of newspaper inside it, with the announce-ment of the death of Heather Jock. "At Bridge of Weir upon the 13th instant, William Brodie, at the age of eighty-two, known through the West of Scotland to all as Heather Jock."

So Heather Jock would strive no more with life, with people just as foolish if more wicked than himself, struggle no more against the difficulties of English concert pitch and be with "Annie Laurie" and the other puny dead who erstwhile plied his trade. Then I remembered where I saw him last—at an old house in Scotland perched on a rock above the Clyde and set about with trees, the avenue winding about through woods and crossing a little stream on bridges made the most of by landscape-gardeners' art. I saw the yew-trees under which John Knox is said to have preached and dealt with heresy and superstition, like the man he was, driving out all that kindly paganism which is mingled with the Catholic faith, and planting in its stead the stern, hard, hyper-Caledonian faith which bows the knee before its God in a temple like a barn, and looks upon the miserable east end of Glasgow as a thing ordained by God. The tulip-tree, the yellow chestnut, and the laurels tall as houses all came back to me, the little garden with its curious stone vases and the tall hollyhocks. I saw the river with the steamers passing between the fairway marks, saw Dumbarton Castle on its rock and wondered how it could have been the seat of Arthur's Court, as wise men tell. Again I recollected that one day upon the sands I found the outside covering of a cocoanut and launched it on the Clyde just opposite to where the roofless house of Ardoch stood,[8] and watched it vanish into nothing, after the fashion of an Irish peasant woman on the quay at Cork watching the vessel take her son away, and just as sure as she of the return.

Then it occurred to me that Heather Jock had been a different character from what he really was, and that there had been something noble and adventurous in his career. That he had, somehow, fought against convention, and preferred, after the fashion of Sir Thopas,[9] to "liggen in his hood,"[10] and go about the world a living protest against the folly of mankind. But, God pardon me, for that way exegesis lies, with finding out of hidden, mysterious esoteric motives for common actions, after the fashion which would astonish many, who, if they came to life again, would find those worshipping who, in life, were their most bitter foes.

Nothing of moment was in the other letters, and when the neighbours mustered, armed with spears and rusty guns, *lazo* and *bolas*, but each man mounted on a first-rate horse and leading another to run away upon in case of danger, I mounted a *picazo*, which I kept for such occasions, knowing he was a horse "fit for God's saddle," and taking my rifle with me unloaded, not from superior daring, but because I had no cartridges.

Just at the crossing of the Guaviyú, close to a clump of *espinillo de olor*,[11] we found the body, cut and hacked about so as to be almost unrecognisable, but holding in the hand a tuft of long black hair, coarse as a horse's tail, showing the dead man had behaved himself up to the last like a true Christian.

At the fandango after the funeral, during the hot night, and whilst the fire-flies flickered amongst the feathery *tacuarás*, and lit the metallic leaves of the orange-trees occasionally with their faint bluish light, above the scraping of the cracked guitar, above the voices of the dancers when they broke into the chorus of the *gato*, above the neighing of the horses shut in the corral for fear of Indians, I seemed to hear the jangling of the dead fool's bells, and listen to the minstrelsy, such as it was, of the hegemonist of Bridge of Weir.

(From *The Ipané*, 1899)

NOTES

1. *Scotice*, Scottish style or fashion.
2. See "A Survival," note 4.
3. One of the Scottish leaders defeated at the Battle of Halidon Hill (1333), during the reign of David II, which led to the surrender of Berwick.
4. *schauchlin*, loose and mis-formed, i.e. knock-kneed.
5. *faux bossu*, literally, a false hunchback.
6. *Papingoe*, literally, a parrot, but also a wooden bird shot in a yearly trial of shooting skill. The name is also used for the annual Papingoe Ball held to celebrate the shooting of the papingoe.
7. David Riccio, Mary Queen of Scot's Italian secretary and counsellor, murdered in 1566 by the Protestant Lords.
8. Ardoch is, of course, Graham's family home near Dumbarton. This is quite an accurate description of the house and its grounds.
9. In "The Tale of Sir Thopas" from Chaucer's *Canterbury Tales*.
10. *liggen in his hood*, to talk nonsense, to blether. cf. lag, i.e. to fall behind, to be backward (mentally).
11. Fragrant spiky bush like the hawthorn.

MISS CHRISTIAN JEAN

Two pictures hang upon my study wall, faded and woolly, but well stippled up, the outlines of the hills just indicated with a fine reed pen, showing the water, coloured saffron, deepening to pink in the deep shadows of the lake. Although one picture is a sunset and the other done as it would seem at sunrise, they show a country which even yet is undefiled by any human step.

So accurately is the dark brown tree set in position on the border of the fleecy lake, one feels an artist, superior to mere nature, has been about the task. The castle on the mountain top, in one of the two masterpieces, is at the bottom of the hill in its compeer, and in the two a clear blue sky throws a deep shadow over the unruffled water, on which float boats with tall white sails, progressing without wind.

Still, with their frames, which are but fricassées of gingerbread well gilt, to me they say a something all the art of all the masters leaves unsaid.

A masterpiece speaks of imagination in its maker; but those pale blue-grey hills and salmon-coloured pinkish lakes, castles which never could have been inhabited, boats sailing in a calm, and trees that seem to rustle without breeze, set me reflecting upon things gone by, and upon places of which I once was part, places which still ungratefully live on, whilst that of me which lived in them is dead.

A long low Georgian room, in which the pictures hung, with its high mantelpiece, its smell of damp and Indian curiosities, and window looking out on the sunk garden underneath the terraces, the sides of which were honeycombed by rabbits, rises in my view, making me wonder in what substance of the body or the mind they have been stamped.

How few such rooms remain, and how few houses such as that, to which the dark and dampish chamber, with its three outside walls, and deep-cut mouldings on the windows and the doors, was library. We called it "bookroom," in the Scottish way, although the books were few and mostly had belonged to a dead uncle who had bought them all in India, and on their yellowing leaves were stains of insects from the East, and now and then a grass or flower from Hydera-bad or Kolapur (as pencilled notes upon the margin said), transported children to a land so gorgeous that the like of it was never seen on earth. These books were all well chosen, and such as men read fifty years ago—Macauley's *Essays*, with the *Penny Cyclopaedia*, Hume, Smollett, Captain Cook, *The Life of Dost Mohammed*, Elphinstone's *Cabul Mission*, with Burckhardt's *Travels*, enthralling Mungo Park, and others of the kind that at hill stations in the rains, or in the plains during the summer, must have passed many an hour of boredom and of heat away for their

dead purchaser. The rest were books of heraldry and matters of the kind, together with a set of Lever and of Dickens, with plates by Cruikshank or by
Hablot Brown. One in particular set forth a man upon a horse, with a red fluttering cloak streaming out in the wind, galloping in the midst of buffaloes with a
long knife between his teeth. But books and furniture and Indian curiosities, with
the high Adams chimney-piece and portraits of the favourite hounds and horses
of three generations, were, as it were, keyed up to the two water-colours, one of
which hung up above a cabinet sunk far into the wall and glazed, the other over a
low double door, deep as an embrasure.

All through the house the smell of damp, of kingwood furniture, and roses
dried in bowls, blended and formed a scent which I shall smell as long as life
endures. This may, of course, have been mere fancy; but often in the old houses
some picture or some piece of furniture appears to give the keynote to the rest.
But it seemed evident to me that, in some strange mysterious way, the pictures,
outstanding in their badness, had stamped themselves upon the house more than
the Reynoldses and Raeburns on the walls, though they were pictures of my
ancestors, and the two water-colours represented no known landscape upon
earth. They entered into my ideas so strongly (though they were unobtrusive in
themselves) that, looking from the window-seat in the deep bay of the sunk
window in the dining-room, across the terraces, over the sea of laurels, beyond
the rushy "parks," and out upon the moss and the low lumpy hills that ran down
to the distant lake, almost divided into two by a peninsula set with dark pine trees
and with planes, the landscape seemed unfinished and lacking interest without
the castles and the chrome-laden skies of the twin masterpieces.

It may be, too, that the unnatural landscape caused me to form unnatural
views of life, finding things interesting and people worthy of remark whom
others found quite commonplace, merely upon their own account, and not from
the surroundings of their lives. So every one connected with the house of the
two works of art became mixed up somehow with them in a mysterious way, as
well as things inanimate and trees, the vegetation and the white mist which half
the year hung over moss and woods, shrouding the hills and everything in its unearthly folds, making them strange and half unreal, as is a landscape in a dream.

Perhaps the fact that the house stood just at the point where Lowlands end
and the great jumble of the Highland hills begins, and that the people were compounded of both simples, Saxon and Celtic mixed in equal parts, gave them and
all the place an interest such as clings to borderlands the whole world over, for
even forty years ago one talked of "up above the pass" as of a land distinct from
where we lived. Down from those regions wandered men speaking a strange
tongue, shaggy, and smelling of a mixture of raw wool and peat smoke, whose
dogs obeyed them in a way in which no dog of any man quite civilised, broken
to railways and refreshment-rooms, obeys his master's call. The bond of union
may have been that both slept out in the wet dew, huddling together in the
morning round the fire for warmth, or something else, the half-possession of

some sense that we have lost, by means of which, all unknown to themselves, the drover and his dog communicated. Communion, very likely, is the word, the old communion of all living things, the lost connection between man and all the other animals, which modern life destroys.

But, be that as it may, the men and dogs seemed natives, and we who lived amongst the mosses and the hills seemed strangers, by lack of something or by excess of something else, according to your view.

The herds of ponies that the men drove before them on the road fell naturally into the scheme of nature; sorrels and yellow chestnuts, creams and duns, they blended with the scrubby woods and made no blot upon the shaggy hills. Instinctively they took the long-forgotten fords, crossing below the bridges, and standing knee-deep in the stream, the water dripping from their ropy tails and burdock-knotted manes. The herds of kyloes too have gone, which looked like animals of some race older than our own. The men who drove them, with their rough clothes of coarse grey wool, their hazel crooks, and plaids about their shoulders, whether the wind blew keenly or midges teased in August, all have disappeared. Their little camps upon the selvedge of the roads are all forgotten, although I know them still, by the bright grass that grows upon the ashes of the fires. Or have they gone, and are the hills brown, lumpy, heather-clad, and jewelled after rain by myriad streams, merely illusions; and is it really that I myself have gone, and they live on, deep down in the recesses of some fairy hill of which I am not free?

Men, too, like my friend Wallace of Gartchorrachan, have disappeared, and I am not quite sure if we should bless the Lord on that account. All through Menteith, and right "across the hill" as far as Callander and Doune, he was well known, and always styled Laird Wallace, for though our custom is to call men by the title of their lands, thus making them *adscripti glebae*[1] to the very soul, the word Gartchorrachan stuck in our throats, although we readily twist and distort the Gaelic place-names in our talk just as the Spaniards mutilate the Arab words, smoothing their corners and their angles out in the strong current of their speech.

Dressed in grey tweed with bits of buckskin let into the shoulders of his coat, for no one ever saw him leave his house without a gun, he was about the age that farmers in the north seem to be born at—that is, for years he had been grey, but yet was vigorous, wore spectacles, and his thick curly hair was matted like the wool upon a ram, whilst from his ears and nostrils grew thick tufts of bristles, just as a growth of twigs springs from the trunk of an old oak tree, where it has got a wound.

His house was like himself, old, grey, and rambling, and smelt of gun oil, beeswax, and of camphor, for he was versed in entomology, and always had a case of specimens, at which he laboured with a glass stuck in his eye, reminding me of Cyclops or of Polyphemus, or of an ogre in a story-book. Botany and conchology and generally those sciences, which when pursued without a method soon became trifling and a pastime, were his joys, and he had cabinets in which the specimens reposed under a heavy coat of dust, but duly ticketed each with its Latin name.

He spoke good English as a general rule, and when unmoved, as was the custom with the people of his class and upbringing, but often used broad Scotch, which he employed after the fashion of a shield against the world, half in a joking way and half against the sin of self-revealment which we shun as the plague, passing our lives like pebbles in a brook, which rub against each other for an age, and yet remain apart.

In early life he had contracted what he called a "local liassong," the fruit of which had been a daughter whom he had educated, and who lived with him, half as his daughter, half as housekeeper. Her father loved her critically, and when she not infrequently swept china on the floor as she passed through the drawing-room (just as a tapir walks about a wood, breaking down all the saplings in its path), he would screw up one eye, and looking at her say, "That's what you get from breeding from a cart-mare, the filly's sure to throw back to the dam."

Withal, he was a gentleman, having been in the army and travelled in his youth, but had not got much more by his experience than the raw youth of whom his father said, "Aye, Willie's been to Rome and back again, and a' he's learnt is but to cast his sark aince every day." But still he was a kindly man, the prey of any one who had a specious story, the providence of all lame horses and of dogs quite useless for any kind of sport, all which he bought at prices far above the value of the most favoured members of their race.[2]

His inner nature always seemed to be just struggling forth almost against his will, mastering his rough exterior, just as in pibrochs, after the skirling of the pipes has died away, a tender melody breaks out, fitful and plaintive, speaking of islands lost in misty seas, of things forgotten and misunderstood, of the faint, swishing noise of heather in the rain moved by the breeze at night, and which through minor modulations and fantastic trills ends in a wild lament for some Fingalian hero, like the wind sighing through the pines.

Nothing was more congenial to his humour than to unpack his recollections of the past, seated before the fire, an oily black cigar which he chewed almost like a quid between his teeth, and with a glass of whisky by his side.

After expatiating upon the excellencies of his lame, jibbing chestnut mare, that he had bought at Falkirk Tryst from a quite honest dealer, but which had gone mysteriously so lame that even whisky for his groom had no effect in curing her, he usually used to lament upon the changes which the course of time had brought about. All was a grief to him as it is really to all of us, if we all knew it, that some particular landmark of his life had disappeared. No one spoke Gaelic nowadays, although he never in his life had known a word of it. The use of "weepers"[3] and crape hat-bands by the country-folk on Sunday was quite discontinued, and no one took their collie dogs to church. Coffins were now no longer carried shoulder-high across the hills from lonely upland straths, as he remembered to have seen them in his youth. Did not some funeral party in his childhood, taking a short cut on a frozen loch, fall through and perish to a man?—a circumstance he naturally deplored, but still regretted, as men of older generations may have regretted highwaymen, as they sat safely by their fire. Although he never fished, he was quite certain no one now alive could busk a fly as well as a departed worthy of his youth, one Dan-a-Haltie, or make a withy basket or those osier loops which formerly were stuck between the divots in a dry-stone dike, projecting outwards like a torpedo netting, to stop sheep jumping from a field. Words such as flauchtered feal and laroch were hardly understood; shepherds read newspapers as they lay out upon the hill, the Shorter Catechism had been miserably abridged, and the old fir-tree by the Shannochill was blasted at the top.

All these complaints he uttered philosophically, not in a plaintive way, but as a man who, at his birth, had entered as it were into a covenant with life just as it was, which he for his part had faithfully observed, but was deceived by fate.

Then when he had relieved his mind he used to laugh and, puffing out the smoke of his thick black cigar, which hung about the tufts which sprung out of his nostrils, just as the mist hangs dank above a bog, he would remark, "I'm haverin'," as if he was afraid of having to explain himself to something in his mind. On these occasions, I used to let him sit a little, and usually he would begin again, after a look to see if I had noticed the gag he suddenly had put upon himself, and then start off again. "Ye mind my aunt, Miss Christian Jean?" I did, eating her sweetmeats in my youth, and trembling at her frown.

"Ye never heard me tell how it was I kisted her," he said, and then again fell into contemplation, and once again began. "My aunt, Miss Christian Jean, was a survival of the fittest—aye, ye know I am in some things quite opposed to Darwin, the survival of the potter's wheel in the Fijis and several other things . . . aye, haverin' again . . . or the most unfitted to survive.

"She was a gentlewoman, . . . yes, yes, the very word is now half ludicrous, ye need not smile, . . . lady is a poor substitute. Tall, dark, and masculine, and with a down upon her upper lip that many a cornet of dragoons, for there were cornets in those days, might well have envied, she was a sort of providence, jealous and swift in chastisement, but yet a providence to all the younger members of her race who came across her path.

"I see her now, her and her maid, old Katherine Sinclair, a tall, gaunt Highland woman, who might easily have walked straight from the pages of *Rob Roy*, and her old butler, Robert Cameron, grey and red-faced, and dressed eternally in a black suit, all stained with snuff, a pawky sort of chiel, religious and still with the spirit of revolt against all dogmatism which modern life and cheap and stereotyped instruction has quite stamped out to-day. My aunt kept order in her house, that is as far as others were concerned. Each day she read her chapter, in what she styled the Book, not taking over heed how she selected it, so that the chapter once was duly read. It happened sometimes that when she came into the room where, as my cousin Andrew used to say—ye mind that he was drowned in one of those Green's ships, fell from aloft whilst they were reefing topsails in a dark night somewhere about the Cape.

"I've heard him say he could come down the weather-leach of a topsail, just like a monkey, by the bolt ropes. . . . Where was I, eh? Aye, I mind, he used to say that my aunt's prayers reminded him of service in a ship, with all hands mustered; so as I said, my aunt would sometimes open up the book and come upon a chapter full of names, and how some one begat another body and sometimes upon things perfectly awesome for a maiden lady to read aloud, for 'twas all one to her.

"Then the old butler would put his hand up to his mouth and whisper, 'Mem, Miss Christian, Mem, ye're wandered,' and she would close the book, or start again upon another chapter and maybe twice as long.

"My aunt and her two satellites kept such good order that a visitor from England, seeing her neat and white-capped maids file in and take their seats facing the menservants, expressed her pleasure at the well ordered, comely worship, and received the answer, 'Yes, my dear, ye see at family prayers we have the separation of the sexes, but I understand when they meet afterwards at the stair foot, the kissing beats the cracking of a whip.'

"Poor Aunt Christian, I used to shiver at her nod, and well remember when a youth how she would flyte me when I pinched the maids, and say, 'Laddie, I canna' have you making the girls squeal like Highland ponies; it is not decent, and decency comes next after morality, sometimes, I think, before it, for it can be attained, whereas the other is a counsel of perfection set up on high, but well out of our reach.'

"A pretty moraliser was my poor aunt, almost a heathen in her theory, guided by what she said were natural laws, and yet a Puritan in practice, whereas I always was a theoretic Puritan, but shaped my life exclusively by natural laws, as they appear to me.

"Let ministers just haver as they will, one line of conduct is not possible for nephews and for aunts. Take David, now, the man after the Lord's own heart, and ask yourself what would have happened if his aunt ... aye, aye, I'm wandered from my tale . . . I ken I'm wandering.

"Well, well, it seemed as if my aunt might have gone on for ever, getting a little dryer and her face more peakit, as the years went by and her old friends dropped off and left her all alone. That's what it is, ye see; it's got to come, although it seems impossible whilst we sit talking here and drinking—that is, I drinking and you listening to me talk. One wintry day I was just sitting wiping the cee-spring of a gun, and looking out upon the avenue, when, through the wreaths, I saw a boy on a bit yellow pony-beast come trotting through the snow.

"It was before the days of telegrams, and I jaloused that there was something special, or no one would have sent the laddie out on such a day, with the snow drifted half a yard upon the ground, the trees all white with cranruch like the sugar on a cake, and the frost keen enough to split a pudding stone and grind it into sand.

"I sent the laddie to the kitchen fire, and ripped the envelope, whilst the bit pony rooted round for grass and walked upon the reins. The letter told me that

my aunt had had a fit, was signed by 'Robert Cameron, butler,' and was all
daubed with snuff, and in a postcript I was asked to hurry, for the time was short,
and to come straight across the hill as the low road was blocked by the snow
drifting and nobody could pass. I harnessed up my mare—not the bit blooded
chestnut I drive now"—this was the way in which he spoke of the lame cripple
which had conveyed him to my house—"but a stout sort of Highland mouse-
coloured beastie that I had, rather short backit, a little hammer-headed, and with
the hair upon the fetlocks like a Clydesdale. . . . Maun, I think ye dinna' often see
such sort of beasts the now." I mentally thanked God for it, and he again launched
out into his tale.

"An awful drive, I'm tellin' ye! I hadna' got above Auchyle—ye mind, at the
old bridge just where yon English tourist coupit his creels,[4] and gaed to heaven,
maybe last summer—when I saw I had a job. The snow balled in the mare's feet
as big as cabbages, and made her stotter in her gait, just like a drunken curler
ettlin' to walk upon a rink. I had to take her by the head till we got on the flat
ground, up about Rusky. Man, it was arctic, and the little loch lay like a sheet of
glass that had been breathed upon, with the dead bulrushes and reeds all sticking
through the ice! The island in the loch seemed but a blob of white, and the old
tower (I dinna' richtly mind if, at one time, it belonged to some of your own
folk) loomed up like Stirling Castle or like Doune in the keen frosty air. The little
firwood on the east side of the old change-house—that one they called Wright,
or some such name, once keepit—was full of roe, all sheltering like cows, so cold
and starved they scarcely steered when I passed by and gave a shout to warm my
lungs and hearten up the mare; and a cock capercailzie, moping and miserable, sat
on a fir tree like a barn-door fowl. I ploutered on just to where there used to be a
gate across the road, where ye see Uamh Var and the great shoulder of Ben Ledi
stretching up out by the pass of Leny and the old chapel of St. Bryde. It was fair
awesome; I did not rightly know the landscape with the familiar features blotted
out. I very nearly got myself wandered just in the straight above the Gart, for all
the dikes were sunk beneath the snow, and the hedge-tops peeped up like box in
an old cabbage-garden. At last I reached the avenue, the mare fair taigled, and the
ice hanging from her fetlocks and her mane and wagging to and fro. The ever-
greens were, so to speak, a-wash, and looked like beds of parsley or of greens, and
underneath the trees the squirrels' footsteps in the snow seemed those of some
strange birds, where they had melted and then frozen on the ground. Across the
sky a crow or two flew slowly, flapping their wings as if the joint oil had been
frozen in their bones and cawing sullenly.

"On the high steps which led up to the door the butler met me, and as he
took my coat, said, 'Laird, ye are welcome; your poor dear auntie's going. Hech,
sirs, 'twill be an awfu' nicht for the poor leddy to be fleein' naked through the air
towards the judgement-seat. Will ye tak speerits or a dish o' tea after your cold-
some drive, or will I tak' ye straight in to your aunt? I'm feared she willna' know
you. But His will be done, though I could wish He micht hae held His hand a
little longer; but we must not repine. I've just been readin' out to her from the

old Book, ye ken, passin' the time awa' and waitin' for the end.'

"All day my aunt lay dozing, half-conscious and half-stupefied, and all the day the butler, sitting by the bed, read psalms and chapters, to which she sometimes seemed to pay attention, and at others lay so still we thought that she was dead. Now and again he stopped his reading, and peering at his mistress with his spectacles pushed up, wiped off the tears that trickled down his face with his red handkerchief, and, as if doubting he were reading to the living or the dead, said, 'Nod yer heid, Miss Christian,' which she did feebly, and he, satisfied she understood, mumbled on piously in a thick undertone.

"Just about morning she passed away quite quietly, the maids and butler standing round the bed, they crying silently, and he snorting in his red pocket-handkerchief, with the tears running down his face. The gaunt old Highland waiting-woman raised a high wail which echoed through the cold and silent house, causing the dogs to bark and the old parrot scream, and the butler stottered from the room, muttering that he would go and see if tea was ready, closing the door behind him with his foot, as if he feared the figure on the bed would scold him, as she had often done during her life, if it slammed to and made a noise.

"All the week through it snowed, and my aunt's house was dismal, smelling of cheese and honey, yellow soap, of jam, of grease burnt in the fire, and with the dogs and cats uncared for rambling about and sleeping on the chairs. The cold was penetrating, and I wandered up and down the stairs quite aimlessly, feeling like Alexander Selkirk in the melancholy house,[5] which seemed an island cut off from the world by a white sea of snow. None of Aunt Christian's friends or relatives could come, as all the roads were blocked; even her coffin was not sent till a few hours before the funeral, the cart that brought it stalling in the snow, and the black-coated undertaker's men carrying it shoulder-high through the thick wreaths upon the avenue.

"The servants would not have a stranger touch the corpse, and the old butler and myself kisted my aunt, lifting her body from the bed between the two of us. A week had passed and she looked black and shrunken, and as I lifted her, the chill from the cold flesh struck me with horror, and welled into the bones. I could not kiss her as she lay like a mummy in the kist, for the shrunk face with the white clothes about the chin was not the same Aunt Christian's, whom I had loved and before whom I trembled for so many years, but changed somehow and horrible to see.

"The butler did, looking at me, as I thought, half reproachfully as I stood silently, not once crying but half stupefied, and then as she lay shrunken and broken on the white satin lining of the kist, we stood and looked at one another, just as if we had been partners in a crime, till they began to hammer down the lid. A drearsome sound it makes. One feels the nails are sticking in the flesh, and every time ye hear it, it just affects ye more than the last time, the same as an earthquake, as I mind I heard a traveller say one day in Edinburgh. What the old butler did, I do not mind; but I just dandered out into the garden, and washed my hands in snow, not that I felt a skunner at my poor Aunt Christian's flesh, but somehow I had to do it, for ye ken 'twas the first time."

Laird Wallace stopped just as a horse props suddenly when he is fresh and changes feet, then breaking into Scotch, said: "I have talked enough. That's how I kisted my Aunt Christian Jean, puir leddy, a sair job it was, and dreich.... Thank ye, nae soddy, I'll tak' a drop of Lagavoulin." Then lighting a cigar, he said, "Ring for my dog-cart, please," and when it came he clambered to the seat, and pointing to his spavined mare, said, "Man, a gran' beast, clean thorough-bred, fit to run for her life" (and this to me who knew her); then, bidding me good-night, drew his whip smartly on her scraggy flank, and vanished through the trees.

(From *His People,* 1906)

NOTES

1. *adscripti glebae,* tied to the land.
2. Graham could be describing himself here in this portrait.
3. *weepers,* strips of muslin on the cuffs of coats as a sign of mourning, often covered with crape.
4. *coupit his creels,* came to grief.
5. The adventures of Alexander Selkirk (1676-1721) on the island of Juan Fernández (1704-09) provided the material for Daniel Defoe's *Robinson Crusoe* (1719).

THE BEGGAR EARL

Many a shadowy figure has flitted through the valley of Menteith. Just as the vale itself is full of shadows, shadows that leave no traces of their passage, but, whilst they last, seem just as real as are the hills themselves, so not a few of those who have lived in it seem unsubstantial and as illusive as a ghost.

Perhaps less real, for if a man detects a spectre with that interior vision dear to the Highlanders and to all mystics, Highland or Lowland, or from whatever land they be, he has as surely seen it for himself, as if the phantasm was pictured on the retina of the exterior eye.

Pixies, trolls, and fairies, the men of peace, the dwellers in the Fairy Hill that opens upon Hallowe'en alone, and from which issues a long train, bringing with them our long-lost vicar Kirke of Aberfoyle. True Thomas, and the rest of all the mortals who forsook their porridge three times a day, for the love of some elf queen, and have remained as flies embedded in the amber of tradition, are in a way prosaic. Men have imagined them, enduing them with their own qualities, just as they have endued their gods with jealousy and hate. Those born in the ordinary, but miraculous, fashion of mankind, who live apparently by bread alone, and yet remain beings apart, not touched by praise, ambition, or any of the things that move their fellows, are the true fairies after all.

Such a one was the beggar earl. All his long life he lacked advancement, finding it only at the last, as he died, like a cadger's pony, by a dykeside in the snow. That kind of death keeps a man's memory fresh.

Few can tell to-day where or what manner died his ancestors—the mail-clad knights who fought at Flodden, counselled kings with the half-Highland cunning of their race, and generally opposed the Southrons, who, impotent to conquer us in war, yet have filched from us most of our national character by the soft arts of peace. A mouldering slab of freestone here and there, a nameless statue of a crusader with his crossed feet resting upon his dog, in the ebenezerised cathedral of Dunblane; a little castle on a little reedy island in a bulrush-circled lake, some time-stained parchments in old muniments[1] preserve their memory, ... to those who care for memories, a futile and a disappearing race.

His is preserved in snow. Nothing is more enduring than the snow. It falls, and straight all is transfigured. All suffers a chromatic change; that which was black or red, brown, yellow or dark grey, is changed to white, so white that it remains for ever stamped on the mind, and one recalls the landscape, with its fairy woods, its stiff, dead streams, its suffering trees and withered vegetation, as it was on that day.

So has the recollection of the beggar earl remained, a legend, and all his humble life, his struggles and his fixed, foolish purpose been forgotten; leaving his death as it were embalmed in something of itself so perishable that it has had no time to die.

No mere success, the most vulgar thing that a man can endure, would have been so lasting, for men resent success and strive to stifle it under their applause, lauding the result, the better to belittle all the means. His life was not especially eventful, still less mysterious, for the poor play out their part in public, and a greater mystic than himself has said, "The poor make no noise."[2]

Someone who knew him said he was "a little man; a little clean man, that went round about through the country. He never saw him act wrong.... He was—just a man asking charity. He went into farmhouses and asked for victuals; what they would give him; and into gentlemen's houses."

This little picture, drawn unconsciously, shows us the man he was after ill-fortune overtook him. For a brief season he had been well known in Edinburgh. In 1744, when he was studying medicine, he suddenly appeared at the election of a Scottish peer and told the assembly who he was, and claimed the right to vote.

From that time till his death, he never dropped his claim, attending all elections of a Scottish peer till he got weary of the game. Then disillusion fell on him, and he withdrew to beg his bread, and wander up and down his earldom and the neighbouring lands, until his death.

Once more he came into public view, in the year 1747, when he published his rare pamphlet, *The Fatal Consequences of Discord*, dedicated to the Prince of Wales. In it he says "that there can be no true unity without religion and virtue in a State."

This marks him as a man designed by nature to be poor, for unity and virtue are not commodities that command a ready sale.

He had not any special gift but faith, and that perhaps sustained him in his wanderings. Perhaps he may have thought that he would sit some day in a celestial senate, and this belief consoled him for his rejection by an earthly house of peers. One thing is certain, even had the House of Lords, that disallowed his claim, although he voted several years in Edinburgh, approved him as a peer, it would not have convinced him of his right one atom more; for if a man is happy in conviction, he had it to the full.

It is said he bore about with him papers and pedigrees that he would never sell. No bartering of the crown for him, even for bread. A little, grey, clean-looking man, mounted upon an old white pony, falling by degrees into most abject poverty and still respected for his uprightness, and perhaps a little for his ancestry, for in those days that, which to us is but a mockery, was real, just as some things, which with us are valued, in those days would have been ridiculous.

So through the valley of Menteith, along the Endrick, and by Loch Lomond side, past the old church at Kilmaronock, through Gartocharn, and up and down the Leven, he took his pilgrimage.

Over the wild track on the Dumbarton moor, and past the waterfall at the head of the glen of Galingad, he and his pony must have wandered many times, reflecting that the lands he passed over should have been all his own, for he was really Earl of Menteith by right and by descent, no matter though his fellow peers refused to recognise him. He talked at first, in any house he came to, of his rights, and people, having little news to distract them in those days, were no doubt pleased to hear him and to inveigh against injustice in the way that those who had themselves received it all their lives are always pleased to talk.

So does a goaded ox lower his head and whisk his tail, and then, after a glance thrown at his fellow, strain once again upon the yoke. Then, when the novelty was over, they would receive his stories with less interest, driving him back upon himself, until most likely he bore his wrongs about with him, just as a pedlar bears his pack, in silence and alone. So did he, when the first efforts to obtain his title and his rights had spent their force, quit Edinburgh, as if it had been a city of the plague, when there was any election of a peer.

Whilst he was wandering up and down the parishes of Kilmaronock and of Port, Scotland was all convulsed with the late rising of '45. Parties of soldiers, and bands of Highlanders retreating to the north, must have passed by him daily, and yet he never seems to have had the inclination to change sides. Staunch in his allegiance to the Goverment, and with a faith well grounded in the Protestant Succession, as his pamphlet shows, most probably he was a Church and State man, as he would have said, up to his dying day.

Of such, as far as kings and rulers are concerned, are the elect, and thrones are founded on this unquestioning belief, more strongly than on armies or in Courts.

As the years passed, and he still wandered up and down Menteith, losing by degrees the little culture that his studies had implanted in him when he attended the Edinburgh schools, the farmers must have begun to treat him first as one of themselves, and then just as they would have treated any other wandering beggarman. Still, on the few occasions when he had to write a letter he always signed "Menteith," especially to begging letters, and the signature, no doubt, consoled him many a time for a refusal of his plea.

Few could have known all the traditions of the district as did the wandering earl; but he most probably, living amongst them, thought them not in the least remarkable, for it needs time and distance to make old legends interesting.

He and his pony must have been familiar figures on the roads, and when he came to a wild moorland farm, no doubt they welcomed him, expecting news from the outside world, and were a little disappointed when he sat silent in the settle, gazing into the smouldering peats, brooding upon his wrongs.

At such times, most likely he drew out his cherished papers from his wallet and pored upon them, though he must long ago have known them all by heart, and as he read them all his pride in his old lineage revived, and the long day upon hill tracks may have seemed light to him as he sat nodding by the fire. His hosts, with the old-fashioned hospitality of those times, would set before him a great bowl of porridge, which he must often only have eaten for good manner's sake, and then gone off to sleep beside his pony on the straw.

How many years he wandered through the mosses and the hills, how many times he saw the shaws in April green upon the Fairy Hill, or the red glow upon the moor in autumn, is not quite clear; but all the times he never once forsook his wanderings. Offers were made him, by many of his friends, to settle down; but either the free life held something for him that no mere dwelling in a house could give, or else he thought himself more likely to attain his object by being always on the road, travelling, as it were, like a Knight of the Holy Grail, towards some goal unseen that fascinated him, still always further on.

No doubt the darksome thickets by loch sides, in which he and his pony must have passed so many summer nights, were pleasanter than a smoke-infested Highland shieling. Sleeping alone in them he could hear all the mysterious voices of the night; hear wild ducks whirring overhead, the cries of herons in the early morning, the splash made by the rising trout, and watch the mist at dawn creeping upon the water as he lay huddled in his plaid.

All our old tracks, so long disused, but visible, to those who look for such things, by their white stones on which so many generations of brogue-clad feet have passed, and by the dark green grass that marks them as they meander across uplands or through the valleys, he must have known as well as did the drovers coming from the north.

Lone wells, that lie forgotten nowadays, but of which then the passers-by all knew and drank from, he too had drunk from, lying upon his chest, and with his beard floating like seaweed in the water as he lay.

Mists must have shrouded him, as he rode through the hills, and out of them strange faces must have peered, terrible and fantastic to a man alone and cut off from mankind.

Possibly to him the faces seemed familiar and more kindly than were those he generally saw upon his pilgrimage. If there were fairies seated on the green knolls, he must have seemed to them one of themselves, for certainly he was a man of peace.

Cold, wind and rain and snow must have beat on him as they do upon a tree, but not for that did he once stay his wanderings up and down. As age drew on him it was observed that by degrees he seldom left his native parish, Kilmaronock, where he was known and understood by all.

There is a tract of moorland, high-lying and bleak, from which at the top you see Loch Lomond and its islands lying out as in a map beneath. The grey Inch Cailleach, and dark Inch Murren with its yews float in the foreground like hulks of ships, and the black rock of Balmaha rises above a little reedy bay. Just at the bleakest part of the bare moor the wandering earl was seen by some returning drovers on a cold winter's night. Light snow was falling, and as they passed him on the wild track that leads down to the Vale of Leven, huddled up on his pony, they spoke to him but he returned no answer, and passed on into the storm. All night it snowed, and in the morning, when the heritors were coming to the old kirk of Bonhill parish, they found him with his back against a dry-stone dyke, and his beloved parchments in his hand. Not far away his old white pony, with the reins dangling round his feet, stood shivering, and in the snow where he had thrust his muzzle deeply down to seek the grass were some faint stains of blood.

(From *A Hatchment*, 1913)

NOTES

1. *muniments*, documents, title-deeds, preserved as evidence of rights or privileges.
2. Graham knew the work of the Spanish mystics, like St. John of the Cross and St. Teresa, and he was fascinated by mysticism. cf. his life of Antonio Conselheiro, *A Brazilian Mystic* (1920). This mystical reference to the poor is very obscure and may well be Graham's own paraphrasing of another proverb or biblical quotation. It certainly echoes the words of the Book of Ecclesiastes (IX, 16): "The poor man's wisdom is despised, and his words are not heard."

A FISHERMAN

The steamer scrunched against the pier, the gangway plank was drawn back slowly, and with as great an effort as if it had weighed a ton, by the West Highland tweed-clad semi-sailors, semi-longshore men. The little groups of drovers separated, each following its fugleman to the nearest public-house. The ropes were cast off from the belaying pins and whisked like serpents over the slippery slime-covered boards. A collie dog holding on to one of them by its teeth was dragged to the very edge, amongst a shower of Gaelic oaths.

Then with a snort and plunge the "Isleman" met the south-west swell coming up past Pladda from the Mull. The wandering Willie, with his fiddle in a green baize bag, stripped off its cover, and got to work in the wild wind and drizzling rain, at reels, strathspeys, laments, and all the minor music which has from immemorial time been our delight in Scotland, although, no doubt, it is as terrifying to the Southern as when the bagpipes skirl. His dog beside him, a mere mongrel, looking like a dirty mop, and yet with something half pathetic, half ridiculous about him, sat holding round his neck a battered can for pence. The fiddler, bandy-legged and dressed in heather mixture tweed, which gave out fumes of peat reek, snuff, and stale whisky, stood by the forebitts, and round him clustered all the heterogeneous "heids and thraws" of the population of the West Highlands, Glasgow and Greenock, and the other towns upon the Firth of Clyde. Gently the steamer glided through the Kyles of Bute, left Toward Point on her port bow, and headed for Dunoon. And as she steamed along, passing the varied scenery of mist-capped mountain and of stormy loch, the peaks of Arran in the distance like a gigantic saddle hung outlined in the clouds. The passengers, for the most part, seemed to see nothing but each other's clothes and personal defects, after the fashion of so many travellers, who, with their shells of prejudice borne on their backs as they were snails, go out to criticise that which they could have seen to just as great advantage in their homes. Amongst them was a man dressed in a greasy "stan' o' black," who, at first sight, appeared to be what we in Scotland call a "goin' aboot body," and recognise as having quite a status in the land. His clothes, originally black, had borne the labour, whisky, and the rain of many a funeral. He did not seem a townsman, for he had that wizened, weather-beaten look which, once a sailor, never leaves a man this side of the grave. At once you saw that he had made his bread in ships, or boats, or in some way upon that element on which those who go down to it in brigs "smell hell," as the old shellback said who heard the passage in the Bible on the wonders of the deep.

Hard bread it is; damned hard, as the old admiral told his sacred majesty, the fourth William, who asked him whether he had been bred up to the sea.

The nondescript, at least, cared not an atom for the others on the boat, but seemed to know each inlet, stone, and islet on the coast. He carried a geranium cutting in a little pot, hedged round with half a newspaper to shield it from the wind, and as the sun fell on the hills of "Argyle's bowling-green," broke out into a rhapsody, half born of whisky and half of that perfervidness which is the heritage of every Scot.

" 'There shall be no more sea,' no a wise like saying of John, though he was sort o' doited in Patmos; what had the body got against the sea?"

"I followed it myself twal year. First in an auld rickle o' a boat, at Machrihanish, and syne wi' the herrin' fishers about Loch Fyne. Man, a gran' life the sea. Whiles I am sorry that I left it; but *auri sacra fames*,[1] ye mind. Nae mair sea! Set John up. But the mountains, mountains will remain. Thank the Lord for the mountains."

No one responding to his remarks, he turned to me, observing that I looked an "eddicated man."

"Aye, ou aye, I mind I made a matter of five hundred pund at the herrin' fishin', and then, ye ken, I thocht I saw potentialities (gran' word, potentiality) of being rich, rich beyond the dreams of avarice, as that auld carle, Dr. Johnson, said. Johnson, ye ken, he that keepit a skule, and ca'ed it an academy, as auld Boswell said. A sort o' randy body yon Boswell, man, though he gied us a guid book.[2] Many's the time I hae lauched over it. Puir, silly deevil, but with an eye untill him like a corbie for detail. Details, ye ken, are just the vertebrae of the world. Ye canna do without detail. What did I do? Losh me, I had most forgot. Will ye tak' an apple? It'll keep doun the drouth. Scotch apples are the best apples in the world, but I maun premise I like apples sour, as the auld leddie said.

"Na—well, ye're maybe right, apples are sort o' wersh without speerits. Bonny wee islands, yon Cumbraes, the wee yin just lik a dunter's heid, the big yin, a braw place for fishin'.

"Whitin' bay, ye ken, just beyond where the monument for they puir midshipmen stands. An awfu' coast, I mind three laddies, some five and thirty year syne, from up aboot England gaein' oot in a lugsail boat from the Largs. Ane o' they easterly haars cam' on. They just come doon like a judgment of God on this coast—ye canna escape them, nor it. Aye weel, I'll no say no, a judgment, a special judgment o' divine providence, just fa's like a haar, fa's on the just and the unjust alike. Na, na, I'm no meanin' any disrespeck to providence, weel do I ken which side my bannock's buttered. . . . The laddies, the easterly wind just drave them aff the coast, in a wee bit boatie, and had it no' been ane o' them was a sailor laddie, they would ne'er a' won back. Wondrous are His ways, whiles He saves those that never would be missed, and whiles. . . . Do I no believe in the efficacy o' prayer. Hoots aye, that is I'm no sure. Whiles a man just works his knees into horn wi' prayin' for what might profit him, that is, profit him in this world ye see, and providence doesna steer for a' his prayin'. Whiles a man just puts up a sipplication for some speeritual matter, and the Lord just answers him before the man is sure he wants the object of his prayer.

"The Cumbraes, sort o' backlyin' islands, but the folk that live on them hae a guid conceit. Sort o' conceity, the bit prayer, the minister in Millport used to pit up for the adjawcent islands o' Great Britain and Ireland, ye'll mind it, ye that seem to be a sort o' eddicated man.

"Yer lookin' at the bit gerawnium. Sort of tragical that gerawnium, if you regard the matter pheelosophically. I tell't you that I aince made a bit o' money at the herrin' fishin'. Shares in a boat or twa. Man, I was happy then, a rough life the fishin', but vera satisfyin'. Just an element o' gambling aboot it that endears it to a man. Aye, ou aye, the sea, I ken it noo, I see why I lik't the life sae weel. I felt it then though, just like a collie dog feels the hills, although he doesna ken it. I always fancy that collies look kind o' oot o' place in Glesca.

"A collie dog, ye ken, would rather hear a West Hielandman swear at him in Gaelic than an English leddie ca' him a' the pets in the world. It's no his fault, it's no the swearin' that he likes, but just the tone o' voice. A gran' language the Gaelic, profanity in it just sounds like poetry in any other tongue.

"Weel, a fisherman is just like a collie dog, he'd rather hear the tackle run through the sheaves o' the blocks than a' the kists o' whistles in the Episcapalian churches up aboot Edinburgh. And then the sea, dam't I canna tell why I still ettle to get back to it. It took ma fayther, maist o' ma brithers, and the feck o' a' ma folk. It's maybe that, it's the element o' uncertainty there again, but dam't I dinna right know what it is, except that when ye aince get the salt doon into the soul, ye ken, ye canna get it oot again. That is, no' on this side the grave. I wouldna have left it, had it not been ma mither, threep, threepin' on me . . . aye, and the *auri sacra fames*.

". . . Bonny the Largs looks, eh? Gin it's no the view of Cuchullin, the hills of Arran frae the Largs is the brawest view in Scotland. That is for a man that likes the sea. But I see I'm wearyin' ye wi' ma clash. Ye'd maybe like to see the *Herald*. . . . I hae Bogatzky in my bawg; Bogatzky's *Golden Treasury*,[3] but maybe it's no greatly read in your body. Fine old-fashioned book Bogatzky, nae taint o' latter-day Erastianism aboot it. Na, na, I'se warrant ye the man compiled Bogatzky gied his congregation mony a richt shake abune the pit. Tophet,[4] ye ken, the real old, what I might ca' the constitutional Tophet, before they hung thermometers aboot the walls, in case the temperature should gae ower high."

The steamer, after plunging uneasily beside the pier at Largs for sufficient time to let a knot of drovers, each with his dog led by a piece of twine, and holding in their hands hooked hazel sticks, reel off towards the town, and to allow the passengers (who did not mark it) space to view the beauties of the place, the little river brawling through the town, and the long bit of sea-swept grass on which goats pasture fixed to chains, and get a living on the scanty herbage, eked out with bottles, bones and sardine tins, turned eastward once again towards the Clyde.

She ran past Fairlie, with its cliffs all clothed in oak and hazel copse. The passengers by this time being "michtily refreshed," as was the chairman of the curling club at Coupar-Angus after his fifteenth tumbler, threw sandwich bags and bottles overboard, and took to dancing on the deck. The elders gathered into knots, talked politics, religion, or, with much slapping of red hands upon their knees, enjoyed indecent tales, after the fashion of the Puritan, who, though his creed enjoys a modest life, yet places no embargo on the speech. So it is said an Irishman in Lent, meeting a friend who remarked he was drunk, rejoined, "Sure, God Almighty never set a fast upon the drink."

My philosophic friend and I watched the athletic sports, and when the lassies skirled as partners pinched them, or in the joy of life, which manifests itself in divers ways, and usually in some unseemly fashion when the two sexes meet, he wagged a moralising head and freely poured out his philosophy.

"Man, Rabbie, . . . ye'll hae Burns . . . Rabbie kenned his countrymen. A fine, free, fornicatin', pious folk we are. Man, Rabbie kent us better than he kent himsel', I sometimes think. Aye, ou aye, ye canna mak' a saint o' Rabbie. Saints, ye ken, are weel enough in books, but sort o' weary bodies to live wi', they must hae been, the feck o' them. I didna tell ye aboot the bit gerawnium. I hae it in the cabin, for fear they cattle micht sit doon on it; ye mind auld Walter Scott, the time he pouched the glass George IV drank oot o', and then fair dang it into flinders on the road hame? Kind o' weak o' Scott, pouchin' yon glass; a bonny carle, yon George, to touch folk for the King's evil . . . but ou aye, the gerawnium, I mind it.

"Ye see a' my potentialities of growing rich werena just realised. I wrocht twa year in Glesca, ane in Edinburgh, syne sax in Brig o' Weir, whiles takin' a bit flutter on the Stock Exchange. Rogues they fellies on the Exchange, ettlin' to mak' their siller without honest toil. Na, na; I ken what ye're goin' to say—if I had won, I wouldna' hae misca'ed them. Pairfectly reasoned, sir; but then ye ken, when a man loses, the chap that get his siller is aye a rogue. Weel, weel, many's the time I wished masel back at Tobermory in the bit boat, wi' the bonny wee-tanned lug, fishin', aye, like the Apostles. Weel, I ken why the Lord found His first followers amongst fishermen. Simple folk, ye see, and wi' the gamblin' element weel developed; no like yer hinds—slave, slavin' at the ground—but oot upon the lake, yon sea of Galilee, ye mind; a sort o' loch, just like Loch Fyne, as I ae thocht. When ye sit in the boat, keepin' her full and by, fetchin' the sea, your eye just glancin' on the waves, it kind o' maks ye gleg to risk a wee. Nae fears we'll get another preacher like the Lord; but if we did, there wouldna be a fisher-man, from Tobermory doun to the Cruives o' Cree, that wouldna follow him. I'se warrant them. Dour folk, the fishers, but venturesome; and a' the time I wrocht aboot thae stinkin' towns, I ettled to get back. I aye went aince a year to see our mither; she just stops aboot twa mile west of Tobermory, and I aye tak back ane of they gerawniams in a pot. Why do I no stop there when I win back, ye say? Aye, there's the mystery of it, the sort o' tragedy as I was tellin' ye when we cam through the Kyles.

"Ye see . . . spot yon lassie wi' the sunset hair, ane o' the lang backit, short-leggit West Highland kind, built like a kyloe, just gars me think upon yon woman of Samaria . . . I'm haverin' . . . weel, the fack is I canna stop at hame. Tak' a West Hielan' stirk, and put him in a park, doon aboot Falkirk, or in the Lothians, and maybe, at the first, he doesna' thrive, misses the Hielan' grass maybe, and the gran' wind that blaws across the sea. Syne, he gets habeetuated, and if ye take him back to the north, maybe he couldna bide. That's just ma ain case, sir.

"Weel do I mind the auld braw days; a herrin' never tastes sae weel as just fresh caught and brandered in the boat. I mind yon seinin' too, sic splores we had, aye and a feck o' things come back to me when I am in the toon. The peat reek, and a' the comfortable clarty ways we had; the winter nights, when the wind blew fit to tak' aff the flauchter feals o' the old cottage. I mind them a'. That is, I dinna care to mind."

And as we talked, the steamer slipped past Wemyss Bay, left the Cloch Lighthouse on the left hand, and passed by Inverkip, slid close by Gourock, and then opened up the valley of the Clyde. Greenock with all its smoky chimneys rose in view, sending a haze of fog into the air. The timber in the ponds upon the shore surged to and fro against the railings as the steamer's swell lifted it slowly, and then settled down again to season in the mud. Dumbarton Rock showed dimly, and the river narrowed; the fairway marks showing the channel like a green ribbon winding through mud banks, as the vessel drew towards the pier.

Gathering their packages and parcels, and smoothing out their clothes, the passengers passed down the gangway, laughing and pushing one another in their haste to get away.

The man with the geranium in the pot still lingered, looking back towards the sea. Then, gathering up his traps and tucking his umbrella underneath his arm, prepared to follow them.

"Good-bye," he said, "we hae had a pleasant crack, I'll just be off and daunder up the toon. Doddered and poor, and a wee thing addicted to strong drink, strong drink, ye ken, speerits, that maketh glad the heart o' man; neither a fisher nor a townsman, a sort o' failure, as ye may say, I am. Good-bye, ye seem a sort o' eddicated man.... Na, na, I will na drop it, never fear. I broacht it a' the way from Tobermory, and ye ken, sir, Greenock is no' a guid place for gerawniums after all."

He stumbled out along the gangway plank, his rusty "stan o' black" looking more stormworn and ridiculous than ever in the evening sun. Holding his flower-pot in his hand, wrapped round with newspaper, he passed out of my sight amongst the crowd, and left me wondering if the flower in the pot would live, and he return, and die in Tobermory by the sea.

(From *Success*, 1902)

NOTES

1. *auri sacra fames*, the blessed greed for gold.
2. James Boswell (1740-95), who wrote his famous *Life of Samuel Johnson* (1791), and also a *Journal of a Tour to the Hebrides* (1785).
3. Karl Heinreich von Bogatzky (1690-1774), German hymn-writer, author of *Golden Treasury of God's Children* (1718).
4. *Tophet*, place of punishment for the wicked, i.e. Hell.

A TRAVELLER

He stood, a square, grey figure in the hall, and, looking upward at the pictures of my grim-visaged ancestors in their full-bottomed wigs, said, "Bonny scenery, aye, bonny scenery." The criticism was as novel as it was unexpected, and was the introduction to a bickering friendship which extended over years.

His greasy cap and crisp grey hair which melted into one another, hodden grey clothes, and greenish flannel shirt, but with one touch of colour in his bright red cheeks, like apples tinged with frost, made him look like the stone which, in the district where he lived, was known as the "auld carlin wi' the bratty plaid."

"Laird, I hae travel't it, yes, fack as death, richt through frae up aboot Balfron."

A man may make the circuit of the world in as short space of time as it seems good to him, and yet not earn the title of a "soople traveller," for "travelling" means to walk. Thus we refer to pedlars by the name of "travelling merchants," and tramps as "gaein' aboot" or "travelling bodies," saving thereby their pride and ours, and not contributing to wear out shoe-leather any the faster by the mere application of the word. But, still, in using it, we usually extend our pity to the traveller, who is a sort of a survival of the times when all men rode, if only on West Highland ponies schauchling through the mud. Used by a poor man, it generally infers that he is going to ask a favour, or, by a tenant to his landlord, that the times are bad.

"Laird, I just travel't it. Thank ye, nae soddy, laird," and as he spoke he drained a good half-tumbler of raw whisky to the dregs, in such a quiet, sober, and God-fearing way, it seemed an act of prayer.

Of all the tenant farmers it has been my luck to meet and chaffer with, none could exceed the traveller in making a poor mouth. Seasons were always backward, markets bad, and sheep had foot-rot or the fluke, the "tatties" were diseased—"Man, laird! I felt the smell of yon field out by Gartchurachan whenever I cam forward to the trough-stone, ye ken, fornent the Hosh."

The act of God was instant at his farm, tirling the slates or hashing up the rhones, leaving the sarking bare, so that the snaw bree seepit thro' upon the stirks.[1] "I just tak' shame to pit horse in yon rickle o' a stable, and a' the grips are fair dune in the byre. Laird, I just biggit a' the steadin', that is, I drave the stanes and drainit a' the land to ye. Siccan a farm for tile! Man, I hae pit in more than ten thousand since last back en', and still she's wet, wet as Loch Lomond. I'm just tellin' ye, ye'll maybe hae to tak' it back and try it yersel', for I am just beat wi' it. . . . What? tak' it off my hands at Martinmas! Na, na, I'll fecht awa' in it, though

I'll hae to hae a wee reduction, or maybe a substantial ane, just to encourage me to carry on my agricultural operations. Aye, dod aye, I'm sayin' it."

His farm was grey and square, with the house planted down upon the road, leaving an angle which ran out from the farmyard, planted with cabbages and with some flowers which wrestled with the wind. No tree grew near the place, which, high and desolate, stood solitary, exposed to the full fury of the south-west wind. An air of neatness without homeliness pervaded everything. Carts with their shafts upright stood under sheds, and on a rope, stretched from the stable to the byre, hung braxy sheep, their bodies black and shrunken, their skins, new flayed and pink, fluttering about like kites.

But if the roadside farm was dreary in itself, a mere corral of coarse grey stones topped by blue slates, the distant hills atoned for all shortcomings in the foreground of the view.

From the high moorland platform where Tombreak seemed to be stuck down like a child's house of bricks, the Grampians rose, making a semicircle to the north and west. Lumpy, and looking like misshapen vegetables, monstrous and brown, their chain was broken here and there by peaks, and here and there by mountain burns which glistened on their sides as streaks of foam gleam white upon a horse's flanks. Ben Ledi and Schaehallion to the east, with Stuc-a-Chroin, Ben Voirlich, Ben A'an, and Ben Venue; nearer Ben Dearg and Craigmore, and to the west Ben Lomond rising solitary, a vast blue cone about whose top floated a vapoury cloud, as if the soul of the volcano long extinct hovered about its once accustomed haunts, stood sentinels, frowning down on the mossy strath, set with its lumpy hillocks grown with stubbly oak, and on the still blue lake with the grey priory and the castled isle. Far to the north snow-capped Ben More, with its twin paps, peeped out between the shoulders of the bolder hills, showing its beauties timidly, and at the faintest shift of wind retreating back into the mist—that veil which shrouds the Highlands in its mystery, shutting them off for ever from the south.

Below the farm straggled the village of Balfron, a long grey ribbon in the mist. Nearer it showed a Scottish toun all bare of flowers, but cosy in its clartiness, in which barefooted children ran about and played at "bools," wiping their noses on their coat sleeves, or went to school wearing their boots uneasily, as ponies from the far-off islands of the north hobble along in the first dignity of shoes.

Above the toun with its ancestral trysting-tree clamped round with iron hoops, its antiquated toll-house, now turned sweet-shop, and in whose windows fly-blown toffy and flat-looking ginger beer winked at the passer-by, who knew, perhaps, that there was liquor more alluring to be had inside—the Campsies rose, a wall of green, broken but by the Corrie of Balglas. Their grassy sides and look of pastoral quiet made a sharp contrast with the Highland hills, only ten miles away. The two hill ranges were as far apart as is a northern shepherd, wrapped in his plaid and "sheltering awee" behind a rock whilst his dog slumbers at his feet, his coat all wet with mist, and a gull-followed southland ploughman labouring at his craft.

Upon the plateau, with the hills to the north and south, the wind raged ceaselessly, and many a weary mile upon the moors after his sheep my tenant must have "travelled" before his face took on the dark red polish which, starting out from his grey aureole of hair and Newgate frill, looked like a red bottle in a chemist's window when you passed him in the gloaming on the road. Long contact and familiarity with sheep had given him something of the grace of a West Highland wether, which he resembled somewhat in his mind; for, in a land in which most men are cautious, not delivering their souls without due hedging, manward and Godward, as befits a Scot, he stood out easily the first. Prudence in his case almost amounted to a mania, so that in any case a bargain must have been a torture to him; for if he lost, he naturally cursed God and man, and if he gained by it, bewailed himself for having lost the chance of getting better terms. No word he spoke without a qualifying clause. Thus the best harvest ever known to man, to him was "no that bad," and a fine Clydesdale horse "a bonny beast, but no well feathered on the pastern joints."

No Ayrshire cow but was "a wee thing heich abune the tail," which dictum he would modify, and, sighing say, "but we are a' that," and thus humanity and all the race of cows were either justified or stood arraigned, according to your taste.

As was to be expected from a man so gifted for success amongst the men with whom he lived, he was "well doing," that is, he had amassed some little money, chiefly by "travellin'" about to cattle markets and picking up cheap beasts. In fact, he was an instance of the Scots proverb, that "the gangin' foot aye picks up something, if it is but a thorn." No one who saw him walin' his way across the moors leading his collie by a piece of common string, with his long hazel shepherd's crook thrust through his arms behind his back, making him look like a trussed fowl, or driving home some of his purchases through a mist upon the muddy roads, could ever think of him and death as having anything in common that should one day make them friends. So like the stubbly oaks he looked, which grew in the Park Wood upon his farm, and which themselves had braved a thousand tempests and a hundred pollardings, that he seemed likely to endure as long as they. But your cursed cold or heart disease, or his neglect in taking whisky at set hours, or something which no doctor can foresee, proved his undoing, and he departed "travellin'" to a tryst, his collie following at his heels, and his long shepherd's staff in hand, willing and eager for the coming deal.

Tough, knarred, and kindly, with his apple cheeks and his thick fell of crisp grey hair, his hodden clothes and cheery smile, no matter whether he had got the best of his opponent in a bargain or the worst, he took away with him some of my life and the kind memories of the whole countryside aboot Balfron.

Ben Lomond and Ben Ledi still look down upon the carse; in the Park Wood the twisted oaklings rustle in the breeze, and by Tombreak the wind sweeps ceaselessly.

"Andra" is gone, his collie dog perchance comes to another whistle, and his roan Iceland pony mare maybe ekes out her life in a fish-hawker's cart; but her lost owner, I would like to think, there in the spheres, is "travellin'," if only "goin' aboot," for it may well be that they hold no trysts where he dwells now; but still I know that it is ill to stay "the gangin' foot" after a lifetime of the road.

(From Progress, 1905)

NOTES

1. "unroofing the tiles or damaging the gutters, and leaving the wood above the rafters bare, so that the melted snow seeped through on to the cattle."

A RETAINER

"Laird, ye ken ane o' my forbears gaed to Bannockburn wi' the Graemes."
Though my retainer always insisted that this forbear was "nigh upon seven feet
high," and used to add, "men nowadays run awfie small," he would himself with
his inadequate six feet and four or five inches have wielded a good spear.

Indeed, no man could possibly have had a better spearsman at his back in the
old days.

Tall, dark, and with a fell of hair that grew down low upon his forehead and
met his curling beard, which grew so thick upon his face, if you had dropped a
pin upon it, it would have never touched the skin, his twinkling grey eyes looked
out suspiciously and yet with humour on the world. His upper lip was always
shaved, that is to say, upon the "Sabbath morn," and bore throughout the week a
crop of stubble on it, so that, had it not been an article of faith with him to shave
it on the Sunday, he might as well have thrown away his razor, though I can
never fancy him with a moustache. He had, I think, a vague idea that to have
grown it would have been a sort of poaching on the customs of the "gentry,"
though if a long descent can make a gentleman, surely the fact of the grim
forbear who had gone to Bannockburn should have entitled him to be so styled,
even although the warrior ancestor may have been legendary. Most ancestors do
not bear looking at too closely, not only for their moral worth, but for their
authenticity, and my retainer's had done as much for him, as if he had, after the
manner of most Scottish worthies, hall-marked his passage through the world by
witnessing a charter, for he lived up to him, according to his lights.

Born just before the railway penetrated the remoter districts, he had,
although he never knew it, preserved a flavour of an older world.

His speech was harsh and dialectic but yet not vulgar, and in his voice you
heard that cadence, as of a Gaelic song, natural to those born near the Highland
line. Whether he ever knew it I know not, but he appeared to me a little wasted
in a world which had no special function for such men, as he was to perform.
Walking beside a cart, towering above the horse, or sitting on the cramped iron
seat of some new reaper, cutting the corn upon his boggy fields, he seemed a
little out of place, too fine a figure for the work, not that he was especially intelli-
gent, beyond a certain "pawky" humour, the inheritance of nearly everyone who
tills the soil in our bleak, kindly North, but because a manhood such as his
imparts a dignity to its possessor quite as impossible to explain as humour, but
seen at the first glance.

Huge and athletic as he seemed to me in later life, in childhood he loomed
gigantic, and illness, death, or age appeared in his case as impossible as they would
have been to a mountain or to the world itself.

Seated beside his father, his very counterpart, but bent and grey, he used to keep my eyes focussed upon him, half against my will, during long hours in the church. It seemed a miracle how his great hands, in which the soil had entered, as it were, below the skin and dyed them dark as peat, could "whummle o'er" the pages in the "Book," and as I sat desperately waitin for "saxteenthly and seventeenthly," and often cheated by the preacher, who always seemed to have a "few words in conclusion," extending over twenty minutes, in reserve, I used to envy his composure as he sat as little moved as is a rock upon a moor during a shower of rain. As I look back through the long vista of the years, it does not strike me that he was religious to a great degree, though such a constant worshipper in church. In fact, I think he was one of the class of commentators who would not give "five minutes of the clash of the kirkyard for all the sermons in the world." It may be that in this I am unjust, for in things spiritual he did not venture an opinion, although on politics he thought he was a Radical, that is, with reservations, as are most of us, for I remember that on one occasion he remarked he "was na sure ould Wully Gladstane had done richt when he gave votes to the farm labourers" ... for, as he said, "yon class o' cattle is not eddicated up to it." It would have been a work of supererogation to have told him, that what he had just said was what was urged against his own class once upon a time, for he would certainly have answered: "Aye ou aye, prejudice juist dies hard," or something of the sort, with the assurance of a man who knows that he is right.

His house, just on the edge of a wild moss, was suited to him, for certainly it had no outward sign of any inward grace, as it stood gaunt and square, its grey stone walls and green-grey slates gave it that air of self-assertion which I suppose it had to have to face the climate, just as a Scotchman who is lacking in it is a Scotchman lost.

Needless to say, no flowers climbed up the porch, no garden broke the look of sternness of the place.

The only sacrifice, that is, if sacrifice it could be called, upon the altar of aestheticism were two small rowan trees which grew on each side of the iron gate which opened on the gravel path that led up to the house, and had been made to form an arch. I think that in his heart of hearts my retainer looked upon this as foolishness and waste of time, for once when I directed his attention to it, he muttered "havers of the wife's," and turned the conversation with a remark that sheep "were back at the October Tryst," or something of the sort.

Though not a grumbler, or a man who ever asked for a reduction of his rent, my retainer never would allow that any season could be a good one for the crops. Markets were always "back," during the many years I knew him; potatoes always either were diseased or just were sickening for it; the neeps had tae-and-finger, and the hogs wintering upon his farm either had foot-rot or the fluke.

None of these statements did he advance with an ulterior object, but simply threw them out for what they might be worth, either as pleasant subjects to discourse upon, or as a sort of formula with which to enter into conversation in an agreeable way.

This habit, and his enormous hands, and feet encased in boots like barges, heavily soled and tacketed, his homespun clothes and soft black hat (he lived before the age of caps), were but one side of him, the side that he turned outward to the world.

Not having Gaelic, he had lost the gift of picturesque expression, the birth-right, as it seems, of every Highlander, even the dullest of his race. Deep in his mind, however, there seemed to seethe a mixture of hard Lowland Scotch ideas and a half Celtic spirit of revolt, not against powers that be, but against life as we all know it, striving for mastery.

This made him ever in hot water with his fellows, but, on the other hand, took him off into a fantastic world, not that of elves and fairies, of wraiths and second sight, but to a sphere in which all the occurrences of daily life were magnified till they became as interesting as they might well be, or perhaps really are, if we could see them in his way.

During the whole course of his life he was, as he said, "sair ta'en up wi' horse," and yet had the worst horses in the district on his farm.

Floods, frosts, and snows were deeper, fiercer, and more intense, when he recounted them, than anyone had ever known them, and yet in all his dealings with his fellows he was honest to a fault, so that it may have been he either was a poet without the gift of words, or that the spirit of the strange, wild district where he lived worked in his soul, whilst the affairs of life, sordid and common-place, but yet compelling, influenced his mind.

The village, close to where he lived, was rent asunder by feuds between the churches, which, as the difference between them was infinitesimal, rendered their quarrels almost as bitter as those between the Spaniards and the Moors.

Often the battle raged on little matters, such as the appointment of a school-teacher or the like, and my retainer, having taken as it were the shilling of the Free Kirk, duly embroiled himself with almost everybody, offending just as much his co-religionists by too great violence as he outraged his enemies by his attacks.

At last he found himself left all alone, the one sincere and honest man in the whole district branded as an intriguer and a liar.

So he retired to his marshy fields, and passed his time between the plough-stilts and his own ingle-neuk, but never missing kirk on Sundays, where he sat silently, his hair a little greyer, and his hands a little more like roots of trees, turning the criticising gaze of the old-fashioned members of his race upon the preacher, and ostentatiously looking up all the texts he quoted, with a loud rustle of pages, reminding one of dry leaves falling in a wood.

All the strange waifs and strays, goin'-aboot bodies and the like, who forty years ago travelled the upland districts in the North, drifted up to his farm in the same way steel filings jump to a magnet, and he, although he bitterly complained about their presence and the small depredations that they made, was always ready to throw open barns and outhouses for them to pass the night.

Perhaps the district, with its wide mosses and enshrouding mists, its mouldering ruins of the past, mysterious-looking tarns lost in the hills, and its slow-flowing black-streamed river, upon whose bosom bubbles that seemed to rise up from the centre of the earth were ever bursting, was his chief friend, for no one could have pictured him in any other place. The great iron gin he dug out of the moss, and which he called a wolf-trap, and the claymore he found when casting peats, and which by a quite natural process soon became Rob Roy's, were his chief treasures. The one I have inherited, and the other, which he sold to a travelling antiquary, was perhaps the sole occasion in which he got the best of a bargain in his life. His all-embracing feuds, extending from his nearest neighbours, with every one of whom he had some question either of "marches" or of "trespass," did not exclude the humblest from his wrath.

The parish gravedigger, he declared, should never bury him, for as he had not been consulted over his appointment, he used to say, "Yon Ramsey canna howk a grave; he mak's them mair like tattie pits, no like a Christian's grave."

Happening to meet him on the road one day long years ago, I asked him whether he had made it up with Ramsey, and received the answer, "Aye, ou aye, time is a sort o' healer. Aye ou aye ... when I dee, Ramsey wull just hae to sort me ... though he is sure to mak' a bummle o' the job!"

Fate, as it happened, was not willing that his grave should be bungled in the way he feared, for, dying in the North, a snowstorm caught the mourners and he was sheughed, as he himself would certainly have said, in a churchyard by a lake, where to this day his rough-hewn headstone moulders in the mist. All round him lie McFarlanes and McGregors, most of whose tombstones simply bear a sword upon them thus setting forth the manner of their lives.

What he will think when he "spangs up" amongst them at the day of judgement I cannot say, for in the days gone by they were sworn foes ... but, as he said himself, "time is a healer" ... and in the meanwhile the little wavelets of the lake break up against the wall of the wild graveyard where he lies, with a faint gurgling sound.

No one, I know, is left in the whole world the least resembling him, so strange a mixture of the present and the past; on the one side a representative of the rough-footed Scots who harried and who reived, and, on the other, of the laborious race of ploughmen (loved of the sea-gulls) who have made Scotland what she is.

Roughness and kindliness so struggled for the mastery in him that they seemed after the fashion of the spirit and the flesh to fight an everlasting battle for the predominance, leaving the struggle fortunately undetermined, so that he still appeared a man, weak and uncertain in his strength, an infant grafted on a giant, such as, no doubt, was his fell ancestor, who gaed to Bannockburn.

(From *Hope*, 1910)

Section V

THE SCOTS ABROAD

EDITOR'S PREFACE

The Wandering Scot has become as much a part of history as the Wandering Jew or the Wandering Scholar. From earliest times the lad of parts emigrated in search of wealth, to teach the world, to convert the heathen, or simply to escape drudgery and unemployment, Her Majesty's prison, or an English landlord. For centuries, one used to be able to say, the sun never set on a part of the empire where there was not a Scot righting the wrongs of the world—or at least talking about it.

Graham confines his sketches of the Scots abroad to the areas he knows best—Latin America and North Africa, in particular. He could have added Canada where, resident for some years, I never cease to wonder at the contribution of Scotia's sons in every walk of life. A Canadian national magazine, in a recent article on the Scots in Canada, dwelt on the power of the "Scottish Mafia" within the Federal Government. It can be truly said that the evolution of Canada could not have taken place without the massive immigration and industrious efforts of Scots of all classes.[1] During a recent long stay in Argentina I was also impressed by the strength, in number, spirit and culture, of the Scots in the River Plate region, survivors or descendants of those who went out over the last hundred years or so to run the railway and telephone systems, to work in the cattle industry, and pioneer the land.[2]

Graham who had travelled in both Americas, the two Africas, throughout Europe and elsewhere, knew men like the surveyor Campbell (of "A Pakeha") in New Zealand, the trader M'Kechnie in the Mediterranean, the Reverend Archibald, the Scottish missionary in Africa, Christie Christison, the Aberdeen sailor in Argentina. Though there is much that is amusing in these stories of the Scots abroad, Graham does not hesitate to take full aim at the exploitation of the New Zealand aborigines by the canny Scots (not to mention their hypocritical licentiousness), the deceitful business practices and anti-Catholic bigotry of the merchant M'Kechnie, the stubborn, dour behaviour of the missionary in Africa, etc. Though not professedly an orthodox believer, and having no brief for dogmatic Catholicism,[3] Graham admired the human qualities and the courage of the men who preached the faith in far-off lands. His comments on the double morality of the Scots, especially in matters commercial and sexual, as revealed in these sketches, add weight to his moralising on the Scottish nature, and link up with his views on the Scottish character as depicted in Section II. But Scots are Scots, whether they live in Argentina, Africa, New Zealand or at home, and many of Graham's best stories are about those who, by nature of the Scots character, are just about to leave or are returning home—even if it is to die.

NOTES

1. See, for example, Douglas Hill, *Great Emigrations: The Scots to Canada*, London, Gentry Books, 1972, and *The Scots Tradition in Canada*, edited by W. Stanford Reid, Toronto, McClelland and Stewart, 1976. From a literary point of view, one should note the novels of John Galt and Frederick Niven.

2. An early description of these achievements is James Dodds' *Record of the Scottish Settlers in the River Plate*, Buenos Aires, Grand & Sylvester, 1897. My own upcoming study, *English-speaking Writers of the River Plate Region*, will embrace much of this, as reflected in the literature, especially of Scottish writers like Cunninghame Graham, Walter Owen and William Shand.

3. He once called himself a "Christian unattached." For a view of his religious attitudes see Ian M. Fraser, "R. B. Cunninghame Graham: A Study of his Social and Religious Outlook," Ph.D. Thesis, University of Edinburgh, 1955.

A PAKEHA[1]

Rain, rain, and more rain, dripping off the sodden trees, soaking the fields, and blotting out the landscape as with a neutral-tinted gauze. The sort of day that we in the land, "dove il dolce Dorico risuona,"[2] designate as "saft." Enter along the road to me a neighbour of some fifty to sixty years of age, one Mr. Campbell, a little bent, hair faded rather than grey, frosty-faced as we Scotsmen are apt to turn after some half a century of weather, but still a glint of red showing in the cheeks; moustache and whiskers trimmed in the fashion of the later sixties; "tacketed" boots, and clothes, if not impervious to the rain, as little affected by it as is the bark of trees. His hat, once black and of the pattern affected at one time by all Free Church clergymen, now greenish and coal-scuttled fore and aft and at the sides. In his red, chapped, dirty, but grey-mittened hands a shepherd's stick —long, crooked, and made of hazel-wood.

"It'll maybe tak' up, laird."

"Perhaps."

"An awfu' spell o' it."

"Yes, disgusting."

"Aye, laird, the climate's sort o' seekenin'. I mind when I was in New Zealand in the sixties, aye, wi' a surveyor, just at the triangulation, ye ken. Man, a grand life, same as the tinklers, here to-day and gane to-morrow, like old Heather Jock.[3] Hoot, never mind your dog, laird, there's just McClimant's sheep, puir silly body, I ken his keel-mark. Losh me, a bonny country, just a pairfect pairadise, New Zealand. When I first mind Dunedin it wasna bigger than the clachan there, out by. A braw place noo, I understan', and a' the folk fearfu' took up wi' horse, driving their four-in-hands, blood cattle, every one of them. There's men to-day like Jacky Price—he was a Welshman, I'm thinking—who I mind doing their day's darg just like mysel' aboot Dunedin, and noo they send their sons hame to be educated up aboot England.

"When? 'Oo aye, I went oot in the old *London* wi' Captain Macpherson. He'd bin the round trip a matter o' fifteen times, forbye a wee bit jaunt whiles after the 'blackbirds' (slaves, ye ken, what we called free endentured labourers) to the New Hebrides. The *London*, aye, 'oo aye, she foundered in the Bay (Biscay, ye ken) on her return. It's just a special providence I wasna a passenger mysel.

"Why did I leave the country? Eh, laird, ye may say. I would hae made my hame out there, but it was just the old folks threap, threaping on me to come back, I'm telling ye. A bonny toon, Dunedin, biggit on a wee hill just for a' the wurrld like Gartfarran there, and round the point a wee bit plain just like the Carse o' Stirling. Four year I wrocht at the surveyin', maistly triangulation, syne twa at shepherdin', nane o' your Australlian fashion tailing them a' day, but on the hame system gaen' aboot; man, I mind whiles I didna see anither man in sax weeks' time."

"Then you burned bricks, you say?"

"Aye, I didna' think ye had been so gleg at the Old Book. Aye, aye, laird, plenty of stra', or maybe it was yon New Zealand flax stalk. The awfiest plant ye ever clapt your eyes on, is yon flax. I mind when I first landed aff the old *London*—she foundered in the Bay. It was just a speecial inter-position . . . but I mind I telt ye. Well, I was just dandering aboot outside the toon, and hettled to pu' some of yon flax; man, I wasna fit; each leaf is calculated to bear a pressure of aboot a ton. The natives, the Maories, use it to thack their cottages. A bonny place, New Zealand, a pairfect pairadise—six-and-thirty years ago—aye, aye 'oo aye, just the finest country in God's airth.

"Het? Na, na, nane so het as here in simmer, a fine, dry air, and a bonny bright blue sky. Dam't, I mind the diggings opening tae. There were a wheen captins. Na, na, not sea captins, airmy captins, though there were plenty of the sea yins doon in the sooth; just airmy captins who had gone out and ta'en up land; blocked it, ye ken, far as frae here to Stirlin'. Pay for it, aye, aboot a croon the acre, and a wee bit conseederation to the Government surveyor just kept things square. Weel, when the diggins opened, some of them sold out and made a fortune. Awfu' place the diggins, I hae paid four shillin' a pound for salt mysel', and as for speerits, they were just fair contraband.

"And the weemen. Aye, I mind the time, but ye'll hae seen the Circassian weemen aboot Africa. Weel, weel, I'm no saying it's not the case, but folk allow that yon Circassians are the finest weemen upon earth. Whiles I hae seen some tae, at fairs, ye ken, in the bit boothies, but to my mind there's naething like the Maories, especially the half-casted yins, clean-limbed, nigh on six feet high the maist o' them. Ye'll no ken Geordie Telfer, him that was a sojer, he's got a bit place o' his ain out by Milngavie. Geordie's aye bragging, bostin' aboot weemen that he's seen in foreign pairts. He just is of opeenion that in Cashmere or there-aboots there is the finest weemen in the warld. Black, na, na, laird, just a wee toned and awfu' tall, ye ken. Geordie he says that Alexander the Great was up aboot Cashmere and that his sojers, Spartans I think they ca'ed them, just intro-mitted wi' the native weemen, took them, perhaps, for concubines, as the scriptures say; but ye'll ken sojers, laird; Solomon, tae, an awfu' chiel yon Solomon. The Maori men were na blate either, a' ower sax fut high, some nigh on seven fut, sure as death, I'm tellin' ye. Bonny wrestlers, tae; man, Donald Dinnie got an unco tirl wi' ane o' them aboot Dunedin, leastwise if it wasna Dinnie, it was Donald Grant or Donald McKenzie, or ane of they champions frae Easter Ross. Sweir to sell their land tae they chaps, I mind the Goverment sent out old Sir George Grey, a wise-like man, Sir George, ane o' they filantrofists. Weel, he just talkit to them, ca'ed them his children, and said that they shouldna resist legeetimate authority. Man, a wee wiry fella', he was the licht-weight champion wrestler at Tiki-Tiki, just up and said, 'Aye, aye, Sir George,' though he

wasna gi'en him Sir George, but just some native name they had for him, we're a'
your children, but no sic children as to gie our land for naething.' Sir George
turnit the colour of a neep, ane o' yon swedes, ye ken, and said nae mair."

"How did they manage it?"

"The Government just arranged matters wi' the chiefs. Bribery, weel a'
weel, I'll no gae sae far as to impute ony corruption on them, but a Government,
a Government, ye ken, is very apt to hae its way.

"Dam't, 'twas a fine country, a pairfect pairadise. I mind aince going oot with
Captin Brigstock, Hell-fire Jock they ca'ed him, after they bushrangers. There
was ane Morgan frae Australlia bail't up a wheen folks, and dam't, says Captin
Brigstock, ye'll hae to come, Campbell. Shot him, yes, authority must be respected, and the majesty o' law properly vendeecated, or else things dinna thrive.
It was in a wood of gora-gora we came on him about the mouth of day. Morgan,
ye ken, was boiling a billy in a sort o' wee clearin', his horse tied to a tree close by,
when Brigstock and the others came upon him. Brigstock just shouted in the
name o' the law and then let fly. Morgan, he fell across the fire, and when we all
came up says he, 'Hell-fire, ye didna gie me ony chance,' and the blood spouted
from his mouth into the boiling pan.

"Deid, 'oo aye, deid as Rob Roy. I dinna care to mind it. But a fine life, laird,
nae slavin' at the plough, but every ane goin' aboot on horseback; and the bonny
wee bit wooden huts, the folk no fashed wi' furniture, but sittin' doon to tak'
their tea upon the floor wi' their backs against the wall. That's why they ca'ed
them squatters. They talk aboot Australlia and America, but if it hadna been for
the old folks I would hae made my hame aboot a place ca'ed Paratanga, and hae
taken up with ane o' they Maori girls, or maybe a half-caste. Married, weel, I
widna say I hae gane to such a length. Dam't, a braw country, laird, a pairfect
pairadise, I'm telling ye;" and then the rain grew thicker, and seemed to come
between us as he plodded on towards the "toon."

(From *Thirteen Stories,* 1900)

NOTES

1. *Pakeha,* the Maori word in New Zealand for a white man.
2. "where the gentle Doric rings out."
3. See Graham's sketch "Heather Jock" (in Section IV) on this "worthy."

M'KECHNIE v. SCARAMANGA

"Man, an awfu'-like thing yon law o' general average. Dod aye, I mind aince being the matter of a hundred pound oot by it."

He paused, and spat reflectively into what he, having traded in his youth to Portland, Maine, St. John's, and Halifax, knew as a cuspidor. His whole appearance showed him at first sight a man who for the most part of his life had sailed out of Aberdeen or Peterhead.

His iron-grey hair was thin upon his head, and made a halo round his brick-dust face on which the sun, the storm, and whisky of full fifty years had done their worst. His beard was stiff and bristly, and grew high upon his cheek, and, underneath the chin, looked like the back of a wild boar or porcupine. His upper lip was shaved and blue, his teeth stained yellow with tobacco juice. Thick tufts of bristles overhung his eyes and sprang from out his ears, and his enormous hands, once muscular and hard with hauling upon ropes, although immense, were soft and flabby, though still freckled by the sun which tanned them in his youth. Upon his middle finger was tattoed a ring, and round his wrist a bracelet which he tried hard to hide by pulling down his cuff. Not that he was ashamed of it, or ever for an instant posed for anything but what he was, but, as he would explain, "Mistress M'Kechnie thocht it didna' look genteel. A woman's clavers, aye ou aye; but then, ye see, Mistress M'K. raises a wild-like turley-wurley whiles, aboot a feck o' things that dinna matter, for I say when a man has got the siller that is the principal." And certainly he had the siller, for from a mere tin-kettle of a tramp, bought upon credit and in which the saying was if you should drop a marlin-spike it would go through her plates, he had attained to the possession of a fleet which peopled every sea.

But though good luck, which he referred to as the "act of Providence," had thus befriended him and seated him in his own private room in the great office, which he once likened to a liner's cabin, the highest praise in his vocabulary, he yet remained at heart the self-same pawky, pious, superstitious, and hard-fisted sailor man that he was when he first sailed in a whaler to the Arctic seas from Peterhead. His friends and his contemporaries knew him as Andrew Granite, whether because of his resemblance to the stone, his character, or simply from his birthplace, or from all combined, no one was sure. But from the Clyde to Timor-Laut, whenever any of his ships was spoken and ran up her number, a smile went round extending from the forecastle to the bridge, and some old shell-back was pretty safe to say, "One of old Andrew's coffins, damn them, a Granite liner; yes, by God; sink like a stone in some place some day, or run upon a shoal marked in no blooming chart; Andrew will grab the insurance money, and then go off to kirk."

Withal, he was a genial, simple, whisky-drinking, pious, and not unkindly man, with all the low-class Scotsman's love for law and pride in never being over-reached, and with a gift of story-telling which a long life at sea had sharpened and improved.

His conversation ran on bottomry, on jettison, demurrage, barratry ("a grand word yon," he would explain), and barnacles. Much had he got to say about Restraint of Princes and the like, of berth notes, back freights, charter party, cessio clause, frustration of adventure, and as to whether frost and rats fell under act of God, or might be held as perils of the sea. Much did he like to dwell upon "diceesions o' the Coorts," quoting with unction Stamforth v. Wells, Hadley v. Baxendale, and Vogeman v. Parkenthorpe, with comments of his own upon the judges, with much about the lunar and the calendar in the vexed question of the "Charter" month, much of the usages of trades and ports, all which he held "redeeklous," deeming them part and parcel of a scheme against the Granite Line. An elder of the kirk "outby Bearsden," where, as he said, "he stopped," he yet believed that Providence was a malicious demon on the watch to do him damage, sending foul winds and snapping shafts of screws, blowing off heads of cylinders and heating brasses in an arbitrary way, as if the power referred to had nothing else to do but watch him and his affairs through a celestial magnifying glass which he kept screwed into his eye after the fashion of a watchmaker when looking at a watch.

The house "outby" where Andrew Granite "stopped" was built of such well-hewn and finely pointed stone as to resemble plaster, so neat were all the joints, so sharp the edges, and though substantial, did not seem designed to live in, but rather as a model from some exhibition of what no house should be. Roofed with dark blue metallic-looking slates, it stood in its own carriage-sweep, which, laid with furnace slag in lieu of gravel, formed as it were a yellow ochre river flowing between the bulwarks of green grass which bounded it, and which, as the possessor said, were "trimmed square by the lifts and braces and ran down sheer into the tide." He used to add that "in a ship, ye ken, ye canna let minavellings lay aboot, an' for a gairdner ye couldna' get a better man nor steadier than an auld sailor, if ye can keep him frae the drink."

Laurels and rhododendrons, the latter "bonny heebrids," as the seafaring "gairdner" called them, stunted and withered by the wind, stood ranged beside the avenue in rows, each with its Latin nickname dangling from a wire upon a piece of tin, as if it was convicted of some crime against its fellows and was doing penance for its sins. Cast-iron hoops contrived to look like withies bordered the road; and to make all things sure, enamelled plates with the inscription "Parties are requested to keep off the grass" reminded people to be cautious how they walked. A battlemented lodge and wrought-iron gate with a huge gilt monogram upon the top stood sentinels at the edge of the domain. Clumps of young spruce trees were disposed at intervals to break the wind, which bent them over opposite the side it blew, and stripped them bare where they caught all the fury of the blast.

The inside of the villa was suitable to its exterior grace.

Plate-glass and varnished yellow pine gave it a sort of likeness to a ship. White fluffy mats lay on the floors, and on the walls were water-colours, so well finished and so smooth that they could easily have been mistaken for the best kind of chromo-lithographs.

Wax fruit and feather flowers, and hummingbirds, looking distorted ghosts of their bright selves, were stuck about upon the mantelpieces, covered with glass shades. A banner-screen with a ship worked in crewels stood before the fire, which in a bright steel grate burned till the twelfth of May, and then until October was replaced by coloured paper shavings so contrived as to present the appearance of a waterfall. Mistress M'Kechnie, a large, high-coloured lady, dressed in black silk and girt about the neck with a gold chain from which a watch was hung which dangled loose or else was stuck into the waistband of her gown, sat in her "droring-room" in state. A large medallion of her lord, with a stout wisp of his stiff hair fashioned into a cable round the edge, was pinned upon her breast. It showed him at the age of thirty, grim and ill-favoured, and had been taken, in the port that he called "Ryo," by an artist who he said had been "an awfu' clever chiel," and certainly should have been heard of in the world of art for his stout realism and adherence to the truth.

The owner of the house sat in his sanctum, which, like the cabin of a ship, had small round windows, and was adorned with books, bound in morocco bindings, which he never read, and with a coloured photograph of her he always called "Mistress M'K." and stood in awe of; for she came of "weel-kenned folk," and had some tocher and a temper which was not always safe "to lippen to."

With cigars lighted, his friends about him and their glasses filled, Mr. M'Kechnie used to give full play to his imaginative mind on many subjects which had appealed to him during the course of his career—as law pleas about ships, soundings in various ports, the absence of all lights on certain coasts, the charms of ladies he had known about the world and his success with them, and other things of a like nature which he discussed more freely when certain that his wife had gone to bed. One tale led to another, but the tale that his friends all loved the best was one he never failed to tell after his second tumbler of stiff toddy, when, with his feet in carpet slippers worked in yellow beads, and with a fox's head in blue in high relief upon the instep, he would light a Trichinopoly cigar, and after, with the story-teller's instinct, having forced his friends to press him, take up his parable.

"Hae ye all got your glasses filled? Weel—aye—I am a sort o' temperate man masel', but speerits, ye ken, are a fair panawcea, that is when taken moderately." To such a proposition no self-respecting Scotsman has an objection, and they all used to fill, and, "paidlin'" with their ladles, inhale the fumes of the hot spirit, puff their cigars, and wait expectantly.

"Ye see, ma freens, law is a kittle sort o' gear, especially sea law, as mony o' ye ken I know fu' weel. But the maist awfu' thing is what they ca' yon general average—ay juist fair redeeklous. Ye ken what Mr. Scrutton says—he's an M.A.

and LL.B. and has juist written the maist compendious work on contrack of affreightment as expressed in charter-parties—a pairfeck vawdy-mecum. Ane ye ca' Mackinnon helpit him, and between the twa they lay ye aff a'maist a'thing that can arise between a charterer and a shipowner upon the sea.

"Charter-party, sort o' dog Laytin, *carta partita* they ca't. In the auld days they juist wrote it in duplicate on a single sheet o' paper, and then divided it by indented edges, each part fitted to the other. That's hoo they got the name 'indenture.'

"A feck o' things ye'll find in Scrutton's book, ma freens, sort o' auncient like. Whiles when I havna' much to do I tak' it doon and lauch, man I lauch ower it till ma heid juist whummles like a sturdy sheep. Oo aye—ye're richt—I'm sort o' wandered.

"Weel, aweel, I'll tell ye now about a wild-like tulzie I had aince with a lash o' Dawgos, a' aboot yon cursed general average. Man, it was this wey, ye ken—whiles I juist wonder that a man like Scrutton—Mackinnon is na blate either—does na' dae something to get the law changed. Na, na, ye could na' richtly look for it; it's the man's bread, ye ken. Aye, I'll heave roond, I'm subject to thae digressions; so was Sir Walter Scott and others I could mention. Ye mind aboot the seventy-twa, or it may be the seventy-five, freights were fairly high and shipowners were ettlin' to mak' some siller. Bad times we are havin' noo—yon cuttin' prices, I juist ca' it cuttin' throats—but in the seventy-five—that's it—I had a boat was gaein' oot to Smyrny wi' a feck o' cotton goods. Somehow or other she just snappit her screw shaft, and if she had na' just by a special providence come across a tramp out o' the Hartlepools, she micht have wandered aboot yon islands just like Ulysses—him thae raise sic' a dirl aboot in Homer; for, ye ken, I ha'e a sort o' tincture o' the humanities.

"The tramp just gi'ed her a tow in to Saloneeky. Losh me, then there cam' the salvage racket, the maist infernal intrikit affair ye ever saw. A man juist has to go to the slaughter like a lamb, if aiver a ship makes fast a cable to any o' his boats. Scrutton has it textually, that unless the charter amounts to a demise—but I'll no deave ye wi' technicalities. Ye'll get it in Sepla v. Rodgers, or Hubbertey v. Holts, and when ye hae it, mickle wiser may ye be.

"Fill up, men, it winna' hurt ye, and there's plenty mair ... ah—yes, yon maitter o' the salvage was sort o' seekenin'.

"The worst thing, though, was that the freighters were a' upon me for demurrage. Sirs me, I was fair gyte, and I juist yokit on Scrutton (the vawdy-mecum, ye mind) as if it had been the Holy Scriptures. Ma heid fair dirled wi' Sangivetti v. Postlethwaite and a heap o' cases very much resembling mine. I thocht I had a bit issue anent the cesser clause, and awa' I went to my awgents in West George Street. I laid my case before them, and they lauch't at me—fair lauch't. They told me the point was clear that I stood liable. Man, I whiles think the very elements are a' against the shipowner. What wi' they cursed strikes drawin' awa' the trade, the employers' liabeelity, and the infernal intrikitness o' the law, a body hasna' got a chance.

"Ye'll mind, Geordie, when we went tae sea thegither, sax-and-forty years ago—it was maist a' wind jammers in thae days?"

The crony thus interpolated took his black oily Burmah cigar out of his mouth and grunted, "I mind weel. A man juist signed for his salt horse and his salt pork, nane o' your tin-bag then," and, after looking at the ceiling, spat into the fire.

"Aye, that's so, a sailor man was a richt felly then. Nane o' yer comin' aboard withoot an airticle o' kit except a knife and a pair o' sea-boots, and slingin' the latter doon the forepeak and fa'ing drunk upon them.

"Na, na, we a' had our bit kists wi' plenty dunnage in them—and as for your employers' liabeelity—set them up—a sailor man juist took his ain life in his hand."

Geordie having grunted something about a long yarn and a rope-maker, Andra' came, as he said, back to his course, and once again took up his tale.

"I juist cabled oot orders to my awgent in Awthens to proceed to Saloneeky to arrange for chartering a vessel to tak' the stuff on to Smyrny; the body juist agreed wi' the captain o' a Greek schooner, ane they ca'ed Scaramangy, heard you ever sic' a name?

"His craft was ane o' they Levantyne-built bits o' things, awfu' gay wi' paint, a kind o' gin-palace afloat, ye ken the things, Geordie? She lookit weel, and my awgent cabled me that, wi' God's blessing, he hoped she would do the trip to Smyrny in aboot three days. I couldna' thole yon' God's blessing' in the cablegram. A man has his ain releegious opinions—ye mind I'm elder in the U.P. kirk outby Milngavie (ye canna' get the richt doctrine here in Bearsden, a mere puir imitation o' the Episcopawlians, a sort o' strivin' after being genteel, I ca' it); but business, ye see, is business. Besides, thae things are better understood, taken for read, as they ca' it up at Westminister.

"Yon blessing in the cablegram cost me a maitter o' some saxteen shillin'— the rates were awfu' high in thae times, ye mind. Saxteen shillin' just expended in a manner I ca' redeeklous, for the Almighty must ha' kent that I was putting up ma ain bit supplication when the cash was at stake.

"Yon Scaramangy had a wild-like crew on board; man, they Greeks dinna sail short-handed, I'se warrant them. Thirteen Dawgos forby himsel', and the bit schooner not above three hundred tons. Heard ye the like?

"I canna' bide a superstitious man, for I aye haud nae ane should stand between a man and Him; if a man wants Him, let him gang straucht, I say— through the Auld Book. Anyhow, Scaramangy had his Madoney—a sort o' shrine, ye see—aft o' the mainmast, and a bit licht burnin' awa' before it nicht an' day; an' awfu' waste o' can'le. Weel aweel—anither Trichinopoly—ye'll na— aiblins anither tot. What! yer done? Geordie, rax me the ginger snaps. Scaramangy—I didna' see him; but I hae seen his like a thoosand times, maist-like dressed in longshore togs, wi' ane o' thae Maneely straws, an' alpacy jacket, an' white canvas shoes—ye'll mind the rig. Maist o' them has a watch-gaird on them like the cable o' a battleship; ye canna' tell a gentleman nooadays, wi' everybody

wearin' their bloody Alberts. No a'thegither bad-like sailors are they Greeks; sort
o' conceity whiles the way they paint their bits o' schooners and their bar-
quentines; maist o' them yallow, wi' a bit pink streak, whiles a blue ane, and sure
to hae a figure-head, some o' they Greek goddesses.—No, Geordie, Sapho was
no' a goddess—she was a poetess, a queer-like ane tae, just went fair demented
ower a felly they ca'ed—— But I'm havering—the humanities, ye ken, tak' an
awfu' grip on a man.

"Scaramangy was most certain to hae had a wee bit curly Maltese dog on
board—I canna' bide them, rinnin' aboot yap, yappin' and filin' the decks. Set
them up; for my ain pairt, I like a cat, or maybe a mongoose—na, na, man, no a
monkey—dirty brutes, the hale rick ma tick o' them; seem to gae into a decline
tae soon as ye pass the forties. Man, I mind ane, I traded a coat and a bit Bible for
him wi' a missionary in the Cameroons. Puir brute, we had na' sighted the Rock
of Lisbon, comin' hame, afore he started hostin'. I had him in the cuddy, and
ettled to mak' him tak' some Scott's Emulsion. It would na' dae, and we had juist
to commit his bit body to the deep, the same as a Christian, just off the Wolf
Rock. I dinna' care to mind it. I lost my ain Johnny the same way. Man, I felt it
sae, I should hae liked to hae the wee deevil stuff't, but his mother said it would
be heathenish.

"Nae doot o' it, yon Scaramangy would foul some other body's cable when
he lifted anchor, and find his throat halliards unrove—they're apt to use them for
a warp, ye ken, or some other kind o' deevilment; but, anyhow, to sea he went in
half a gale o' wind.

"There must hae been an awfu' hagger-snash o' tongues, bad as the Tower
o' Babel, on board the *Aidonia*; that's what they ca'ed her—thae Levantynes
canna' dae a thing withoot a noise.

"Set o' curly-heided Dawgos, with their silver earrings and sashes rowld
round their hurdies—I canna' stan' a sailor man wi' a sash on him, it looks sae
theatrical.

"What happened only the Lord Himself and Scaramangy really ken. The
Lord, for a' He kens, never lets on He hears, and Scaramangy was a naitural
accomplished liar frae his birth.

"What he said was that a pairfect hurricane burst on him, soon as he'd pit to
sea. He couldna' get the topsails aff o' her, as nane o' his dodderin' deevils daur to
gae aloft. So he juist watched them blow clean oot o' the bolt-ropes, and
shortened the lave o' his sails the best he could—by a special interposeetion o'
Providence he didna' lose ony o' his heidsails, though nae doots but he deserved
tae.

"He says he and his cattle were in the awfu'ist peril that they ever ex-
perienced in their lives, the schooner almost on her beam ends, and the seas fair
like to smother her.

"In the nick o' time, what think ye he did, man?

" 'Ran for some harbour,' 'lie to a bittie'; na, na, nae frichts o' him. He juist
pit up a bit sipplication to his Madoney in the companion, and promised her (as if

the painted bitch could hear him) that if she took him safe to Smyrny, that he would sacrifice something valuable as a sign o' gratitude. Heard ye the like o' that?

"God's truth, it mak's me mad to think aboot it—the folly o' the thing—and the gratuitous waste o' valuable property.

"Anyhow, he doddered in to Smyrny some gait or ither, and what d'ye think he done? He an' his men—aye, Geordie, nae doots he had the dawg along wi' them—went barefit oot to a shrine they had, and returned thanks to Him who stills the waves—that is, when He has a fancy tae.

"I dinna altogether disapprove o' that, for prayer, ye ken, is usefu' whiles. Samuel pit up his sipplication to the Lord before he hewit yon Agag, and Joshua when he smote thae Canaanites, and even Paul—a gran' man Paul, sort o' pawky too—lifted a prayer when he was in juist sich a situation as was yon Scaramangy.

"Scaramangy and his Dawgos, when they had done their prayer, went aboard again, unbent their mainsail, and took it ashore and burnt it on the beach. Mad, ye say, Geordie—mad, aye, mad enough, but no on business matters.

"Ye can't think what they did then?

"They gaed awa' up to the British Consulate, and tabulated their claim, under the law o' general average, for the value o' the mainsail; for the devils said, had they no made their vow, the Madoney wouldna' have interfeired, and the vessel would maist certainly hae been lost. No blate, yon Scaramangy—but mercy me, whatna' a conception o' natural laws he must have had! Fancy the Madoney expawtiating in the heavens, watching a storm like a fisherwife watching for her man when an easterly gale springs up, and no to be propeetiated without the promise o' an offerin'!

"After I got the cable, I fair sprang oot o' the hoose, and awa' to West George Street, to my awgents, and they tel't me Scaramangy was domiciled furth o' Scotland, and the case would have to be heard at Smyrny.

"It was juist held that whereas Captain Scaramangy, bein' in peril on the deep, and havin' done everything within his power and in the compass o' good seamanship to save his ship—ma God!—and being at the point o' daith, had recourse to prayer. Furthermore, the Coort bein' o' opinion that the vessel must have foondered had there not been an interposeetion o'a Higher Power, decides that Captain Scaramangy took the proper course, and that his prayer and his vow being both heard and considered favourably by the Madoney, that she thocht fit to save the vessel and the crew.

"Therefore, the Coort held that the vow was instrumental in the first degree, and that the jettison o' the mainsail—which of course wasna' a richt jettison at all—was necessary, and that the shippers were all bound to bear their due proportion o' the loss.

"Appeal—nae frichts o' me. It cost me, one way and another, mair than a hundred pound. Appeal—na, better to lose than to lose mair; that's a Greek proverb—at least I think so, and no a bad yin.

"Yer gauntin', men; weel, weel good nicht to ye—Geordie, rax me doon Scrutton fae aff the top shelf—there's juist a pint or twa anent yon cursed general aiverage I should like to look at before I turn in for the nicht."

(From Progress, 1905)

A CONVERT

From Bathurst to St. Paul's Loanda, right up and down the coast; in every bight; upon the Oil Rivers; down Congo way, in all the missionary stations, in which the trembling heathen had endured his ministrations; in factory and port; by all the traders and chance travellers, no one was more detested than the Reverend Archibald Macrae. All that is hard and self-assertive in the Scottish character, in him seemed to be multiplied a hundredfold. All that is kindly, old-world, and humorous; all that so often makes a Scot more easy to get on with than an Englishman, in the Reverend Archibald was quite left out. Dour and grey-headed, with a stubbly Newgate frill under his chin; dressed in black broadcloth, with a white helmet shadowing his dark red mottled face, a Bible and umbrella ever in his hand or tucked beneath his arm (he said himself he "aye like oxtering aboot the Word o' God"), he stood confessed, fitted to bring a sword rather than peace to every one he met. Withal, not a bad-hearted man, but tactless, disputatious, and as obstinate as a male mule. "I hae to preach the Worrd, baith in an' out o' season, and please the Lorrd I'll do so," was his constant saw.

From the earliest times, the tactless, honest, and aggressive missionary has been a thorn in the flesh of every one upon the coast of Africa. Consuls and traders, captains of men-of-war, all know and fear him, and most likely he has kept back the cause he labours for more than a hundred slave-raiders have done. They kill or enslave the body, but such as was the Reverend Archibald enslave and kill the soul. His station, far up a river which flowed sluggishly through woods of dark, metallic-foliaged trees, was called Hope House. Sent out from Norway all in sections, it had been set up just on the edge of a lagoon from which at evening a thick white vapour rose. A mangrove swamp reached almost to the door, the situation having been chosen by the Reverend Archibald himself to thwart the heads of his society, who not unnaturally wished it should be "located" in a more healthy spot. Painted a staring white, with bright green shutters, none of which fitted the windows they were supposed to shield, without a garden or a patch of cultivated ground, Hope House stood out a challenge to the heathen either to come at once beneath the yoke of the Reverend Archibald and to embrace his demonology, or to entrench themselves more strongly in their befetished faith.

The Reverend Archibald lived what is called a virtuous life—that is, he did not drink, did not sell gin or arms upon the sly, and round about the precincts of Hope House no snuff- and butter-coloured children played. Hard, upright, and self-righteous, he stalked about as if cut out of Peterhead grey granite—a Christian milestone set up on the heathen way, with the inscription: "That road leads to Hell." This he himself was quite aware of, and used to say, "Ye see I hae the Worrd o' God, and if the heathen dinna come to listen to it, they will all burrn."

Still, disagreeable and wrong-headed as he was, the Reverend Archibald was in his way an honourable man. "Conviction," as he said a thousand times, "should follow reasonable airgument." He himself having from his earliest youth argued upon every subject in the heaven above, the earth beneath, and on the water which may or may not be under the earth, was well equipped for battle with the comparatively lightly armed fetish-worshipper of the West Coast of Africa.

Seated in his black horsehair-covered chair, before his table with its legs stuck into broken bottles filled with paraffin to keep off the white ants, and with his Bible covered in shiny cloth before him, the Reverend Archibald passed his spare time looking up texts wherewith to pulverise such of the infidel who in his neighbourhood had conscientiously resisted all his wiles and held by their old faith.

Often in reading over and again the minor prophets—so called, he would explain, "not on account of their less authenteecity, but simply because of the greater brevity of their prophecies"—his Scottish mind was struck with the similarity of the scheme of life of which they treated and that of those with whom he lived. "Yon Zephaniah—he was a gatherer of sycamore fruit, ye ken —would ha' done powerfu' work amongst the heathen on the coast," he would exclaim as he shut up his Bible with a bang and sat down to read Bogatzky's *Golden Treasury*,[1] and smoke his pipe. His library was limited to the aforesaid *Golden Treasury* of damnatory texts, Blair's *Sermons*,[2] and some books by Black, which he read doubtfully, perceiving well that they set out a picture of no life known to the world, but because the scenes were laid in what he called "N.B."[3]

The frequent poring upon these treasures of the literary art, and ponderings upon the precepts of war to the knife with unbelievers, so faithfully set forth by the more ferocious writers in the Old Testament, together with his isolation from the world, had made him even narrower in mind than when he left his village in the East Neuk of Fife. His blunt outspokenness and bluff brutality of manner, on which he prided himself beyond measure, thinking, apparently, that those who save the soul must of necessity wound every feeling of the mind, had set a void between him and all the other Europeans on the coast.

The washed-out, gin-steeped white men of the Oil Rivers turned from him with an oath when he adjured them to become Good Templars; the traders from the interior, when they dropped down the river in their steam launches or canoes, all gave Hope House the widest of wide berths, after the experience of one who, going to his station with his young wife from Europe, was asked if he had "put away yon Fanti gurrl, that was yer sort o' concubine, ye ken." As for the natives who had come beneath his yoke, he treated them, as he thought, in a kindly way, after the fashion that in days gone by the clergy treated the laity in Scotland—that is, as people conquered by raiders from the Old Testament, making their lives a burden for the welfare of their souls. Still, being, as are most missionaries, possessed of medicines and goodwill to use them when his flock fell ill, he had some reputation amongst those who had no money to go out and pay a fetish doctor on the sly. Upon the spiritual side, he was not quite so far removed in sympathy from those to whom he ministered; his God was the mere counterpart of the negroes' devil, and both of them were to be conciliated in the same way, by sacrifice of what the worshipper held dear. But in his dealings with his flock the Reverend Archibald Macrae took no account of isothermal lines. For him, morality, not that he much insisted on it, holding that faith was more important, was a fixed quantity. The shifting and prismatic qualities of right and wrong, by him were seen identical, no matter if the spectrum used were that of Aberdeen or Ambrizette. Occasionally, therefore, he and his flock were at cross purposes, for to the flock it seemed an easy matter to give up their gods, but harder all at once to change the daily current of their lives.

Conviction, it is true, had followed upon reasonable, or at least upon reiterated, "airgument"; but when the Reverend Archibald spoke of what he called "a nearer approximation to the moral code of the Old Book," his catechumens were apt to leave him and retire to the seclusion of the woods. Nothing contributed more to these backslidings than the vicinity of an unconverted chief known by the name of Monday Flatface, who had his "croon" five or six miles beyond Hope House, upon the river side. The chief lived his own life after the way his ancestors had lived before him, accepting gratefully from the Europeans their gin, their powder, and sized cotton cloths, but steadfastly rejecting all their contending faiths. All the exponents of the various sects had tried their hands on him without success. Priests from the neighbouring Portuguese setlements had done their best, flaunting the novel charms of purgatory before the simple negro's eyes, who up till then had known but heaven and hell. The Church of England, backed by the stamp of its connection with the governing powers, had tried its fortune on the chief, holding out hints of Government protection, but without effect. The Nonconformists too had had their turn, and sought by singing hymns and preaching to let in light upon the opinionated old idolater, and had all been foiled. Lastly, the Reverend Macrae, who bore the banner of the Presbyterians, had attacked in force, bringing to bear the whole artillery of North British metaphysics, dangling before the chieftain visions of a future when his children, brought into the fold, should be in spiritual touch with Aberdeen, be fed on porridge, and on Sawbath while away the afternoon in learning paraphrases and wrestling with the Shorter Catechism.

All had been in vain, and Monday Flatface, while taking all that he could get in medicines, cotton cloths, Dutch clocks, and large red cotton parasols, was still a heathen, a polygamist, some said a cannibal upon the sly, and regularly got drunk on palm-tree wine instead of buying gin after the fashion of his brethren who had come into the fold. But above all the rest, the chief was hateful to the missionary in his character of humorist. Naturally, those who leave their country to propagate their individual faith are serious men, and the Reverend Archibald was no exception to the rule. Your serious man has from the beginning of the world added enormously to human misery. Wars, battles, murders, and the majority of sudden deaths are all his work. Crusades for holy sepulchres, with pilgrimages to saints' tombs, leagues and societies to prevent men living after the fashion they consider best, were all the handiwork of serious men. A dull, gold-dusted-over world it would have been by now, had not a wisely constituted all-seeing Providence in general denied brains in sufficient ratio to energy, and allowed success invariably to wait on iteration. So when Chief Monday Flatface took the Reverend Archibald's exhortations to amend his present naughty life, forsake his father's gods, and straight dismiss the wives he had himself with care selected, choosing them fat but comely, and such as best anointed all their persons with palm oil, as a mere joke, the missionary's fury knew no bounds. Had he but tried to persecute, or stepped an atom beyond what the general sentiment of the European traders sanctioned, the way would have been plain. In the one case the dignity of persecution, hitherto withheld, would, like an aureole, have shone above his head, and in the other a complaint to the nearest British governor would have procured a gunboat to bombard the village of the chief. But nothing of the sort occurred, and the old chief persisted in still flourishing like a green mangrove tree, and stopping up his ears to all the arguments of the Reverend Archibald Macrae.

Often they met and talked the matter out in "Blackman English," eked out with Fanti and with Arabic, of which both polemists just knew sufficient to obscure their arguments upon their disagreeing faiths. Still, as not seldom happens in the case of well-matched enemies, a sort of odd respect, mingled with irritation, gradually grew up between the adversaries. Naturally, neither the chief nor yet the missionary advanced a step towards the conversion of the other infidel. Their simple, bloody creeds, softened in the one case by the increase of indifference which even in East Fife has modified the full relentlessness of the Mosaic dispensation, and on the other by the neighbourhood of European forts and factories, gave them a starting point in common on which they could agree. Each looked upon the other as a keen sportsman looks on some rare bird or beast which he hopes one day may fall before his gun, but which he wishes to escape from every other sportsman in the world except himself. Often the chief would ask the missionary to work a miracle to satisfy his doubts. Sorely the Reverend Archibald at times was tempted to display magnesium wire, or to develop photographs, in short to bag his game by pseudothaumaturgic art; but, having the true sportsman's instinct, always refrained, entrenching himself safely behind his dictum that "conversion should ensue after a reasonable airgument." The chief, on his part, was quite ready to be baptised, if he could see some evidence of the missionary's supernatural power; holding quite reasonably that "airgument" did not quite meet the case in questions of faith. Still he had promised that, if he should ever change his mind, none but the Reverend Archibald should admit him to the fold.

So on the rivers and the coast things jogged along in the accustomed way.

Steamers arrived and hung outside the bars, fleets of canoes came down from the remoter streams to trade, and in the open roadsteads lighters took the goods, and krooboys staggered through the surf, whilst objurgating Scottish clerks, note-book in hand, counted the barrels and the bales. The sun loomed through a continual mist, and sheets of rain caused a white vapour to enshroud the trees, whose leaves seemed to distil a damp which entered to the bones. The traders strove with whisky and with gin to fight off fever and to pass the time, till they could make sufficient money to go home and rear their villas near their native towns.

Years passed, and up and down the coast, at factories and garrisons, upon the hulks, and amongst travellers who, coming from the interior, stayed at Hope House, forced by necessity to ask for hospitality, a rumour made its way. Over their gin, or stretched out smoking in their hammocks during the long hot hours after the second breakfast, traders and merchant skippers, Scotch clerks, and the occasional globe-trotters who waited for steamers in the various ports to take them home to write their ponderous tomes upon the countries they had seen as a swallow sees the land he passes over in his winter hegira, all agreed that a great change had come upon the Reverend Macrae. Not that his outward man had altered, for his beard still bristled like a scrubbing-brush; his face, with years and long exposure to the sun, had turned the colour of "jerked" beef; his clothes still hung upon him as rags hang upon a scarecrow in the fields, and still he faithfully "oxtered aboot the word of God," although the book itself, originally given to him by his mother in East Fife, had grown more shiny and more greasy with the lapse of years. But certainly a change had come to the interior man. Occasionally, and almost as it were apologetically, he would quote texts from the New Testa-ment, and in his steel-grey eye the gleam as of a gospel terrier was softened and subdued. Though he was still as ardent to convert the heathen as before, his methods were more human, and, to the amazement of every one upon the coast, he sometimes said, "Perhaps the patriarchs were whiles sort of a' rash in their bit methods wi' yon Canaanites."

The miserable converts saw the change with joy, and convert-like were quick to take advantage of it, and to revert by stealth to practices which, before, the Reverend Archibald would have instantly put down. They dared to appear on Sawbath at Hope House without the "stan' o' black" with which the Reverend Archibald had provided them. Only the women clung tenaciously to European dress, cherishing in special their red parasols; but holding them in-variably turned from the sun, which beat upon their well-oiled faces, melting the palm oil and causing it to drop upon their clothes.

Traders and brother missionaries came by degrees to drop into Hope House to smoke and talk, and to endeavour to find out the reason of the change. But, as the Reverend Archibald never spoke about himself, their curiosity might have been fruitless, had not a brother worker on his journey home asked for an explanation, saying that, as he thought, "the Lord Himself often worked changes in the heart of man for providential ends." Dressed in pyjamas of grey flannel, his feet stuck into carpet slippers, and seated in a hammock which he kept swinging with his toes, the Reverend Archibald, after thrice spitting in contemplative fashion on the floor, and, after having killed a mosquito on his forehead with a bang, looked round and started on his tale.

"Ye see," he said, "ma freends, as the Arabs say, we are a' in His hands. That which has been the pride of a man's life—in my case it was airgument—may prove at last to be a stumbling-block, for we are all as worrms in His hand. Airgument, airgument, a weel discussed and reasonable airgument, was aye my pride. By it, I thoct to do a mighty worrk before the Lorrd. But He, nae doot for reasons of His ain, has made me see the error of my ways, that is, has shown me that there are things man's reason canna touch."

He paused and wiped the sweat from off his brow, spat thoughtfully, sighed once or twice, and having asked his friends if they would take Kops' ale or ginger beer, resumed his parable.

"Ye mind old Monday Flatface? Many's the crack on speeritual matters we have had, the chief and I, in days gone by. Sort o' teugh in opinions the chief, a weary body for a man to tackle, and one I hoped wi' the Lord's grace to bring into the fold. Aye, aye, ye needna' laugh, I ha'ena pit ma raddle⁴ on him, as ye a' know, yet. May be though, mon, ae keel-mark would do us baith. Weel, weel, the chief and I had bargained that if he got grace I should baptise him. A bonny burdie he would hae lookit at the font wi' his sax wives. Polygamy, ye ken, has its advantages, for I would have convertit a' the seven at once. One evening I was just got through wi' catechising some of the younger flock, when doon the river cam an awfu' rout o' drums, tom-toms, ye ken, and horns a' routing, and the chief's war-canoe tied up opposite the hoose. The chief came out, an' I was thinkin' of some text to greet him wi', airgument, ye ken . . . I think I tellt ye . . . when I saw at once that there was something wrong. He lookit awfu' gash, and wi'oot a worrd, he says 'Big wife she ill, think she go die, you pray piece for her, and if she live, you pour the water on my head.' I told him that was no the way at all we Christians did things, but I would come and see his wife and bring some medicine and try what I could do. A' the way up the river the drums went on, man, it faired deaved me, and, when we reached the "croom," in a' my twenty years' experience of the coast I ne'er saw sic a sight. Baith men and women were a' sounding horns, blowing their whistles, and shaking calabashes full of peas. The ground was red wi' blood, for the misguided creatures had sacrificed sheep, poultry, and calves—an awfu' waste o' bestial, ye ken, forby sae insanitary, and, as ye say, not of the slightest use. At the chief's hut the wives and children made an awfu' din, roarin' and gashin' themselves wi' knives, just like the priests of Baal in the Old Testament. Right in the middle of the floor lay the 'big wife' insensible, and, as I judged, in the last stage of a malignant fever. The chief, holdin' me by the airm, says, 'Save her, pray to your God for her, and if she lives I will believe.'

"Humanity, humanity, shame to me as a Christian, that I say it, but 'tis just the same, no matter if the skin is white or black. We a' just pray when we are wantin' onything, and when we've got it, dinna thank the granter o' the prayer.

"I pushit through the folk, and felt the woman's pulse, and syne, prisin' her mouth open a bit wi' a jack-knife, I gied her some quinine. Then I knelt doon and wrestled in prayer wi' a' ma heart, for the tears just rolled off the old chief's face. Sair I besought the Lord to show me His power, if He thought fit to do so; but prayer, ye ken, is often answered indirectly, and as the night wore on the chief aye askit me, 'Will your God heed you?' and the woman aye got worse. An awful position for a minister of God to be placed in, as ye may understand. Syne Flatface roused himsel', and saying, 'I will call then on my God and sacrifice to him after the manner of my fathers,' stotted outside the house. The drums and whistles and the horns raised a maist deafening din, and in the hut the smell of perspiration and palm oil was sort o' seekenin'. After a spell o' prayer the chief came in, sweatin' and ashy grey, his hand bound up and carrying a finger which he had chappit off upon the altar of his gods. It garred me skunner⁵ when he laid it on the sick woman's breast, and once again I sunk upon my knees, prayin' the Lord to hear the heathen's prayer. Ye ken, mon, his faith in his false gods was just prodeegious, and I felt that a staunch Christian had been lost in the old man. Long did I wrastle, till aboot the dawn, but got nae answer, that is directly, and the woman aye got worse. Just as the day was breaking, and the false dawn appearing in the sky, the chief said, 'I will pray again, and once more sacrifice.' When he came in he stottered in his gait and laid another finger beside the other on his wife. Ma heart just yearned to him, and I yokit prayin' as if I had been askin' for my ain soul's grace, and syne our prayers were heard."

As he talked on, the night had worn away, the frogs ceased croaking, and the white tropic mist which comes before the dawn had drifted to the house and shrouded all the verandah in its ghostly folds. Long shivers of the tide crept up the river, oily and supernatural-looking, and little waves lapped on the muddy banks, making small landslips fall into the flood with an unearthly sound. The listeners shivered over their temperance drinks, and once again the Reverend Archibald began.

"Maist like she had the turn; it might have been the effect of the quinine, or of the prayers, or it may be the Lord had looked in approbation on the sacrifice. I canna say, but from that time the woman mended, and in a week was as well. Ah . . . Flatface, weel no, he's still a heathen, though we are friends, and whiles I think his God and mine are no so far apart as I aince thocht."

He ceased, and from the woods and swamps rose the faint noises of the coming day, drops fell from the iron roof upon the planks of the verandah with a dull splashing sound; the listeners, shaking the missionary by the hand, dispersed, and he, looking out through the mist, was comforted by the confession of his weakness and the relation of his doubts.

(From *Progress*, 1905)

NOTES

1. See "A Fisherman," note 3.
2. The 5-volume *Sermons of Hugh Blair* (1777-1801), Scottish divine and Professor of Rhetoric (1718-1800).
3. Probably William Black (1841-98), Scottish novelist and journalist, who wrote in his later years novels like *Macleod of Dare* (1878), *White Heather* (1885) and *In Far Lochaber* (1888). "N.B." is an abbreviation of North Britain, a term Graham uses sometimes in his sketches to designate Scotland.
4. i.e. *ruddle*, a substance used for marking sheep. Cf. Thomas Hardy's famous ruddleman in *Far from the Madding Crowd* (1874). This marking substance, keel, was also used by cloth-cutters.
5. "It made me sick with disgust."

CHRISTIE CHRISTISON

Of all the guests that used to come to Claraz's Hotel, there was none stranger or more interesting than Christie Christison, a weather-beaten sailor, who still spoke his native dialect of Peterhead, despite his thirty years out in the Plate. He used to bring an air into the room with him of old salt fish and rum, and of cold wintry nights in the low latitudes down by the Horn. This, too, though it was years since he had been at sea.

Although the world had gone so well with him, and by degrees he had become one of the biggest merchants in the place, he yet preserved the speech and manners of a Greenland whaler, which calling he had followed in his youth.

The Arctic cold and tropic suns, during the years that he had traded up and down the coast, had turned his naturally fair complexion to a mottled hue, and whisky, or the sun, had touched his nose so fiercely that it furnished a great fund of witticism amongst the other guests.

Mansel[1] said that the skipper's nose reminded him of the port light of an old sugar droger, and Cossart had it that no chemist's window in Montmartre had any *flacon*, bottle you call him, eh? of such resplendent hue. Most of them knew he had a history, but no one ever heard him tell it, although it was well known he had come out from Peterhead in the dark ages, when Rosas terrorised the Plate,[2] in his own schooner, the *Rosebud*, and piled her up at last, somewhere on the Patagonian coast, upon a trip down to the Falkland Islands. He used to talk about his schooner as if she had been one of the finest craft afloat; but an old Yankee skipper, who had known her, swore she was a bull-nosed, round-sterned sort of oyster-mouching vessel, with an old deck-house like a town hall, straight-sided, and with a lime-juice look about her that made him tired.

Whatever were her merits or her faults, she certainly had made her skipper's fortune, or at least laid the foundation of it; for, having started as a trader, he gradually began to act, half as a carrier, half as a mail-boat, going to Stanley every three months or so with mails and letters, and coming back with wool.

Little by little, aided by his wife, a stout, hard-featured woman from his native town, he got a little capital into his hands.

When he was on a voyage, Jean used to search about to get a cargo for his next trip, so that when the inevitable came and the old *Rosebud* ran upon the reef down at San Julian, Christie was what he called "weel-daein," and forsook the sea for good.

He settled down in Buenos Aires as a wool-broker, and by degrees altered his clothes to the full-skirted coat of Melton cloth, with ample side-pockets, the heather mixture trousers, and tall white hat with a black band, that formed his uniform up to his dying day. He wore a Newgate frill of beard and a blue necktie, which made a striking contrast with his face, browned by the sun and wind, and skin like a dried piece of mare's hide, through which the colour of his northern blood shone darkly, like the red in an old-fashioned cooking apple after a touch of frost.

Except a few objurgatory phrases, he had learned no Spanish, and his own speech remained the purest dialect of Aberdeenshire—coarse, rough and racy, and double-shotted with an infinity of oaths, relics of his old whaling days, when, as he used to say, he started life, like a young rook, up in the crow's-nest of a bluff-bowed and broad-beamed five-hundred barrel boat, sailing from Peterhead.

Things had gone well with him, and he had taken to himself as partner a fellow-countryman, one Andrew Nicholson, who had passed all his youth in Edinburgh in an insurance office. Quiet, unassuming, and yet not without traces of that pawky humour which few Scots are born entirely lacking in, he had fallen by degrees into a sort of worship of his chief, whose sallies, rough and indecent as they often were, fairly convulsed him, making him laugh until the tears ran down his face, as he exclaimed, "Hear to him, man, he's awfu' rich, I'm tellin' ye."

Christie took little notice of his adoration except to say, "Andra man, dinna expose yourself," or something of the kind.

In fact, no one could understand how two such ill-assorted men came to be friends, except perhaps because they both were Scotchmen, or because Andrew's superior education and well-brushed black clothes appealed to Christison.

He himself could not write, but knew enough to sign his name, which feat he executed with many puffings, blowings, and an occasional oath.

Still he was shrewd in business, which he executed almost entirely by tele-gram, refusing to avail himself of any code, saying, "he couldna stand them; some day ye lads will get a cargo of dolls' eyes, when ye have sent for maize. Language is gude enough for me, I hae no secrets. Damn yer monkey talk."

His house at Flores was the place of call of all the ship captains who visited the port. There they would sit and drink, talking about the want of lights on such and such a coast, of skippers who had lost their ships twenty or thirty years ago, the price of whale oil, and of things that interest their kind; whilst Mrs. Christison sat knitting, looking as if she never in her life had moved from Peterhead, in her grey gown and woollen shawl, fastened across her breast by a brooch, with a picture of her man, "in natural colouring." Their life was homely, and differed little from what it had been in the old days when they were poor, except that now and then they took the air in an old battered carriage—which Christison had taken for a debt—looking uncomfortable and stiff, dressed in their Sunday clothes. Their want of knowledge of the language of the place kept them apart from others of their class, and Christison, although he swore by Buenos Aires, which he had seen emerge from a provincial town to a great city, yet cursed the people, calling them a "damned set of natives," which term he generally applied to all but Englishmen.

Certainly nothing was more unlike a "native" than the ex-skipper now turned merchant, in his ways, speech, and dress. Courtesy, which was innate in natives of the place, was to him not only quite superfluous, but a thing to be avoided, whilst his strange habit of devouring bread fresh from the oven, washed down with sweet champagne, gained him the nickname of the "Scotch Ostrich," which nickname he accepted in good part as a just tribute to his digestive powers, remarking that "the Baptist, John, ye mind, aye fed on locusts and wild honey, and a strong man aye liked strong meat, all the worrld o'er."

In the lives of the elderly Aberdeenshire couple, few would have looked for a romantic story, for the hard-featured merchant and his quiet home-keeping wife appeared so happy and contented in their snug villa on the Flores road. No one in Buenos Aires suspected anything, and most likely Christison would have died, remembered only by his tall white hat, had he not one day chosen to tell his tale.

A fierce *pampero* had sprung up in an hour, the sky had turned that vivid green that marks storms from the south in Buenos Aires. Whirlfire kept the sky lighted till an arch had formed in the south-east, and then the storm broke, blinding and terrible, with a strange, seething noise. The wind, tearing along the narrow streets, forced everyone to fly for refuge.

People on foot darted into the nearest house, and horsemen, flying like birds before the storm, sought refuge anywhere they could, their horses, slipping and sliding on the rough, paved streets, sending out showers of sparks as they stopped suddenly, just as a skater sends out a spray of ice. The deep-cut streets, with their raised pavements, soon turned to watercourses, from three to four feet deep, through which the current ran so fiercely that it was quite impossible to pass on foot. The horsemen, galloping for shelter, passed through them with the water banking up against their horses on the stream side, though they plied whip and spurs.

After the first hour of the tempest, when a little light began to dawn towards the south, and the peals of thunder slacken a little in intensity, men's nerves became relaxed from the over-tension that a *pampero* brings with it, just as if nature had been overwound, and by degrees was paying out the chain.

Storm-stayed at Claraz's sat several men, Cossart, George Mansel, one Don José Hernández[3] and Christie Christison. Perhaps the *pampero* had strung up his nerves, or perhaps the desire that all men feel at times to tell what is expedient they should keep concealed, impelled him, but any rate he launched into the story of his life, to the amazement of his friends, who never thought he either had a story to impart, or if he had that it would ever issue from his lips.

"Ye mind the *Rosebud?*" he remarked.

None of the assembled men had ever seen her, although she still was well remembered on the coast.

"Weel, weel, I mind the time she was well kent, a bonny craft. Old Andrew Reid o' Buckieside, he built her, back in the fifties. When he went under, he had to sell his house of Buckieside. I bought her cheap.

"It's fifteen years and mair, come Martinmas, since I piled her up. . . . I canna think how I managed it, knowing the bay, San Julian, ye ken, sae weel.

"It was a wee bit hazy, but still I thought I could get in wi' the blue pigeon going.

"I mind it yet, ye see you hae to keep the rocks where they say they ganakers all congregate before they die, right in a line with yon bit island.

"I heard the water shoaling as the leadsman sung out in the chains, but still kept on, feeling quite sure I knew the channel, when, bang she touches, grates a little, and sticks dead fast, wi' a long shiver o' her keel. Yon rocks must have been sharp as razors, for she began to fill at once.

"No chance for any help down in San Julian Bay in those days, nothing but ane o' they *pulperías* kept by a Basque, a wee bit place, wi' a ditch and bank, and a small brass cannon stuck above the gate. I got what gear I could into the boat, and started for the beach.

"Jean, myself, three o' the men, and an old Dago I carried with me as an interpreter.

"The other sailormen, and a big dog we had aboard, got into the other boat, and we all came ashore. Luckily it was calm, and the old *Rosebud* had struck not above two or three hundred yards from land. Man, San Julian was a dreich place in they days, naething but the bit fortified *pulpería* I was tellin' ye aboot. The owner, old Don Augusty, a Basque, ye ken, just ca'ed his place the 'Rose of the South.' He micht as well have called it the 'Rose of Sharon.' Deil a rose for miles, or any sort of flower.

"Well, men, next day it just began to blow, and in a day or two knockit the old *Rosebud* fair to matchwood. Jean, she grat sair to see her gae to bits, and I cursit a while, though I felt like greetin' too, I'm tellin' ye. There we were sort o' marooned, a' the lot of us, without a chance of getting off maybe for months; for in these days devil a ship but an odd whaler now and then ever came nigh the place. By a special mercy Yanquetruz's band of they Pehuelches happened to come to trade.

"Quiet enough folk yon Indians, and Yanquetruz himself had been brocht up in Buenos Aires in a mission school.

"Man, a braw fellow! Six foot six at least, and sat his horse just like a picture. We bought horses from him, and got a man to guide us up to the Welsh settlement at Chubut, a hundred leagues away.

"Richt gude beasts they gave us, and we got through fine, though I almost thocht I had lost Jean.

"Yanquetruz spoke English pretty well, Spanish of course, and as I tellt ye, he was a bonny man.

"Weel, he sort o' fell in love wi' Jean, and one day he came up to the *pulpería*, and getting off his horse, a braw black piebald wi' an eye like fire intil him, he asked to speak to me. First we had *caña*, and then *carlón*, then some more *caña*, and yon *vino seco*, and syne some more *carlón*. I couldna richtly see what he was driving at. However, all of a sudden he says, 'Wife very pretty, Indian he like buy.'

"I told him Christians didna sell their wives, and we had some more *caña,* and then he says, 'Indian like Christian woman, she more big, more white than Indian girl.'

"To make a long tale short, he offered me his horse and fifty dollars, then several ganaker skins, they ca' them *guillapices,* and finally in addition a mare and foal. Man, they were bonny beasts, both red roan piebalds, and to pick any Indian girl I liked. Not a bad price down there at San Julian, where the chief could hae cut all our throats had he been minded to.

"... Na, na, we werna' fou, just a wee miraculous. Don Augusty was sort o' scared when he heard what Yanquetruz was saying, and got his pistol handy and a bit axe he keepit for emergencies behind the counter. Losh me, yon Yanquetruz was that ceevil, a body couldna tak fuff at him.

"At last I told him I wasna on to trade, and we both had a tot of square-faced gin to clean our mouths a bit, and oot to the *palenque,* where the chief's horse was tied.

"A bonny beastie, his mane hogged and cut into castles, like a clipped yew hedge, his tail plated and tied with a piece of white mare's hide, and everything upon him solid silver, just like a dinner-service.

"The chief took his spear in his hand—it had been stuck into the ground— and leaning on it, loupit on his horse. Ye ken they deevils mount frae the off-side. He gied a yell that fetched his Indians racing. They had killed a cow, and some of them were daubed with blood; for they folk dinna wait for cooking when they are sharp set. Others were three-parts drunk, and came stottering along, with square-faced gin bottles in their hands.

"Their horses werna tied, nor even hobbled. Na, na, they just stood waiting with the reins upon the ground. Soon as they saw the chief—I canna tell ye how the thing was done—they didna mount, they didna loup, they just melted on their beasts, catching the spears out of the ground as they got up.

"Sirs me, they Indians just took flight like birds, raising sich yellochs, running their horses up against each other, twisting and turning and carrying on in sich a way, just like fishing-boats running for harbour at Buckie or Montrose.

"Our guide turned out a richt yin, and brocht us through, up to Chubut wi'out a scratch upon the paint.

"A pairfect pilot, though he had naething in the wide world to guide him through they wild stony plains.

"That's how I lost the *Rosebud,* and noo, ma freens, I'll tell you how it was I got Jean, but that was years ago.

"In my youth up in Peterhead I was a sailorman. I went to sea in they North Sea whaling craft, Duff and McAlister's, ye ken. As time went on, I got rated as a harpooner ... mony's the richt whale I hae fastened into. That was the time when everything was dune by hand. Nane of your harpoon guns, nane of your dynamite, naething but muscle and a keen eye. First strike yer whale, and then pull after him. Talk of yer fox hunts ... set them up, indeed.

"Jean's father keepit a bit shop in Aberdeen, and we had got acquaint. I cannot richtly mind the way o' it. Her father and her mother were àye against our marryin', for ye ken I had naething but my pay, and that only when I could get a ship. Whiles, too, I drinkit a wee bit. Naething to signify, but then Jean's father was an elder of the kirk, and maist particular.

"Jean was a bonny lassie then, awfu' high-spirited. I used to wonder whiles, if some day when her father had been oot at the kirk, someone hadna slippit in to tak tea with her mither . . . I ken I'm haverin'.

"Weel, we were married, and though we lo'ed each other, we were aye bickerin'. Maistly aboot naething, but ye see, we were both young and spirited. Jean liket admiration, which was natural enough at her age, and I liket speerits, so that ane night, after a word or two, I gied her bit daud or two, maybe it was the speerits, for in the morning, when I wakit, I felt about for Jean, intending to ask pardon, and feelin' a bit shamed. There was no Jean, and I thocht that she was hidin' just to frichten me.

"I called, but naething, and pittin' on ma clothes, searchit the hoose, but there was naebody. She left no message for me, and nane of the neighbours kent anything aboot her.

"She hadna' gone to Aberdeen, and though her father and me searchit up and doon, we got no tidings of her. Sort o' unchancy, just for a day or two. However, there was naething to be done, and in a month or so I sold my furniture and shipped for a long cruise.

"Man, a long cruise it was, three months or more blocked in the ice, and then a month in Greenland trying to get the scurvy out of the ship's company, and so one way or another, about seven months slipped past before we sighted Peterhead. Seven months without a sight of any woman; for, men, they Esquimaux aye gied me a skunner wi' their fur clothes and oily faces, they lookit to be baboons.

"We got in on a Sabbath, and I am just tellin' ye, as soon as I was free, maybe about three o' the afternoon, I fairly ran all the way richt up to Maggie Bauchop's.

"I see the place the noo, up a bit wynd. The town was awfu' quiet, and no one cared to pass too close to the wynd foot in daylight, for fear o' the clash o' tongues. I didna care a rap for that, if there had been a lion in the path, same as once happened to ane o' the prophets—Balaam, I think it was, in the Old Book. I wouldna hae stood back a minute if there had been a woman on the other side.

"Weel, I went up to the door, and rappit on it. Maggie came to it, and says she, 'Eh, Christie, is that you?' for she aye kent a customer. A braw, fat woman, Maggie Bauchop was. For years she had followed the old trade, till she had pit awa' a little siller, and started business for hersel'.

"Weel she kent a' the tricks o' it, and still she was a sort of God-fearin' kind o' bitch . . . treated her lassies weel, and didna cheat them about their victuals and their claithes. 'Come in' she says, 'Christie, my man. Where hae ye come from?'

"I tellt her, and says I, 'Maggie, gie us yer best, I've been seven months at sea.'

"'Hoot, man,' she says, 'the lassies arena up. We had a fearfu' spate o' drink yestreen, an awfu' lot of ships is in the port. Sit ye doon, Christie. Here's the Old Book to ye. Na, na, ye needna look at it like that. There's bonny pictures in it, o' the prophets . . . each wi' his lass, ye ken.'

"When she went out, I looked a little at the book—man, a fine hot one, and then as the time passed I started whistlin' a tune, something I had heard up aboot Hammerfest. The door flees open, and in walks Maggie, looking awfu' mad.

"Christie,' she skirls, 'I'll hae na whistlin' in ma hoose, upon the Sabbath day. I canna hae my lassies learned sich ways, so stop it, or get out.'

"Man, I just lauch at her, and I says, 'The lassies, woman. Whistlin' can hardly hurt them, considerin' how they live.'

"Maggie just glowered at me, and 'Christie,' she says, 'you and men like ye may defile their bodies; but whilst I live na one shall harm their souls, puir lambies, wi' whistlin' on His day. No, not in my hoose, that's what I'm tellin' ye.'

"I laughed, and said, 'Weel, send us in ane o' your lambies!' and turned to look at a picture of Queen Victoria's Prince Albert picnickin' at Balmoral. When I looked round a girl had come into the room. She was dressed in a striped sort of petticoat and a white jacket, a blouse I think ye ca' the thing, and stood wi' her back to me as she was speaking to Maggie at the door.

"I drew her to me, and was pulling her towards the bed—seven months at sea, ye ken—when we passed by a looking-glass. I saw her face in it, just for a minute, as we were sort o' strugglin'. Ma God, I lowsed her quick enough, and stotterin' backwards sat down upon a chair. 'Twas Jean, who had run off after the bit quarrel that we had more than a year ago. I didna speak, nor did Jean say a word.

"What's that you say?

"Na, na, ma ain wife in sichlike a place, hae ye no delicacy, man? I settled up wi' Maggie, tellin' her Jean was an old friend o' mine, and took her by the hand. We gaed away to Edinburgh, and there I married her again. Sort of haversome job, but Jean just wanted it, ye ken. How she came there I never asked her.

"Judge not, the Ould Book says, and after all 'twas me gien' her the daud. Weel, weel, things sort of prospered after that. I bought the *Rosebud*, and as ye know piled her up and down at San Julian, some fifteen years ago.

"I never raised ma hand on Jean again. Na, na, I had suffered for it, and Jean, if so be she needed ony sort of purification, man, she got it, standing at the wheel o' nichts on the old schooner wi' the spray flyin', on the passage out.

"Not a drop, thanky, Don Hosey. Good nicht, Mr, Mansel. Bongsoir, Cossart, I'm just off hame. Jean will be waiting for me."

(From *Charity*, 1912)

NOTES

1. George Mansel, one of Graham's friends in the early days in the River Plate area, to whom he dedicated *Thirteen Stories*.
2. Juan Manuel Rosas (1793-1877), bloody dictator of Argentina (1829-52).
3. Certainly the name, and perhaps the person, of the famous Argentine writer José Hernández (1834-86), author of the great epic poem of the gauchos, *Martín Fierro* (1872), so well known, loved, and oft-quoted by Graham, and published during young Robert's first visit to the Plate region in the 1870s.

Section VI

SCOTTISH STORIES

EDITOR'S PREFACE

All the pieces in this section are examples of what might loosely be called a short story, although Graham's genre, the sketch, is never as easily or clearly defined as that. Of those sketches that approximate most to the traditional concept of a short story, "Beattock for Moffat" is probably the best known, and certainly the most pathetic. Some might feel it rather sentimental, even maudlin. However, since it was written within the decade of his anti-Kailyard blast, sentimentality was certainly not the author's intention.

Almost every story, like every situation in Section III, is about death, and all the protagonists die—the foreign princess married to the Fifer (in "A Princess"), the wandering sailor-laird in "Casteal-na-Sithan," and the old-time spinsters in "Ha Til Mi Tuliadh." In these sketches too Graham has much to say about the changing times, the disappearance of old values, and the bleak, hard character of the Scottish people *and* the Scottish countryside, which in a sense precipitate the death of these lonely people. It is significant that the only one who survives is the visiting Spaniard from Galicia (in "At the Ward Toll"), who moves on through the misty and mysterious atmosphere.

I have chosen to end this section, and thus the anthology, with "Brought Forward," which, although certainly not the best of Graham's sketches—there is a certain artificiality in the proletarian conversations—rounds off the journey and makes a fitting conclusion to the cycle. The section opens with the return of the dying Scot to Moffat, passes through Menteith and Fife, and ends, in "Brought Forward," with the sketch set in Glasgow, its protagonist ready, in typical Scots fashion, to depart his homeland. Graham, as a radical M.P., was familiar with, and sympathetic to, the mentality and aspirations of the working class.[1] Though philosphically a pacifist, and in principle hostile to the 1914 War, Graham too went off to that horrible carnage.

In conclusion, one would like to think that, despite his many views of the Scots that have appeared in these sketches, the final picture which is presented of the reserved Scot quietly going off to war, without fanfare or rhetoric, to avenge the death of a friend, is perhaps the most typical—even if he is almost surely going off to die, albeit courageously.

NOTES

1. See my articles in *Tribune* and *The Bibliotheck* mentioned in the Introduction.

BEATTOCK FOR MOFFAT

The bustle on the Euston platform stopped for an instant to let the men who carried him to the third class compartment pass along the train. Gaunt and emaciated, he looked just at death's door, and, as they propped him in the carriage between two pillows, he faintly said, "Jock, do ye think I'll live as far as Moffat? I should na' like to die in London in the smoke."

His cockney wife, drying her tears with a cheap, hem-stitched, pocket handerkechief, her scanty town-bred hair looking like wisps of tow beneath her hat, bought from some window in which each individual article was marked at seven-and-sixpence, could only sob. His brother, with the country sun and wind burn still upon his face, and his huge hands hanging like hams in front of him, made answer.

"Andra," he said, "gin ye last as far as Beattock, we'll gie ye a braw hurl back to the farm, syne the bask air, ye ken, and the milk, and, and—but can ye last as far as Beattock, Andra?"

The sick man, sitting with the cold sweat upon his face, his shrunken limbs looking like sticks inside his ill-made black slop suit, after considering the proposition on its merits, looked up, and said, "I should na' like to bet I feel fair boss, God knows; but there, the mischief of it is, he will na' tell ye, so that, as ye may say, his knowledge has na commercial value. I ken I look as gash as Garscadden.[1] Ye mind, Jock, in the braw auld times, when the auld laird just slipped awa' whiles they were birlin' at the clairet. A braw death, Jock ... do ye think it'll be rainin' aboot Ecclefechan? Aye ... sure to be rainin' aboot Lockerbie. Naè Christians there, Jock, a' Johnstones and Jardines, ye mind?"

The wife, who had been occupied with an air cushion, and having lost the bellows, had been blowing into it till her cheeks seemed almost bursting, and her false teeth were loosened in her head, left off her toil to ask her husband "If 'e could pick a bit of something, a porkpie, or a nice sausage roll, or something tasty," which she could fetch from the refreshment room. The invalid having declined to eat, and his brother having drawn from his pocket a dirty bag, in which were peppermints, gave him a "drop," telling him that he "minded he aye used to like them weel, when the meenister had fairly got into his prelection in the auld kirk outby."

The train slid almost imperceptibly away, the passengers upon the platform looking after it with that half foolish, half astonished look with which men watch a disappearing train. Then a few sandwich papers rose with the dust almost to the level of the platform, sank again, the clock struck twelve, and the station fell into a half quiescence, like a volcano in the interval between the lava showers. Inside the third class carriage all was quiet until the lights of Harrow shone upon the left, when the sick man, turning himself with difficulty, said, "Good-bye, Harrow-on-the-Hill. I aye liked Harrow for the hill's sake, tho' ye can scarcely ca' yon wee bit mound a hill, Jean."

His wife, who, even in her grief, still smarted under the Scotch variant of her name, which all her life she had pronounced as "Jayne," and who, true cockney as she was, bounded her world within the lines of Plaistow, Peckham Rye, the Welch 'Arp ('Endon way), and Willesden, moved uncomfortably at the depreciation of the chief mountain in her cosmos, but held her peace. Loving her husband in a sort of half antagonistic fashion, born of the difference of type between the hard, unyielding, yet humorous and sentimental Lowland Scot, and the conglomerate of all races of the island which meet in London and produce the weedy, shallow breed, almost incapable of reproduction, and yet high strung and nervous, there had arisen between them that intangible veil of misconception which, though not excluding love, is yet impervious to respect. Each saw the other's failings, or, perhaps, thought the good qualities which each possessed were faults, for usually men judge each other by their good points, which, seen through prejudice of race, religion and surroundings, appear to them defects.

The brother, who but a week ago had left his farm unwillingly, just when the "neeps were wantin' heughin' and a feck o' things requirin' to be done, forby a puckle sheep waitin' for keelin',"[2] to come and see his brother for the last time, sat in that dour and seeming apathetic attitude which falls upon the country man, torn from his daily toil and plunged into a town. Most things in London, during the brief intervals he had passed away from the sick bed, seemed foolish to him, and of a nature such as a self-respecting Moffat man, in the hebdomadal enjoyment of the "prelections" of a Free Church minister could not authorise.

"Man, saw ye e'er a carter sittin' on his cart, and drivin' at a trot, instead o' walkin' in a proper manner alangside his horse?" had been his first remark.

The short-tailed sheep dogs, and the way they worked, the inferior quality of the cart horses, their shoes with hardly any calkins worth the name, all was repugnant to him.

On Sabbath, too, he had received a shock, for, after walking miles to sit under the "brither of the U.P. minister at Symington," he had found Erastian hymn books in the pews, and noticed with stern reprobation that the congregation stood to sing, and that, instead of sitting solidly whilst the "man wrastled in prayer," stooped forward in the fashion called the Nonconformist lounge.

His troubled spirit had received refreshment from the sermon, which, though short, and extending to but some five-and-forty minutes, had still been powerful, for he said:

"When yon wee, shilpit meenister—brither, ye ken, of rantin' Ferguson, out by Symington—shook the congregation ower the pit mouth, ye could hae fancied that the very sowls in hell just girned. Man, he garred the very stour to flee aboot the kirk, and, hadna' the big Book been weel brass banded, he would hae dang the haricles fair oot."

So the train slipped past Watford, swaying round the curves like a gigantic serpent, and jolting at the facing points as a horse "pecks" in his gallop at an obstruction in the ground.

The moon shone brightly into the compartment, extinguishing the flickering of the half-candle power electric light. Rugby, the station all lit up, and with its platforms occupied but by a few belated passengers, all muffled up like race horses taking their exercise, flashed past. They slipped through Cannock Chase, which stretches down with heath and firs, clear brawling streams, and birch trees, an out-post of the north lost in the midland clay. They crossed the oily Trent, flowing through alder copses, and with its backwaters all overgrown with lilies, like an *aguapey* in Paraguay or in Brazil.

The sick man, wrapped in cheap rugs, and sitting like Guy Fawkes, in the half comic, half pathetic way that sick folk sit, making them sport for fools, and, at the same time, moistening the eye of the judicious, who reflect that they themselves may one day sit as they do, bereft of all the dignity of strength, looked listlessly at nothing as the train sped on. His loving, tactless wife, whose cheap "sized" handkerchief had long since become a rag with mopping up her tears, endeavoured to bring round her husband's thoughts to paradise, which she conceived a sort of music hall, where angels sat with their wings folded, listening to sentimental songs.

Her brother-in-law, reared on the fiery faith of Moffat Calvinism, eyed her with great disfavour, as a terrier eyes a rat imprisoned in a cage.

"Jean, wumman," he burst out, "to hear ye talk, I would jist think your meenister had been a perfectly illeeterate man, pairadise here, pairadise there, what do ye think a man like Andra could dae daunderin' aboot a gairden naked, pu'in soor aipples frae the trees?"

Cockney and Scotch conceit, impervious alike to outside criticism, and each so bolstered in its pride as to be quite incapable of seeing that any thing existed outside the purlieus of their sight, would soon have made the carriage into a battle-field, had not the husband, with the authority of approaching death, put in his word.

"Whist, Jeanie wumman. Jock, dae ye no ken that the *odium theologicum*[3] is just a curse—pairadise—set ye baith up—pairadise. I dinna' even richtly ken if I can last as far as Beattock."

Stafford, its iron furnaces belching out flames which burned red holes into the night, seemed to approach, rather than be approached, so smoothly ran the train. The mingled moonlight and the glare of the iron-works lit the canal beside the railway, and from the water rose white vapours as from Styx or Periphlegethon.[4] Through Cheshire ran the train, its timbered houses showing ghastly in the frost which coated all the carriage windows, and rendered them opaque. Preston, the Catholic city, lay silent in the night, its river babbling through the public park, and then the hills of Lancashire loomed lofty in the night. Past Garstang, with its water-lily-covered ponds, Garstang where, in the days gone by, Catholic squires, against their will, were forced on Sundays to "take wine" in Church on pain of fine, the puffing serpent slid.

The talk inside the carriage had given place to sleep, that is, the brother-in-law and wife slept fitfully, but the sick man looked out, counting the miles to Moffat, and speculating on his strength. Big drops of sweat stood on his forehead, and his breath came double, whistling through his lungs.

They passed by Lancaster, skirting the sea on which the moon shone bright, setting the fishing boats in silver as they lay scarcely moving on the waves. Then, so to speak, the train set its face up against Shap Fell, and, puffing heavily, drew up into the hills, the scattered grey stone houses of the north, flanked by their gnarled and twisted ash trees, hanging upon the edge of the streams, as lonely, and as cut off from the world (except the passing train) as if they had been in Central Africa. The moorland roads, winding amongst the heather, showed that the feet of generations had marked them out, and not the line, spade, and theodolite, with all the circumstance of modern road makers. They, too, looked white and unearthly in the moonlight, and now and then a sheep, aroused by the snorting of the train, moved from the heather into the middle of the road, and stood there motionless, its shadow filling the narrow track, and flickering on the heather at the edge.

The keen and penetrating air of the hills and night roused the two sleepers, and they began to talk, after the Scottish fashion, of the funeral, before the anticipated corpse.

"Ye ken, we've got a braw new hearse outby, sort of Epescopalian lookin', we' gless a'roond, so's ye can see the kist. Very conceity too, they mak' the hearses noo-a-days. I min' when they were jist auld sort o' ruckly boxes, awfu' licht, ye ken, upon the springs, and just went dodderin' alang, the body swinging to and fro, as if it would flee richt oot. The roads, ye ken, were no nigh hand so richtly metalled in thae days."

The subject of the conversation took it cheerfully, expressing pleasure at the advance of progress as typified in the new hearse, hoping his brother had a decent "stan' o' black," and looking at his death, after the fashion of his kind, as it were something outside himself, a fact indeed, on which, at the same time,, he could express himself with confidence as being in some measure interested. His wife, not being Scotch, took quite another view, and seemed to think that the mere mention of the word was impious, or, at the least, of such a nature as to bring on immediate dissolution, holding the English theory that unpleasant things should not be mentioned, and that, by this mean, they can be kept at bay. Half from affection, half from the inborn love of cant, inseparable from the true Anglo-Saxon, she endeavoured to persuade her husband that he looked better, and yet would mend, once in his native air.

"At Moffit, ye'd 'ave the benefit of the 'ill breezes, and that 'ere country milk, which never 'as no cream in it, but 'olesome, as you say. Why yuss, in about eight days at Moffit, you'll be as 'earty as you ever was. Yuss, you will, you take my word."

Like a true Londoner, she did not talk religion, being too thin in mind and body even to have grasped the dogma of the sects. Her Heaven a music 'all, her paradise to see the king drive through the streets, her literary pleasure to read lies in newspapers or pore on novelettes which showed her the pure elevated lives of duchesses, placing the knaves and prostitutes within the limits of her own class; which view of life she accepted as quite natural, and as a thing ordained to be by the bright stars who write.

Just at the Summit they stopped an instant to let a goods train pass, and, in a faint voice, the consumptive said, "I'd almost lay a wager now I'd last to Moffat, Jock. The Shap, ye ken, I aye looked as at the beginning of the run home. The hills, ye ken, are sort o' heartsome. No that they're bonny hills like Moffat hills, na', na', ill-shapen sort of things, just like Borunty tatties, awfu' puir names too, Shap Fell and Rowland Edge, Hutton Roof Crags, and Arnside Fell. Heard ever onybody sich like names for hills? Naething to fill the mooth. Man, the Scotch hills jist grap ye in the mooth for a' the world like speerits."

They stopped at Penrith, which the old castle walls make even meaner, in the cold morning light, than other stations look. Little Salkeld, and Armathwaite, Cotehill, and Scotby all rushed past, and the train, slackening, stopped with a jerk upon the platform at Carlisle. The sleepy porters bawled out "Change for Mary-port," some drovers slouched into carriages, kicking their dogs before them, and, slamming to the doors, exchanged the time of day with others of their tribe, all carrying ash or hazel sticks, all red-faced and keen-eyed, their caps all crumpled, and their great-coat tails all creased, as if their wearers had laid down to sleep full dressed, so as to lose no time in getting to the labours of the day. The old red sandstone church, with something of a castle in its look, as well befits a shrine close to a frontier where in days gone by the priest had need to watch and pray, frowned on the passing train, and on the manufactories whose banked-up fires sent poisonous fumes into the air, withering the trees which, in the public park, a careful council had hedged round about with wire.

The Eden ran from bank to bank, its water swirling past as wildly as when "The Bauld Buccleugh" and his moss-troopers, bearing "the Kinmount" fettered in their midst, plunged in and passed it, whilst the keen Lord Scroope stood on the brink amazed and motionless.[5] Gretna, so close to England, and yet a thousand miles away in speech and feeling, found the sand now flying through the glass. All through the mosses which once were the "Debateable Land" on which the moss-troopers of the clan Graeme were used to hide the cattle stolen from the "auncient enemy," the now repatriated Scotchman murmured feebly "that it was bonny scenery" although a drearier prospect of "moss hags" and stunted birch trees is not to be found. At Ecclefechan he just raised his head, and faintly spoke of "yon auld carle, Caryle, ye ken, a dour thrawn body, but a gran' pheelo-sopher," and then lapsed into silence, broken by frequent struggles to take breath.

His wife and brother sat still, and eyed him as a cow watches a locomotive engine pass, amazed and helpless, and he himself had but the strength to whisper "Jock, I'm dune, I'll no' see Moffat, blast it, yon smoke, ye ken, yon London smoke has been ower muckle for ma lungs."

The tearful, helpless wife, not able even to pump up the harmful and unnecessary conventional lie, which, after all, consoles only the liar, sat pale and limp, chewing the fingers of her Berlin gloves. Upon the weather-beaten cheek of Jock glistened a tear, which he brushed off as angrily as it had been a wasp.

"Aye, Andra' " he said, "I would hae liket awfu' weel that ye should win to Moffat. Man, the rowan-trees are a' in bloom, and there's a bonny breer upon the corn—aye, ou aye, the reid bogs are lookin' gran' the year—but Andra', I'll tak' ye east to the auld kirk-yaird, ye'll no' ken onything aboot it, but we'll hae a heartsome funeral."

Lockerbie seemed to fly towards them, and the dying Andra' smiled as his brother pointed out the place and said, "Ye mind, there are no ony Christians in it," and answered, "Aye, I mind, naething but Jardines," as he fought for breath.

The death dews gathered on his forehead as the train shot by Nether-cleugh, passed Wamphray, and Dinwoodie, and with a jerk pulled up at Beattock just at the summit of the pass.

So in the cold spring morning light, the fine rain beating on the platform, as the wife and brother got their almost speechless care out of the carriage, the brother whispered, "Dam't, ye've done it, Andra', here's Beattock. I'll tak' ye east to Moffat yet to dee."

But on the platform, huddled on the bench to which he had been brought, Andra' sat speechless and dying in the rain. The doors banged to, the guard step-ping in lightly as the train flew past, and a belated porter shouted, "Beattock, Beattock for Moffat," and then, summoning his last strength, Andra' smiled, and whispered faintly in his brother's ear, "Aye, Beattock—for Moffat?" Then his head fell back, and a faint bloody foam oozed from his pallid lips. His wife stood crying helplessly, the rain beating upon the flowers of her cheap hat, rendering it shapeless and ridiculous. But Jock, drawing out a bottle, took a short dram and saying, "Andra', man, ye made a richt gude fecht o' it," snorted an instant in a red pocket handkerchief, and calling up a boy, said, "Ring, Jamie, to the toon, and tell McNicol to send up and fetch a corp." Then, after helping to remove the body to the waiting room, walked out into the rain, and, whistling "Corn Rigs" quietly between his teeth, lit up his pipe, and muttered as he smoked "A richt gude fecht—man aye, ou aye, a game yin Andra', puir felly. Weel, weel, he'll hae a braw hurl onyway in the new Moffat hearse."

(From *Success,* 1902)

NOTES

1. *Garscadden*, a suburb of Glasgow.
2. "turnips were needing thinned and a lot of things requiring to be done, as well as a crowd of sheep waiting to be marked."
3. *odium theologicum*, theological hatred.

4. Rivers of the Underworld in classical mythology. Periphlegethon makes sense logically and etymologically, and is not an unintelligent deviation on Graham's part from what was probably Pyriphlegethon, i.e. the fire-burning river.

5. Graham is describing here the famous border incident of 1596, when the English captured William Armstrong of Kinmont. When the Scottish Warden, Sir Walter Scott of Buccleuch, crossed the border and rescued "Kinmont Willie," Elizabeth demanded of James VI, without success, the handing over of the "bold Buccleugh."

HA TIL MI TULIADH[1]

All was unchanged, and Nature cared not, being occupied with sun and moon and stars, the tides, the mists, the dew, rain, snow, the fall and reproduction of the leaf, and the great mysteries, the cause of which evades and always has evaded man. She smiled, as she does sometimes at a funeral, sending a glimpse of sun upon a coffin-plate, so that the cold-nipped mourners read the age of the deceased whilst they stand peering down into the grave, as in a blaze of light.

All was unchanged.

The two tall lime trees towered above the rough field-gate contrived of poles running through horseshoes wedged into their trunks.

The leaves just swept the roof, and in the evening air they seemed to sigh for the departed, who for so many years had watched them green in April bursting into life, and glorious in autumn as they fell carpeting the road, and piled upon the level doorstep with its concentric pattern drawn in chalk. The rush-thatched byre, upon whose roof grew fumitory and corydalis, looked just as it had looked for forty years, and the low door flanked by great tufts of golden-rod and of angelica, and painted blue, was shut for ever on its late owners and on me. Through it, from earliest childhood, as I passed, I led my ponies, tying them in the dark beside the cow to the tall uprights which in Highland cowsheds serve for stalls.

Two sisters, almost the last survivors of an ancient race, had lived for years in the old cottage by the reedy lake. Descendants of the retainer of a feudal chief, their ancestors had been hereditary ferrymen, for, in the days of old, caste, now confined to India and the East, was spread throughout the world.

In what rough coracle or boat their remote ancestors had ferried over to the island, men dressed in skins, no one can say, for from the dawn of history in Menteith marauding clansmen, coming with a *creagh* from the laigh, had been rowed over to the castle in the isle by some one of their race.

In the deep bay, rush-locked and clear, they or their father had constructed a rude pier of stones and wattles, to which a boat was tied, the paint all sun-cracked, and with an inch or two of water in the well.

So in the days gone by, in houses occupied by gentlemen whose pedigrees were longer than their purse, an antiquated carriage, used as a roosting-place by hens, slowly decayed in some gaunt coach-house given up to damp.

Carriage and boat were evidence of better times, a link with days of glory long departed, drawing a smile or tear, according to the point from which the man who saw them looked upon the world.

So in the cottage the two sisters lived—relics of days when men were civil in their speech, had time, and did not spare it in its use. They never travelled far, but, for all that, they knew the world in which they lived themselves in all its niceties. Constrained by poverty to work, the sisters yet appeared two ladies in distress, not fallen in fortunes, though their Potosí was but the little croft and garden with "its hantle of sour plumtrees," but, so to speak, having suffered wrong from Nature, which had not placed them free from all necessities at birth. Not that they lacked advancement either, for in their heart of hearts they held themselves the equals of the highest in the land—a tacit claim which all admitted but their equals, in the old-fashioned district where they lived. Raw-boned and rather hard of feature, the eldest had the soft Highland voice and manner, which somehow seems not to belong to modern life, and places the possessor of them in a world outside the present age. The younger, gentle and delicate, had never married, must have been pretty in her youth, and lived her life subordinated to her sister, admiring her, and in her turn being admired and cherished by her in a half-tender and half-peremptory way.

Their father was an ancient Celt who formed a link with olden times, being compounded of quite different essences and stronger simples than men of latter days. Born as he was, just where the Highlands and the Lowlands touch, he had amalgamated much of the characteristics of the two. His manners were all High-land, his knowledge of the world partly his own and partly that of the Low Country, as we style the realm of bogs and marshy fields that swells and billows like a sea up to the lumpy range of tawny hills that cuts them from the north, and, till the days of railways, formed a bar as strong and as insuperable as is a navigable river, or indeed the sea. Short, and in later years bent almost double, but to the last alert upon his legs, time and the rain, which when it ceases for a fortnight is the theme of prayers in church, had turned him a light fern colour, and his clothes, and hair—originally grey (for no one living could remember when his head was brown)—had weathered to a lichen-looking green, and his blue twinkling eyes, not bleared with age, could, as he said himself, "discern a gentleman almost a mile away." Gentry and gentlemen, by which he understood those of old family, for money could not make, nor the want of it mar, in his opinion, were the chief objects of his creed.

"The Queen can mak' a duke, she canna' mak' Lochiel," he would observe with pride, not that the limitation of the royal power rejoiced him, for he held, as do Mohammedans, that he who reigned did so by right divine, but it seemed to him evident, or else the prayer for those "set over us and under Him" had been of no account.

Withal, he was himself a gentleman, if natural good-breeding makes one, conjoined with courtesy in speech. Upon a visit, when he had showed you round his croft, with what an air he used to offer you fruit in a cabbage leaf, saying, "Will ye tak' berries, laird," or "leddy," as the case might be, thus exercising hospitality in its best sense, by giving what he had without false shame or with excuses for his poverty. One ate them, listening all the time to local lore, dis-torted through the vision of his years, and rendered picturesque partly by want of education and partly by the way he touched his subject, embroidering and adorning it with sidelights of his own, just as an artist draws from what he sees in his own brain, and neither copies nor extenuates his theme.

Seated upon the gunwale of his boat, and talking volubly in the soft Highland accent, which makes you think that you knew Gaelic once upon a time, the landscape all unchanged, the scrubby oak copse straggling up the hill, the bracken yellowing in the autumn breeze, and leaves of sycamores, mottled and black, like trout in moorland burns, all falling softly round about, whilst the white mist crept up and hung the castle and the chapel in the air, making the great stag-headed chestnuts in the Isle of Rest look like gigantic antlers thrown against the sky, the things and men of which he spoke became alive again and the long, broken link with the old world was welded into shape. You heard unmoved, and as a thing quite natural, and which it seemed had happened to yourself, how he had walked to Eglinton to see the tournament, taking three days to do it, in the rain; had slept beneath the trees, had seen it all, especially the Emperor of the French, "Napoleon Third, ye ken," the Queen of Beauty carried through the mud, and then tramped back again.

Who, in these days of education and of common sense, made manifest and plain by copy-book, would .do the like, out of pure love of sport, lightness of heart, or the sheer devilment of youth?

All the old legends of the Borderland he knew—with much about Rob Roy, who as he used to say was "better in a tuilzie than a fight, for all his skill o' fence, and they long arms o' his, ye mind, he could untie the garters frae his hose without a stoop or hogging up his back." He talked about the man just as if he were alive, so naturally and without effort, having heard all he told you from his grandfather, that it would not have startled you on looking round to see Red Robert in the flesh come trotting down the hill, his target at his back, and his long Spanish "culbeir" in his hand, humming a waulking song or whistling a strathspey.[2]

All the old legends of the district and his lore of times gone by he left his daughters, which, working in their minds and coming to the surface in their speech, stranded them lonely in the world, without a fellow, just as a glacier boulder in a glen must feel deserted in the tall heather where it lies, far from the hills and stones.

The younger sister first departed, going on before to tell their father that the world was changed, and that no place was left for them or theirs, and that the osprey built no more in the old chestnuts which the monks had planted round the grey priory in the isle, and that the trees themselves were growing balder and more sere. The elder lingered on alone, brisk but alert, driving her cow down to the mossy "park," and stepping east to church when it was fine, not following the road, but going through the fields (though it took longer by them), perhaps from the hereditary Highland habit of avoiding stones in days when every man made his own brogues at home. In summer time she took into her house artists and fishermen, and those whom the fine weather drives into the country for a time, and who lounge through their time smoking and bored, but conscious it is right to do as others do, and therefore satisfied. They thought her odd, and she esteemed them common, but "awfa' clever folk, ye ken; ane o' them painted me a bit picture o' ma sister from a fotygraph, ane o' they dagyriotypes, ye mind them, done on glass, which I have by me since it was ta'en back aboot sixty-three, the time o' yon review at Paisla', the verra image o' her, laird, I'm tellin' ye." The effort of the limner's art (to which even a "dagyriotype" on glass was preferable) hung in her little parlour, resplendent with megilp, shining with poppy oil, and setting forth the patient with a grin upon her face, and with the clothes in fashion forty years ago, themselves not beautiful, rendered ridiculous by newness, just as a play of the same time appears to us absurd, not that our own are better, but because folly is a changing quantity and different in degree.

Our friendship, fast but intermittent, lasted many years, and the byre door through which my ponies used to pass became too small to lead my horse through and so we generally talked outside the house, not that we said much, for she was growing deaf, and I knew all her stories years ago, but it pleased both of us, and when I mounted and rode off she used to stand, holding her hand above her eyes, after the fashion of a sailor on a pier, looking out seaward, even when not a sail is on the sea.

Her death was in the olden style, after the fashion she had lived—so to speak, not premeditated, but natural, just as a tree dies at the top, decaying downwards, till it is gone almost before those who have known it all their lives are well aware of its decease. The neighbours told me, for I was absent in that region which folks in Menteith call "up aboot England," that she was "travellin'" from church, felt ill upon arriving at her house, took to her bed, and "sleepit bonnily awa,'" upon the following day. A man, that is a man who feels the ancient Highland spirit in his blood, would like to die with his boots on, but for a woman this was the nearest thing to sudden death, and quite became the last of an old violent race of men.

In the old churchyard by the lake, amongst the Grahams and the Macgregors, some of whom have swords upon their headstones, for all their trademark and memorial of their lives, she sleeps. With pride of race and Scottish thoughtfulness she left sufficient to erect a stone, in which is cut her name, her sister's, that of her father, and those of many of her clan. It stands in the wet grass, close to the wall of the kirkyard, a sort of landmark in the history of Menteith, showing a page turned down—a page on which but few could read, even before the book was shut for the last time. To bid her sleep in peace is but a work of supererogation, after full eighty years of life. Those who remain tossing and turning upon life's uneasy pillow stand more in need of such a wish.

So I "stepped west," and, coming to the Highland cottage by the lake, found the door shut, the hearthstone cold, the garden eaten up with weeds, the flauchtered feals upon the cowhouse roof fallen from the poles, and the old boat, hauled up upon the beach, paintless and blistering in the sun. No cow fed in the little rushy park. Even the withies which had once confined the gate were burst and swinging in the wind. The door was shut, shut against me, and shut upon the last of my old friends. So, sitting down upon the step, on which no longer was a pattern laid in chalk, I smoked and meditated, seeing a long procession pass upon the road, all riding ponies which grew larger towards the end, until a man upon a horse brought up the rear. They stopped before the house, which seemed to have turned newer, and in which a fire of peats burned brightly on the hearth. Then, from the door ... but ... I will return no more (*Ha til mi tuliadh*). He who waits at the ferry long enough will get across some time.

(From *His People,* 1906)

NOTES

1. "I will return no more."
2. Red Robert is another name for Rob Roy MacGregor; the culbeir is a long, steel-bladed weapon, derived from the Spanish word *culebra*, meaning a snake; to waulk or wauk cloth is to "full" it or make it hard—hence wauking or waulking songs were sung to accompany the work of fulling the cloth.

CAISTEAL-NA-SITHAN

It was indeed a castle of the elves. Over all, hung an air of melancholy. From the deserted lodge, behind the high, beech hedge, which shut the place off from the lake, the avenue led through a sea of billowy mounds, on which grew trees as thickly as in the tropics, some dead and some decaying, some broken off by storms and left to die or live just as they chose.

Moss had spread like a carpet over the deeply rutted road.

Here and there by its side stood foreign shrubs, some of them growing rankly, and others which had died years ago, standing up dry and sere, inside their iron cages, as a dead body in a life-belt floats upon the sea. The bracken met the lower branches of the trees and formed a screen, through which rabbits had made their runs, like little railway tunnels.

They fed upon the mossy grass outside, retreating slowly when they were alarmed, conscious they were at home and that a passer-by was an intruder into their domain. Where the trees fell, they lay and rotted, covered with lichens and with a growth of ferns that sprang from the dead bark.

The neglected woods seemed to have bred a strange and hostile air. Instinctively one looked around, as if some power of nature, which cultivations kills, was still unchecked, had just declared a war upon mankind, and was about to open its attack.

The passing of a roe through the deep underwood, a passage ordinarily so fairy-like and light, there sounded ominous, and the sharp cracking of a decaying twig under its flying feet, or the soft rustling of its body through the ferns, sent a thrill through the listener, as if some monstrous creature of a dream were going to appear.

Even in summer everything seemed dank, and in the peaty soil the water oozed beneath the footsteps, making the ground seem treacherous and false.

Sometimes at sunset, when a red gleam fell on the top of oaks, turned all the bracken fiery, and lighted up the overhanging hills which peeped above the tops of the high trees, the air of menace was dispelled and a breath from the outer world brought back security. When the last gleams had vanished, and a cold, chilly air, especially before the autumn frost, crept through the brakes and stirred the frozen tufts of bulrushes in the black, awful-looking ponds, fringed with dark rhododendrons, and set about upon one side with towering spruce firs, a panic seemed to creep into the soul.

The thick, white mists that rose up from the pool hung in the trees, and seemed as if they were alive, so stealthily they crept about the branches and twined like serpents, twisting and writhing in the air.

Owls floated like gigantic moths across the avenue, or sat and called to one another in the recesses of the woods. All was so silent and so still, one seemed to feel the waves of sound that floated from their call, just as one hears the whirring of an old eight-day clock before it strikes its bell. In the low park beyond the wood, through which the avenue led to the house, the dun or creamy Highland cattle slept on the hillocks, to shun the draughts of nights. A chilly damp rose from the old bog-land, long since reclaimed, but showing black and peaty where moles had made their hills, which dotted the sour grass at intervals, and in the moonlight looked like animals asleep. A great moss ditch cut the low park in two, and in it the black, frozen water seemed like a stream of pitch. Birches and stunted oaks were set about the fields, their old, gnarled roots laid bare by winter rains, and by the stamping of the cattle in the summer, when they stood underneath the trees to shelter from the flies. Through the long, limb-like roots, rabbits had burrowed, and here and there a heavy stone was left, stuck in the crevices, looking like some lost weapon of the Stone Age, or prehistoric club.

Just where the deep moss ditch crossed underneath the road, a high, iron, double gate barred off the avenue.

Beyond it stretched a gloomy road, winding between dark trees. At night when you rode through it, your horse snorting occasionally when rabbits ran across the path, or birds stirred in the trees, it felt as if you were a thousand miles from help. In front, the dark road wound, as it seemed, interminably, through overhanging trees. Between you and the world was the half-mile or so of the mysterious woods, and the black, sullen ponds.

At last, passing another gate, it led up to a shrubbery. A mossy burn fed a neglected duck-pond, upon whose waters floated feathers, and round whose sides grew tufts of pampas grass. Tall bushes of wygelia and syringa, dead at the sides but vigorous in the middle, with flowering currants, andromeda and rank-growing thickets of guelder-rose and dogwood, concealed the house from view.

The rabbit netting, nailed to the fencing of the park, was broken here and there, and billowed like a sail. Through it the rabbits entered as they pleased, burrowing beneath the bushes, and leaving trails which led up to the lawn. Enormous beeches, and a sycamore or two, growing like cabbages, showed that at one time the neglected policies had been well cared for, and the decayed and mouldering rustic seats, set about here and there, recalled the time when children played upon the lawn, whilst nurses sat and watched them underneath the trees. The house itself, high and steep-roofed, with pepper-boxes at the angles and a wide flight of steps, upon whose parapet [stood] two great iron eagles that once had been all painted in the proper colours of the coat of arms of which they formed the crest, was desolate and drear. The rough-cast plaster, which at one time had covered all the walls, had fallen in patches here and there, leaving great blotches, that looked like maps, upon its sides.

Right opposite the door, a roundel of rank grass, once closely shaven, but now rank and ill-tended, lay like an island in the road. Two whinstone posts, with eight-shaped irons at their sides, for hitching horses to in times gone by, just raised their heads above the turf.

The house door, left ajar, but yet made fast against the world by a confining chain, with the bolt running in a tube, gave just the touch of human interest required to accentuate the melancholy of the forlorn abode.

As one peeped through into the hall, covered with a well-worn oilcloth, and marked the absence of sticks, hats, umbrellas, and all that goes to give a hall a look of being the introduction to a comfortable home, one felt the owner was a solitary man who, in the summer evenings, when the owls hooted faintly in the recesses of the woods and swallows hawked at flies across the lawn, sat on the parapet of the tall flight of broken steps between his iron eagles, and meditated on what might have been, had things gone differently.

Beyond the hall few ever penetrated, for an old woman, holding the door fast in her hand, used to peep out and answer, "The laird is oot," and then, when the chance visitor had turned away disconsolate, flatten her nose against a window and watch him stumble down the road. The great, old Scottish stable, built round a courtyard, with the decaying clock upon its tower, one hand long lost, the other pointing eternally to twelve, stood buried in the trees whose branches swept the slates, showering them down upon the grass in gales, and dripping ceaselessly in rain, till a green lichen grew just underneath the drip.

Most of the doors had gone, and those that still fought on against the rain and wind were kept in place by pieces of coarse leather, roughly nailed on the jambs. Upon the wooden sheathing of the pump, hay seed had sprouted, growing a rank crop of grass, which in its turn had died, and hung all mildewed and with small drops of moisture oozing from the stems.

Such was the place, one of the last examples of the old Scotland which has sunk below the waves of Time. Perhaps not an example to be followed, but yet to be observed, remembered, even regretted in the great drabness of prosperity which overspreads the world.

Few people ever trod the avenue, and even tramps but rarely camped in the deserted woods, though fallen trees were plentiful, and none would have been the wiser if they had stayed a week. The owner, an old sailor who had inherited the place in middle life, had by degrees become such a recluse that sometimes weeks would pass without his being seen. Shut off from all the world, he lived with an old housekeeper, as it were in a wilderness, and if by chance he met a stranger on the road would dive behind the bushes to escape, like a wild animal. Now and then far-off relations would come down to shoot, stopping at some hotel, and now and then a neighbour would drive over, always to be received by the old housekeeper with the same formula, "The laird is oot."

Occasionally he left the country and went abroad, but always to some place near the seaside, where he would pass long hours looking at ships, though without making any friends. Lübeck and Kiel, Riga or Genoa, were his favourite haunts, and those who met him at any of those ports used to report having seen him, dressed in his blue serge suit, and with the air of being the one man left in a depopulated world, in the same way that captains jot down in their log, "In such a latitude, in the first dog-watch, passed a derelict."

By degrees his visits to far-off ports grew rarer, and at last he seldom passed the gates of his neglected grounds, except occasionally on Sundays, when he attended church, reserved and silent, speaking to none, but yet a little critical, after the fashion of a man who had read prayers on board his ship and therefore should know something of the way in which a service ought to be carried on.

On these occasions he would stand a little in the churchyard, looking intently at a sort of pen, surrounded by a broken iron railing, in which his ancestors reposed.

Whether his thoughts ran on the unstability of life, or if he only tried to make a calculation of the probable expense he would incur if he embarked upon repairs, was never known to anyone, although some said he thought of neither, but merely leaned against the rails to pass the time until the congregation had dispersed, and left him free to set off home again.

Everyone speculated on his death, some saying that it would occur some day when he was quite alone out in the woods, and others that he would be found dead in his chair, with the *Pacific Pilot* open in his hand—not a bad book for an old sailor to have consulted, when just about to weigh his anchor. But as it happened, he had to make his landfall unassisted and alone.

A bitter frost, intense and black, had bound the district, congealing the dark waters of the lake into a sheet of glass. Trees groaned and cracked, and in the silent woods a shudder seemed to run through the gaunt avenues, as if they suffered from the cold. Crows winged their way, looking like notes of music on an old page of parchment, across the leaden sky.

High in the air there passed strings of wild geese, and in the stillness of the frost their melancholy cry was heard, till they were almost out of sight.

All nature seemed engaged in a stern fight for life with some calamity, which had attacked it unawares. The very streams stood still to watch the progress of the battle, fast in their bonds of ice.

Somehow or other, after the fashion that in Africa news travels always a day or two ahead of any traveller, it got about the countryside the laird was missing from his home. As, in the little inn, the constable, "the post," one or two farmers, and the innkeeper were talking of the report, the housekeeper was seen hobbling along the road. Coughing and wheezing, she averred she "couldna bide alane, up in yon awfu' house." The laird, it seemed, upon the evening of the commencement of the frost, gone out, as was usual, just before tea-time, but never had come back. She had waited for two days, setting his meals upon the table at the stated hours, and at night putting out a lantern at the front door to guide him to the house. A day and night had broken down her courage, and given her the strength to find her way alone through the deserted avenue, for, as she said, "If she had passed anither nicht alane wi' all they bogles and they howlets, she would have gone fair gyte."

All search was useless. The woods and moors guarded their secret, and, had not chance revealed it, the disappearance of the laird would have been put down as the last eccentricity of an eccentric life.

Fate was not willing that the laird's last resting-place should not be known, for as some boys were skating on one of the black ponds they saw what they took for bird's feathers, frozen in the ice. When they came home, trembling and pale, they said the feathers turned out to be the hair on a man's head, and that below the ice they had seen something that "lookit like a muckle fish, and frichted them to death."

At once the sparse inhabitants of the wild district proceeded to the place, entering the sacred grounds from which they had been debarred for years. Their lanterns, glimmering like glow-worms over the dark pond, and shedding a fantastic light in the black ice, outlining every branch upon the leafless trees, and playing on the clump of rhododendrons on the bank, gave a strange air of unreality to everything around.

One of the boys pointed out the spot, and as the ice was frozen so intensely, on the clear, windless night, they saw beneath it the laird's body, in the same way you can see a fish which has been taken by the frost.

When they had cut it out, framed in a square of ice, he was so life-like, laid upon the bank, in the dim, quavering light of the horn lanterns, that those who saw him always used to say, "You'd hae just thocht the laird was sleepin', if he had na been sae gash."

(From *Charity*, 1912)

AT THE WARD TOLL

The mist had blotted out the moss, leaving the Easter Hill, Gartur, and the three fir trees above the Shanochil, rising like islands out of a dead sea. At times the waves of mist engulfed the islands, and then slowly fell back and left them clear, as if some tide, unseen and unsuspected, had ebbed and then had flowed again, or a volcano underneath the moss had been at first half doubtful of its work and shrouded it in steam till it had taken shape. Great drops of damp hung from the feathers of the larches in the long sheltering plantations on each side of the road. Damp filled up the interstices of spiders' webs that clung between the bents, stretching like fairy rigging between the stems, as a triatic-stay stretches between a schooner's masts. It settled on the heads of grasses, enveloping them as in a veil, making each individual stem look like a little ghost of what it had been in the summer, when it was green with life. Where banks of rushes, now turning brown, emerged out of the shroud of steam, they looked like frozen water weeds protruding from the ice, by a pond's side, during a winter's frost.

The perfume of the spruces and of the beds of moss and blae-berries hung in the moist atmosphere and filled the nostrils with a scent of something older than mankind, keen, subtle, vivifying, and which somehow connected man, by some unseen, uncomprehended essential oil or particle so small no microscope could make it manifest, with the whole universe.

Beyond the moss the five-fold hummocks of Ben Dhu ran out into the rolling waves of mist, as a great cape runs out into the sea. Far off, in the interior ocean of the mist, Ben Ledi showed its topmost ridge, just as the Peak of Tenerife rises among the fleecy clouds of the Trade Winds.

The approaching evening added to the gloom, and night appeared about to fall with double darkness on the wide valley of Menteith. My horse's feet fell with a muffled sound upon the road, as if it had been hollow underneath. Now and again out on the moor the crowing of a grouse was heard, and once an owl floated across the road as silently as thistledown is wafted through the air, like an enormous moth. All was so quiet and mysterious, one seemed to ride enveloped in a shroud which kept one from the world. The spirit of the north was in the air, intangible, haunting and vague, that makes the dwellers in the north vague and intangible, poetic and averse to face the facts of life, with a hard rind covering the softness of their hearts. Gigantic forms rode in the billowy vapours by my side, those Valkyrie which northern poets have discerned, either projected on the mist, as I did on that night, or else projected on the *pia mater* of their brain, round which a mist of vapour always seemed to brood.

The shapes I seemed to see—or saw, for if a man sees visions with the interior sight he sees them, for himself at least, as surely as if he saw them with the outward eye—loomed lofty, and peopled once again Menteith with riders, as it was peopled in the past. The ill-starred earls, their armour always a decade out of fashion, and now and then surmounted by a Highland bonnet set with an eagle's feather, giving them an air half of the Saxon, half of the Celt, their horses lank and ill-groomed, their followers talking in shrill Gaelic, seemed to defile along the road. Their blood was redder than the King's, their purses lighter than an empty bean-pod after harvest, and still they had an air of pride, but all looked "fey" as if misfortune had set its seal upon their race.

They passed and vanished into the mist they once had known so well, and it seemed to me that they all rode, just as if they knew the way as well as they had known it in their lives, towards their ruined castle in the low island of the rush-ringed lake. I did not turn and ride with them, though had I done so I feel sure, upon arriving at the ferry-keeper's hut thatched thick with heather, out of which sprouted corydalis and on whose ridge grew tufts of ragweed, there would have been a place empty and waiting in the decaying, insubstantial boat. Highlanders, driving the *creagh* towards Balquhidder, passed, their moccasin-shod feet leaving as little impress on the mist as they had left in life, upon the tussocks of bent-grass. They urged the phantom cattle with the points of their Lochaber axes; and, last of all, wrapped in his plaid, his thick hair curling close about his hard-lined features, passed one I knew at once by his great length of arm and the red beard, on which the damp shone in a frosty dew, just as it glistened on the coats of the West Highland kyloes that he drove before him on the road. Though for two hundred years he had slept well in the lone graveyard of the deserted church beside Loch Voil, he seemed to know the road as intimately as he had known it in his old foraying days. As he passed by he moved his target forward and his hand stole to his sword, as if he recognised one of his ancient foes. Then he was swallowed up by the same mist that had protected him so often in his life.[1]

The gloom grew thicker, and in the clinging air fantastic noises surged, as if the spirits of the hills, so long oppressed and overcome by modern life and by man's dominance of nature, were abroad and had resumed their sway. All the old legends appeared natural, the second sight a thing so evident, it seemed a madness to deny. The *Bodach Glas*[2] would not have been surprising had he appeared, his head averted and his plaid twisted about him in the ancient fashion of the Isles. London was millions of miles off, lost in reality, and the true world was that I thought I saw on every side, in the grey pall of mist. It seemed that I had ridden miles through the dark, steamy woods. The damp chilled to the bones, and if I put my hand upon my horse I left the imprint of my fingers in the white dew that clustered on his coat. Emerging from the woods, at least upon one side, where the rough moorland pasture stretches out towards the moss, close to the toll-house at the cross-roads, four-square to all the winds, there is an island of old ash trees amongst the firs and spruces, which stands upon a knoll close to a gate. At all times the old trees look strange against the background of dark firs. Upon that evening they appeared gigantic, menacing, and magnified to twenty times their size. As I approached them, glad to have left the gloomy woods, my horse snorted and bounded half across the road. A voice in Spanish hailed me, and a figure moved from the shadow of the trees and stood, dew-damped and shivering, in his light southern clothes.

His olive face had turned an earthy colour with the cold, and it was rendered ghastly-looking by a red sash tied like a comforter about his neck. He told me that at a village which he thought was called "Bocliva,"[3] or something of the sort, he had been informed there lived a gentleman hard by who could speak christian,[4] and he believed that I must be the man. He was, he said, "fasting from all but sin that day, and he esteemed his having come across me almost a miracle, for he felt saved as on a plank, when he had heard me speak."

He knew a "litel Inglis," which he would "spika so that I might hear." Then in that language he informed me that "he had lose the ship in Liz[5] and walka Glasco"; and then, turning again to Spanish, thanked me, and in particular for some cigarettes I gave him, which he declared "were better far than bread when the heart is empty and the feet sore, and that the scent of them was sweeter than the orange flower or than the incense in a church."

He came from Vigo,[6] so he said, and if I went there any time, I had my house in Teis, just past the blacksmith's, and he, though a poor man, was one who could appreciate. Then, after telling me that "Ildefonso López was my servant, and God would pay me," he raised his battered hat and, starting off again upon the road to "walka Glasco," disappeared into the night, singing a tango in a high falsetto voice.

I rode into the open between the rough stone dykes that bound the road beyond the toll, passed the old-fashioned cast-iron milestone on which a hand is moulded pointing the way to Aberfoyle, and, riding cautiously down the stony brae, crossed the Ward bridge and came out on the moor.

White waves of vapour came surging up against the posts that marked the road, and foamed about them, as the surf surges round a rock. Through the thick air the scent of the bog-myrtle penetrated, acrid and comforting, and on the banks of peat the willows trembled as my horse passed them, as if they floated on the moss.

All was as lonely and as northern as before, but the spell had been broken by Ildefonso López in his brief apparition out of the mist and gloom of the October evening, and though I knew I rode along the road towards the Kelty bridge, and marked unconsciously the junipers that grow just by the iron gate that opens on the path towards the Carse, it seemed somehow that I was entering Vigo, by the north channel between the Cies[7] and the high land on which a clump of pine trees overhangs the sea.

The noble bay spread out between the hills, which ran down sheer, right to the water's edge, leaving at intervals just ground enough for a white, little town with red-tiled roofs to lodge itself, half hidden amongst vines.

The fishing boats, brown and with sails as sharp as a shark's fins, dotted the water, and on a tongue of land the town of Bouzas seemed to rock upon the sea, as it lay basking in the sun.

Vigo itself, with its steep, winding streets, its dark-tree'd *alameda*, its mouldering fort, and the decaying hulk of an old ship left derelict upon the sand, appeared, just as I first had seen it thirty years ago. The castles, where the brass guns had sunk upon the ground beside their mouldering carriages, towered above the town.

Chestnut and pine woods almost met the houses, and from the beach the chattering of the fishwives, in their bright red and yellow petticoats, resounded in my ears. Beyond the town the harbour narrowed, and the white oratory of La Guía crowned the pine-clad hill that rises up from the black point of the Cabrón. Still, narrowing till it seemed a lake, the harbour stretched towards the *lazareto*,[8] where under piles of sand that clearly show on a still day, lie the galleons Drake hunted up the bay, until they sank themselves to save the treasure that they held. It passed by Redondela, with its high bridge, and finished at San Payo, from whence as I looked backwards I seemed to see the islands at the harbour mouth float in a sunset, red and glorious, and crossed by bars of purple and of black.

It all appeared to hang outlined and visible upon the vapour rising from the moss, just as a wood appears, projected on the clouds, in the South Pampa on a misty morning, with its roots growing in the sky. Slowly it faded, and as I jogged along, passing the Kelty bridge and turning by the watering-trough into another belt of wood, I almost wondered whether Ildefonso López had been a real man, or but an emanation from the mist, from which he issued out so suddenly, and which had swallowed him again almost as suddenly, upon his lonely way.

(From *Faith*, 1909)

NOTES

1. The red-bearded ghost is, of course, Rob Roy MacGregor.
2. *Bodach Glas*, literally, the "Pale Old Man," i.e. the Devil himself.
3. *Buchlyvie*, a village between Balfron and Arnprior.
4. "Hablar cristiano" means to speak Spanish.
5. *Liz*, Leith, probably.
6. *Vigo*, Spanish port in the province of Galicia, where Graham and his wife lived for two years on his return from Texas in 1881.
7. *Cies*, the islands off the coast.
8. *lazareto*, the area, outside the harbour, where those ships, that might have been in contact with contagious diseases, had to remain in quarantine.

A PRINCESS

Nothing is wilder than the long stretch of sandy coast which runs from the East Neuk of Fife right up to Aberdeen.

Inland, the windswept fields, with their rough walls, without a kindly feal upon the top, as in the west, look grim and uninviting in their well-farmed ugliness.

The trees are low and stunted, and grow twisted by the prevailing fierce east winds, all to one side, just like the trees so often painted by the Japanese upon a fan.

The fields run down until they lose themselves in sandy links, clothed with a growth of bent.

After the links, there intervenes a shingly beach, protected here and there by a low reef of rocks, all honeycombed and limpet-ridden, from which streamers of dulse float in the ceaseless surge.

Then comes the sea, grey, sullen, always on the watch to swallow up the fishermen, whose little brown-sailed boats seem to be scudding ceaselessly before the easterly haar towards some harbour's mouth.

Grey towns, with houses roofed with slabs of stone, cluster round little churches built so strongly that they have weathered reformations and the storms of centuries.

Grey sky, grey sullen sea, grey rocks, and a keen whistling wind that blows from the North Sea, which seems to turn the very air a steely grey, have given to the land a look of hardness not to be equalled upon earth.

One sees at first sight that in the villages no children could have ever danced upon the green. No outward visible sign of any inward graces can be seen in the hard-featured people, whose flinty-looking cheeks seem to repel the mere idea of kisses, and yet down in whose hearts exists a vein of sentiment for which in other and more favoured lands a man might search in vain. As any district, country, or race of men must have its prototype, its spot or person that sums up and typifies the whole, so does this hard, grey land find its quintessence in the town of Buckiehaven, a windswept fisher village, built on a spit of sand.

Its little church is stumpier than all the other little churches of the coast. Its houses are more angular, their crowsteps steeper, and the gnarled plane trees that have fought for life against its withering blasts, more dwarfish and ill-grown. The fisherfolk seem ruddier, squarer, and more uncouth than are their fellows.

Their little wave-washed harbour looks narrower and still more dangerous than the thousand other little harbours that dot the coast from Kinghorn to St. Forts.

Still in the churchyard, in which the graves of mariners, of old sea-captains (who once sailed, drank, and suffered, where their descendants, now sail, drink, and suffer), lie thick, each waiting for the pilot, the headstones looking to the sea, their Mecca, there is an air of rest. The graves all look out seawards, where their hearts lived, and yet most of the denizens returned to lay their bones in the old paroch where in their youth they must have run about, clattering like ponies on the grey causeway stones. Yet there are gravestones which relate that Andrew Brodie or George Anstruther were buried in the deep, and that their monument was raised by Agnes, Janet, or some other sorrowing wife, in the full hope of their salvation, with a text drawn from the minor prophets and unintelligible to any eyes but those of love and faith.

The lettering on the stones is cut so deeply that in that mossless land it looks as fresh as when the widow and the local stonemason stood chaffering for its price, surrounded by her flaxen-headed children, whom in good time the sea would claim, taking them from her as relentlessly as it had claimed her man.

Only a little lichen here and there, yellow and looking like a stain, shows that time and the weather have both wrought their worst and failed to get a hold, so hard the whinstone, and so good the workmanship.

In the low, wiry grass the graves look like a flock of sheep, the rough-built wall keeps them from straying, and the squat cock upon the spire, that creaks so harshly in the wind, looks down upon them and does not crow, because it knows the inmates are asleep.

So they sleep on, sleeping a longer watch below than any that they ever had on earth, when the shrill boatswain's whistle roused them at each recurring period of four hours, or a shout called them all on deck to shorten sail.

All round the churchyard wall are old-world tombs, of worthies of the places—Brodies and Griersons, Selkirks and Anstruthers—adorned with emblems of their trades, as mallets, shears, and chisels, with a death's-head and crossbones crowning all, to show not only that the skeleton had sat unbidden at life's feast, but after a full meal still lingered with his hosts.

The whinstone church, hardly distinguishable from the rocks beside the harbour in colour and in shape, the little burial-ground more like a sheep-pen than a cemetery, the high-pitched house-roofs in the steep stony staircases of streets, all give the idea of a corner of the world to which no stranger could have penetrated except by accident. If such a one there were, he must have felt himself indeed a foreigner in such an isolated spot.

Yet on the south side of the church, set perhaps by accident to catch the little sun that ever shines upon that drear East Neuk, there is a slab let in or stuck against the wall.

Upon the granite tablet, edged round with a suppositious Gothic scroll, cut into flowers like pastry ornaments upon a pie, the letters poorly executed, showing up paltry in their shallowness, beside the lettering of the staunch old tombs amongst the grass, is written, "Here lies Sinakalula, Princess of Raratonga, the beloved wife of Andrew Brodie, Mariner."

What were the circumstances of their meeting the stone does not declare, only that the deceased had been a princess in her native land, and had died in the obscure east-country haven, and had been "beloved."

Nothing, but all—at least all that life has to give.

The simple idyll of the princess and Andrew Brodie, mariner, is writ on the red marble slab, in letters less enduring than their love, badly designed and poorly cut, and destined soon to disappear in the cold rains and steely blasts of the East Neuk of Fife, and leave the stone a blank.

How they met, loved, and how the mariner brought home his island bride, perhaps to droop in the cold north, and how he laid her in the drear churchyard to wait the time when they should be united once again in some Elysian field, not unlike Polynesia, with the Tree of Life for palms, the selfsame opal-tinted sea, angels for tropic birds, and the same air of calm pervading all the air, only the mariner, if he still lives, can say.

The princess, as Andrew Brodie first saw her, must have looked like the fair damsels Captain Cook describes, with perhaps just a slight tincture of the missionary school, but not enough to take away her grace.

Dressed in a coloured and diaphanous sacque, a wreath of red hibiscus round her head, her jet-black hair loose on her shoulders, bare arms and feet, and redolent of oil of cocoanut, she must have seemed a being from another world to the rough mariner.

How he appeared to her is harder to determine, perhaps as did Cortés to La Malinche,[1] or as did Soto to the Indian queen amongst the Seminoles.[2] True, we know what Cortés was like, how he rode like a centaur, was noble, generous, that he knew Latin, as Bernal Díaz says,[3] and Soto was designed by nature to capture every heart. The Scottish sailor possibly appeared as the representative of a strange race, harder and fiercer, but more tender at the heart than her compatriots.

His steel-blue eyes may have appeared to her as hardly mortal; his rough and hairy hands, symbols of strength embodified; his halting speech, a homage to her charms. Then as he must have been an honest and true-hearted man, approaching her with the same reverence with which he would have courted one of the hard-faced, red-headed women of his native place, not in the fashion of the trader or the beach-comber, it must have seemed as if a being, superior by its strength, had thrown its strength aside, all for her love.

When his ship sailed, the sailor may have hidden in the hills, then when her topsails had sunk well beneath the waves, and he was sure the ship would not return, come out of hiding, and strolled timidly along the beach, until some trader or the missionary came out and sheltered him.

Naturally, chiefs and missionaries and all the foreign population looked on his love as an infatuation; but he, setting to work, trading in copra and bêche-de-mer, in coral and the like, gradually made himself a man of consequence. Schooners would come consigned to him, and cargoes of his own lie heaped in barracoons, thatched with banana leaves.

At last, when he had "gathered siller" and become a man of substance—for Brodie certainly was one of those who could not stoop to live upon his wife—he must have gone and seen the missionary. One sees him sweating in his long-shore togs, a palm-tree hat upon his head, toiling along the beach, and rapping at the door. The missionary, most likely a compatriot, bids him come in, and lays the "Word," which he has been translating into Polynesian, upon the table and welcomes him.

"I'm glad to see ye, Andrew. How time goes on. Now you're a man of substance, and will be sending for a wife ... unless, indeed, you might think of Miss McKendrick, the new Bible-reader. A nice-like lass enough. No bonny, but then beauty, ye ken, is not enduring.... What, ye dinna say? I thocht ye had been cured o' all that foolishness. They island girls are a' like children. What sort of looking wife would she be to ye at hame, man Andrew?"

This may have passed, and then the wedding in the mission church, with the dusky catechumens looking stiff and angular in the death-dealing clothes of Christianity, the bride listening to the old-fashioned Scottish exhortation on the duties of her new estate, what time the chief, her father, a converted pagan, thought with regret of the marriage ceremonies that he had witnessed in his youth, so different from these.

It may have been that for a year or two the ill-assorted pair lived happily, the husband trading and watching his men work in his garden, whilst his wife swung in a hammock underneath a tree. As time went by, the recollection of the grey village in East Fife would come back to the husband's mind and draw him northwards, whilst the wife wondered what it was he thought about, and why the steely eyes seemed to look through her as if they sought for something that she could never see.

At last would come the day when he first spoke of going home, timidly, and as if feeling somehow he was about to commit a crime. Her tears and expostulations can be imagined, and then her Ruth-like resolution to follow him across the sea.

The voyage and the first touch of cold, the arrival in the bare and stormy land, the disappointment of poor Andrew, when he found he was forgotten by the great part of his friends, and that the rest despised him for having brought a coloured woman home, all follow naturally.

All the small jealousies and miseries of a provincial town, the horrors of the Scottish Sabbath, the ceaseless rain, the biting wind, the gloom and darkness of the winter, the disappointment of the brief northern summer, the sea, in which none but a walrus or a seal could bathe, must have done their worst upon the island princess, now become in very truth the wife of Andrew Brodie, mariner. One sees her in her unbecoming European clothes, simple and yet accustomed to respect, exposed to all the harshness of a land in which, though hearts are warm, they move so far beneath the surface that their pulsations hardly can be felt, except by those accustomed to their beat.

Then in the end consumption, that consumption that usually attacks a monkey when it passes north of forty, making its end so human and so pitiful, must have attacked her too.

Then the drear funeral, with Andrew and his friends in weepers and tall hats, which the east wind brushed all awry, making them look like ferrets; the little coffin with the outlandish name and date, and "in her thirtieth year" emblazoned on it in cheap brass lettering; and the sloping pile of shingly earth, so soon to be stamped down over the island flower.

Slowly the friends would go, after shaking Andrew by the hand. He, feeling vaguely that he had murdered her whom he loved best, would linger, as a bird hovers for a time above the place where it has seen its mate fall, a mere mass of bloodstained feathers, to the gun.

When he was gone the island princess would be left alone with the wind sweeping across the sea, sounding around the Bass, and whistling wearily above Inch Keith to sing her threnody.

(From *Charity*, 1912)

NOTES

1. Hernán Cortés (1485-1547), Spanish conquistador of Mexico, who defeated the Aztecs. La Malinche, or Doña Marina, was the Indian princess who served as Cortés' interpreter and mistress.
2. Hernando de Soto (*c.* 1500-42), Spanish conquistador, famous for his discovery of the Mississippi.
3. Bernal Díaz del Castillo (1492-1581), Cortés' captain, who wrote his *True History of the Conquest of New Spain*, describing the capture of Mexico by the Spaniards.

BROUGHT FORWARD

The workshop in Parkhead was not inspiriting.[1] From one week's end to another, all throughout the year, life was the same, almost without an incident. In the long days of the Scotch summer the men walked cheerily to work, carrying their dinner in a little tin. In the dark winter mornings they tramped in the black fog, coughing and spitting, through the black mud of Glasgow streets, each with a woollen comforter, looking like a stocking, round his neck.

Outside the dreary quarter of the town, its rows of dingy, smoke-grimed streets and the mean houses, the one outstanding feature was Parkhead Forge, with its tall chimneys belching smoke into the air all day, and flames by night. Its glowing furnaces, its giant hammers, its little railway trucks, in which men ran the blocks of white-hot iron which poured in streams out of the furnaces, flamed like the mouth of hell.

Inside the workshop the dusty atmosphere made a stranger cough on entering the door. The benches, with the rows of aproned men all bending at their work, not standing upright, with their bare, hairy chests exposed, after the fashion of the Vulcans at the neighbouring forge, gave a half-air of domesticity to the close, stuffy room.

A semi-sedentary life quickened their intellect; for where men work together they are bound to talk about the topics of the day, especially in Scotland, where every man is a born politician and a controversialist. At meal-times, when they ate their "piece" and drank their tea that they had carried with them in tin flasks, each one was certain to draw out a newspaper from the pocket of his coat, and, after studying it from the Births, Deaths, and Marriages, down to the editor's address on the last page, fall a-disputing upon politics. "Man, a gran' speech by Bonar Law aboot Home Rule. They Irish, set them up, what do they make siccan a din aboot? Ca' ye it Home Rule? I juist ca' it Rome Rule. A miserable, priest-ridden crew, the hale rick-ma-tick o' them."

The reader then would pause and, looking round the shop, wait for the answer that he was sure would not be long in coming from amongst such a thrawn lot of commentators. Usually one or other of his mates would fold his paper up, or perhaps point with an oil-stained finger to an article, and with the head-break in the voice, characteristic of the Scot about to plunge into an argument, ejaculate: "Bonar Law, ou aye, I kent him when he was leader of the South Side Parliament. He always was a dreary body, sort o' dreich like. No that I'm saying the man is pairfectly illiterate, as some are on his side o' the Hoose there in Westminister. I read his speech—the body is na blate, sort o' quick at figures, but does na take the pains to verify. Verification is the soul of mathematics. Bonar

Law, eh! Did ye see how Maister Asquith trippit him handily in his tabulated figures on the jute business under Free Trade, showing that all he had advanced about protective tariffs and the drawback system was fair redeeklous ... as well as several errors in the total sum?"

Then others would cut in and words be bandied to and fro, impugning the good faith and honour of every section of the House of Commons, who, by the showing of their own speeches, were held to be dishonourable rogues aiming at power and place, without a thought for anything but their own ends.

This charitable view of men and of affairs did not prevent any of the disputants from firing up if his own party was impugned; for in their heart of hearts the general denunciation was but a covert from which to attack the other side.

In such an ambient the war was sure to be discussed. Some held the German Emperor was mad—"a daft-like thing to challenge the whole world, ye see; maist inconsiderate, and shows that the man's intellect is no weel balanced ... philosophy is whiles sort of unsettlin' ... the felly's mad, ye ken."

Others saw method in his madness, and alleged that it was envy, "naething but sheer envy that had brought on this tramplin' upon natural rights, but for all that he may be thought to get his own again, with they indemnities."

Those who had studied economics "were of opinion that his reasoning was wrong, built on false premises, for there can never be a royal road to wealth. Labour, ye see, is the sole creative element of riches." At once a Tory would rejoin, "And brains. Man, what an awfu' thing to leave out brains. Think of the marvellous creations of the human genius." The first would answer with, "I saw ye coming, man. I'll no deny that brains have their due place in the economic state; but build me one of your Zeppelins and stick it in the middle of George Square without a crew to manage it, and how far will it fly? I do not say that brains did not devise it; but, after all, labour had to carry out the first design." This was a subject that opened up enormous vistas for discussion, and for a time kept them from talking of the war.

Jimmy and Geordie, hammering away in one end of the room, took little part in the debate. Good workmen both of them, and friends, perhaps because of the difference of their temperaments, for Jimmy was the type of red-haired, blue-eyed, tall, lithe Scot, he of the *perfervidum ingenium*,[2] and Geordie was a thick-set, black-haired, dour and silent man.

Both of them read the war news, and Jimmy, when he read, commented loudly, bringing down his fist upon the paper, exclaiming, "Weel done, Gordons!" or "That was a richt gude charge upon the trenches by the Sutherlands." Geordie would answer shortly, "Aye, no sae bad," and go on hammering.

One morning, after a reverse, Jimmy did not appear, and Geordie sat alone working away as usual, but if possible more dourly and more silently. Towards midday it began to be whispered in the shop that Jimmy had enlisted, and men turned to Geordie to ask if he knew anything about it, and the silent workman, brushing the sweat off his brow with his coatsleeve, rejoined: "Aye, ou aye, I went wi' him yestreen to the headquarters o' the Camerons. He's joined the kilties richt eneugh. Ye mind he was a sergeant in South Africa." Then he bent over to his work and did not join in the general conversation that ensued.

Days passed, and weeks, and his fellow-workmen, in the way men will, occasionally bantered Geordie, asking him if he was going to enlist, and whether he did not think shame to let his friend go off alone to fight. Geordie was silent under abuse and banter, as he had always been under the injustices of life, and by degrees withdrew into himself, and when he read his newspaper during the dinner-hour made no remark, but folded it and put it quietly into the pocket of his coat.

Weeks passed, weeks of suspense, of flaring headlines in the press, of noise of regiments passing down the streets, of newsboys yelling hypothetic victories, and of the tension of the nerves of men who know their country's destiny is hanging in the scales. Rumours of losses, of defeats, of victories, of checks and of advances, of naval battles, with hints of dreadful slaughter filled the air. Women in black were seen about, pale and with eyelids swollen with weeping, and people scanned the reports of killed and wounded with dry throats and hearts constricted as if they had been wrapped in whipcord, only relaxing when after a second look they had assured themselves the name they feared to see was absent from the list.

Long strings of Clydesdale horses, ridden by men in ragged clothes who sat them uneasily, as if they felt their situation keenly, perched up in the public view, passed through the streets. The massive caulkers on their shoes struck fire occasionally upon the stones, and the great beasts, taught to rely on man as on a god from the time they gambolled in the fields, went to their doom unconsciously, the only mitigation of their fate. Regiments of young recruits, some in plain clothes and in hastily-made uniforms, marched with as martial an air as three weeks' training gave them, to the stations to entrain. Pale clerks, the elbows of their jackets shiny with the slavery of the desk, strode beside men whose hands were bent and scarred with gripping on the handles of the plough in February gales or wielding sledges at the forge.

All of them were young and resolute, and each was confident that he at least would come back safe to tell the tale. Men stopped and waved their hats, cheering their passage, and girls and women stood with flushed cheeks and straining eyes as they passed on for the first stage that took them towards the front. Boys ran beside them, hatless and barefooted, shouting out words that they had caught up on the drill-ground to the men, who whistled as they marched a slow and grinding tune that sounded like a hymn.

Traffic was drawn up close to the kerbstone, and from the top of tram-cars and from carts men cheered, bringing a flush of pride to many a pale cheek in the ranks. They passed on. Men resumed the business of their lives, few understanding that the half-trained, pale-faced regiment that had vanished through the great station gates had gone to make that business possible and safe.

Then came a time of waiting for the news, of contradictory paragraphs in newspapers, and then a telegram, the "enemy is giving ground on the left wing"; and instantly a feeling of relief that lightened every heart, as if its owner had been fighting and had stopped to wipe his brow before he started to pursue the flying enemy.

The workmen in the brassfitters' shop came to their work as usual on the day of the good news, and at the dinner-hour read out the accounts of the great battle, clustering upon each other's shoulders in their eagerness. At last one turned to scan the list of casualties. Cameron, Campbell, M'Alister, Jardine, they read, as they ran down the list, checking the names off with a match. The reader stopped, and looked towards the corner where Geordie still sat working silently.

All eyes were turned towards him, for the rest seemed to divine even before they heard the name. "Geordie man, Jimmy's killed," the reader said, and as he spoke Geordie laid down his hammer and, reaching for his coat, said, "Jimmy's killed, is he? Well, some one's got to account for it."

Then, opening the door, he walked out dourly, as if already he felt the knapsack on his back and the avenging rifle in his hand.

(From *Brought Forward*, 1916)

NOTES

1. *inspiriting*, cheerful or inspiring. This is a good example of Graham's use of archaisms or unusual forms. Though not common, they exist and are always etymologically correct. cf. his use of "endue," "unstability," "beat" (as past particle), "simple" (as a noun), etc.
2. *perfervidum ingenium*, hot-tempered disposition.

GLOSSARY

This glossary is designed solely to help the reader appreciate more the foregoing sketches. It is not meant to be specialist, technical or exhaustive, nor does it try to provide all the alternative meanings of the words and phrases listed. Its express function is related only to the sketches treated in this volume.

abune above
agiotage speculation in stocks and shares
aguapey plant (South America)
aiblins perhaps
alameda avenue (South America and Spain)
aucuba hardy evergreen shrub
aumrie cupboard, pantry
awqua i.e. aqua, usually brandy, or some such liquor

baadan wood
back end late autumn
bail up tie up
ball (of snow) to gather in lumps, stick to feet
barracoon enclosure or barrack used for keeping slaves or convicts
bask dry
bawbee halfpenny, (plural) money
bealach narrow mountain pass
bêche-de-mer sea-slug, delicacy eaten by the Chinese
bent coarse grass near the sea
bicker argue, quarrel
biggit built
birl drink hard
birlinn large rowing boat used by Highland chiefs
bit small, puny
blaeberry bilberry
blate shy; dull, stupid
bogle spectre, bogey
bolas ball-shaped gaucho weapons (Argentina)
bole trunk (of tree)
bool boy's marble, large round stone
boss weak

bouet, bowet hand lantern; moon
braid broad
brake bracken
brander broil
brattle flow noisily (of a stream)
bratty ragged
braxy dead from internal inflammation (of sheep)
breer briar
bummle bungle, blunder
busk dress, prepare

cailleach nun; old woman
calkin part of a horse's shoe
caña rum (South America)
camera obscura dark room
capercailzie woodgrouse, mountain cock
carle fellow, character
carlin man, old man
carlón wine (South America)
carse stretch of flat fertile land near a river
caschrom foot-plough
cauker, caulker iron rim on horse's shoe
chappit chop
cheep chirp, squeak
chiel fellow, character
clachan small Highland village
clartiness dirtiness, untidiness
clarty dirty, untidy
clash gossip, tales
clavers idle talk, gossip
clishmaclaver gossip
compeer crony
copra dried kernel of the coconut
coracle small wickerwork boat covered by waterproof material
corbie raven, crow
coronach funeral song, dirge

corrie hollow in the hillside
cottary group of cottages
cranruch hoar-frost
creagh raid
creaght nomadic cattle
croon top, head, crown
cuachan drinking cup, bowl, goblet
cuddy cabin below the round house (of a boat)
cushat(-doo), cushet wild pigeon

dander, daunder stroll
dang throw violently, drive
darg work
daud strike
deave bother
deil devil
dhu black
dirl fuss
divot piece of turf
dodder dawdle
doited foolish, childish; doting
dreich dull, dismal, grim
drouth thirst
drumly thick, muddy
dunnage material used to help stow things carefully
dunt knock, bang
dunter porpoise

Equisetum horsetail (plant)
ettle try; hanker

falloch thick, bulky
fank enclosure, pen
fash trouble, bother
fay, fey doomed to disaster or death
feal turf
fecht fight
feck many
fell large quantity
filing fouling, defiling
flauchter feals cut turfs
flinders pieces, fragments
fluke parasite insect in the liver (of sheep)
flyte scold
forbear ancestor
fornent opposite
fou drunk
founds foundation (of a building)
freen friend
fricht fear, fright

gait way
ganaker guanaco, savage llama of the pampa (Argentina)
gang go, walk
gar make, cause
garron small horse
gash grim, ghostly, dismal-looking
gato Argentine dance
gaunt yawn
gin if; bolt or lock of window or door
girn weep
glas grey, pale
gleg smart, sharp-eyed, clear-sighted
grap grip
grat wept
greet weep
grip dung-channel in cattle shed
grozet gooseberry
guillapices cover, cloth worn by the Indians (South America)
gyte crazy, mad

haar wet mist or fog
hag wild broken ground
hagg peat hole
haggersnash confusion, mixture (of languages)
hag-taper great mullein (plant)
hantle large number
haricles the pluck of an animal
haver nonsense, talk nonsense
haversome silly, nonsensical
heigh high, tall
het hot
heugh thin (turnips)
hewit cut
higgle argue
hirsel sheep
hob ghost, goblin
hodden homespun, rough-cloth
host cough
houk, howk dig
howlet owl
hourdies, hurdies buttocks
hurl ride, drive

inch island, low-lying land near river or stream
ingle-neuk chimney corner
intil within

jalouse suspect, judge
jaw-box indoor sink

kail-yard cabbage patch attached to cottage
keel-mark coloured marking on sheep
kelpie water-sprite, river-horse
kent known
kist coffin, chest; prepare a corpse for the coffin
kist o' whistles organ
kye cows
kyloe small, long-horned Highland cattle

laigh low (lands), plain
laroch site of a ruined house
lash crowd
lauch laugh
lave rest
laverock lark
lazo lasso (Argentina)
leastwise at any rate, at least
leddy lady
ling rushes, long thin grass
linn pool
lippen trust
lochan loch, lake
loupit jumped
louring threatening
lowse set free

machair, machar, macher bent-grown sandy tracts by the sea
maist most, almost
maun must; man
makar, makkar poet
megilp mixture of linseed oil and turpentine
midden rubbish dump
moss region covered with peat
muckle much, huge
mullein herbaceous plant like foxglove

neep turnip

outby near by
oxter underarm

paidle walk with short steps
palenque hitching post (Argentina)
pampero pampa storm (Argentina)
paroch parish
patroncito boss (diminutive of affection, Argentina)
pawky shrewd, sly

peakit sharp
picazo black horse with white face (Argentina)
plouter flounder
pollard tree that has been cut back or lopped
pownie pony
pricker tailor (pejorative)
prionsa, prionnsa prince
pulpería pampa store-cum-pub (Argentina)
pund pound in money or weight

quairn, quern small stone hand-mill
quey heifer

rap knock
rappit knocked
rax hand, pass (down or over)
reid red
rickle pile, heap
rick-ma-tick, rick ma tick, rickmatick collection, gang, bunch
ruckly rickety, unsteady
rugg and rieve to struggle violently for possession

saft soft
sair sore, sad
sark shirt
schauchlin loose and mis-shapen; splashing
sein(n) sing or play music
selvage, selvedge edge, bank
shaws heads or leaves of vegetables, potatoes, etc.
sheaf wheel of a pulley
sheugh cover over (in a pit, for example)
shieling hut, cottage
shilpit skinny
siccan such a
siller silver, money
skirl shriek
skunner revulsion, disgust
slake wet, daub
smoor extinguish, smother, cover
sneeshin snuff
soddy soda
soople supple
souch, sough sigh, moan
spang leap
spathe sheathing-leaf

splent armour for legs and arms. cf. splint
splore spree, good time
stanch stop the flow of
stan o' black black suit
steading, steding, stedding building land, site, farmhouse and building
steer stir
stirk steer
stook pile, mass, stack
stot stagger
stot(t) young bull or ox
stotter stumble
stoup water jug or pail
stour dust
straucht, straught straight
syne then, since

tacket ticket, hobnail
tacketed hobnailed (boots)
tacuará hard bamboo (Argentina)
tae toe
taigled worn-out
tak full get angry
tarn small mountain lake
taties, tatties potatoes
teind tithe
teugh tough
thack thatch
thole endure
thrawn ill-tempered, disagreeable
threap nag, continually complain
threnody lament for the dead
tirl try, round; pull or strip off (e.g. slates)
tittle detail, anything small

tocher dowry
Tophet hell
tormentil low-growing roscaceous herb
trootie trout
tryst fixed cattle market, fair
trysting tree where lovers meet by agreement
tuilzie, tulzie quarrel, dispute; or touzle, lovers' playing about
turley-wurley whirligig

unco extraordinary

vino seco thick yellow Catalonian wine

wale thrash
wauk, waulk make cloth hard, or "full" cloth
wattle twig
wersh tasteless
whaup curlew
wheen|(a) many
whiles sometimes, at other times
whummle turn over fast, spin
withy willow, especially flexible branches used for binding
wraith apparition, spectre of a living person
wrocht worked
wynd narrow street, lane

yelloch yell, scream
yokit got down to, tackled, undertook

BIBLIOGRAPHY

I. WORKS OF R. B. CUNNINGHAME GRAHAM

This list does not include translations, prefaces to other writers' works, and pamphlets. The books have been listed in order of publication.

Notes on the District of Menteith, London, A. &. C. Black, 1895.
Father Archangel of Scotland, London, A. &. C. Black, 1896.
Mogreb-el-Acksa, London, Heinemann, 1898.
The Ipané, London, Fisher Unwin, 1899.
Thirteen Stories, London, Heinemann, 1900.
A Vanished Arcadia, London, Heinemann, 1901.
Success, London, Duckworth, 1902.
Hernando de Soto, London, Heinemann, 1903.
Progress, London, Duckworth, 1905.
His People, London, Duckworth, 1906.
Faith, London, Duckworth, 1909.
Hope, London, Duckworth, 1910.
Charity, London, Duckworth, 1912.
A Hatchment, London, Duckworth, 1913.
Scottish Stories, London, Duckworth, 1914.
Bernal Díaz del Castillo, London, Eveleigh Nash, 1915.
Brought Forward, London, Duckworth, 1916.
A Brazilian Mystic, London, Heinemann, 1920.
Cartagena and the Banks of the Sinú, London, Heinemann, 1920.
The Conquest of New Granada, London, Heinemann, 1922.
The Conquest of the River Plate, London, Heinemann, 1924.
Doughty Deeds, London, Heinemann, 1925.
Pedro de Valdivia, London, Heinemann, 1926.
Redeemed, London, Heinemann, 1927.
José Antonio Páez, London, Heinemann, 1929.
Thirty Tales and Sketches (selected by Edward Garnett), London, Heinemann, 1930.
The Horses of the Conquest, London, Heinemann, 1930.
Writ in Sand, London, Heinemann, 1932.
Portrait of a Dictator, London, Heinemann, 1933.
Mirages, London, Heinemann, 1936.
Rodeo (selected by A. F. Tschiffely), London, Heinemann, 1936.

The Essential R. B. Cunninghame Graham (selected by Paul Bloomfield), London, Jonathan Cape, 1952.

The South American Sketches of R. B. Cunninghame Graham (selected and edited by John Walker), Norman, University of Oklahoma Press, 1978.

"Beattock for Moffat" and the Best of R. B. Cunninghame Graham, Edinburgh, Paul Harris Publishing, 1979.

II. SELECTED STUDIES—GENERAL

Haymaker, Richard E., *Prince Errant and Evocator of Horizons*, Kingsport, Kingsport Press, 1967.

MacDiarmid, Hugh (pseud. C. M. Grieve), *Cunninghame Graham—A Centenary Study*, Glasgow, Caledonian Press, 1952.

Tschiffely, A. F., *Don Roberto*, London, Heinemann, 1937.

Watts, Cedric and Laurence Davies, *Cunninghame Graham: A Critical Biography*, Cambridge, Cambridge University Press, 1979.

West, Herbert F., *Robert Bontine Cunninghame Graham—His Life and Works*, London, Cranley and Day, 1932.

III. CRITICAL STUDIES ON GRAHAM AND SCOTLAND

Davies, Laurence, "R. B. Cunninghame Graham: The Kailyard and After," *Studies in Scottish Literature* (University of South Carolina), XI, No. 3, January 1974, 156-77.

Grieve, Christopher Murray, *Contemporary Scottish Studies*, First Series, London Leonard Parsons, 1926, 49-57.

MacDiarmid, Hugh (pseud. C. M. Grieve), "The Significance of Cunninghame Graham," originally published in *National Weekly,* 1952; reprinted in *Selected Essays of Hugh MacDiarmid*, ed. Duncan Glen, London, Jonathan Cape, 1969, 121-8.

Mackenzie, Compton, "R. B. Cunninghame Graham: Scottish Nationalist," *Outlook* (Glasgow), Vol. 1, No. 2, May 1936, 21-4.

Niven, Frederick, "Cunninghame Graham," *Library Review*, Vol. 3, Winter 1932, 376-81; reprinted in *Coloured Spectacles*, London, Collins, 1938, 131-4.

Parker, W. M., "A Modern Elizabethan," *Modern Scottish Writers*, Edinburgh & Glasgow, William Hodge, 1917, 195-219.

IV. BIBLIOGRAPHICAL WORKS ON CUNNINGHAME GRAHAM

Walker, John, "A Chronological Bibliography of Works on R. B. Cunninghame Graham (1852-1936)," *The Bibliotheck*, Vol. 9, Nos. 2 & 3, 1978, 47-64.

—— *Cunninghame Graham and Scotland: An Annotated Bibliography,* Dollar, Douglas Mack, 1980.

—— "R. B. Cunninghame Graham: An Annotated Bibliography of Writings About Him," *English Literature in Transition,* Vol. 22, No. 2, 1979, 77-156.

Watts, Cedric Thomas, "R. B. Cunninghame Graham (1852-1936): A List of his Contributions to Periodicals," *The Bibliotheck,* Vol. 4, No. 5, 1965, 186-99.